DURWOOD MERRILL'S FANS SPEAK OUT

"**He's the greatest storyteller in baseball.** And his stories are often metaphors for life's experiences and lessons. He's a wonderful, sensitive person, but he's also a hell of an umpire and performer. The man has a great lust for life. He's an entertainer and a real hot dog. And when I say hot dog, I mean it as a term of endearment."

—Former Umpire Steve Palermo

"Durwood, a lot of people say, is the funniest umpire in all of baseball. I happen to think he's the **funniest man in baseball.** Just watch him on the field sometime and your sides will hurt from laughing so much. He puts a kid's perspective back in the game, and that's what baseball needs."

—George Brett, former All Star

"He's the **Reggie Jackson of umpiring.** You would pay to get into the ballpark just to see Durwood Merrill do his act. He's that good."

—Reggie Jackson

"He's the **best umpire in baseball** over the last five years. He's one of those guys that you like to watch on TV because he puts so much zest into the game."

—Tony LaRussa, Manager, St. Louis Cardinals

More . . .

"Merrill's good-ol'-ump approach has a certain charm . . . Part of him still can't believe he's in the majors. That sense of wonderment infuses Merrill's memories of 20-plus years in the American League."
—*The New York Times Book Review*

"Very, very funny . . . Is there a likable side to umpires? The colorful Merrill . . . proves there is."
—*New Orleans Times-Picayne*

"It all makes for an entertaining read during rain delays."
—*Chattanooga Free Press*

"This is not a book that mercilessly repeats the 'poetry and beauty' of the game. It is an **honest and rather original** look at baseball and its players, managers, and umpires. Merrill has watched the game from the absolutely best seat in the house."

—*Library Journal*

"The book has the **feeling of a session in the umpire's locker room after the game** . . . The opportunity to view the game as it is being played today from the point of view of the men in blue should not be passed up."
—Amateur Baseball Umpire Home Page (a Four Plate rating)

YOU'RE OUT

AND YOU'RE UGLY, TOO!

CONFESSIONS OF AN
UMPIRE WITH ATTITUDE

**Durwood Merrill
with Jim Dent**

Foreword by Ken Griffey Jr.

St. Martin's Paperbacks

YOU'RE OUT AND YOU'RE UGLY, TOO!

Library of Congress Catalog Card Number: 97-36577

ISBN: 0-312-96900-7

Printed in the United States of America

St. Martin's Press hardcover edition/April 1998
St. Martin's Paperbacks edition/April 1999

10 9 8 7 6 5 4 3 2 1

This book is dedicated to the umpires
who wear the blue
for their integrity and commitment
to a grand game

Contents

Acknowledgments

The authors thank associate publisher Pete Wolverton for recognizing the merit of the book. Pete not only provided a guiding light with his editorial direction, but he also lent encouragement and a timely sense of humor. Pete might be the most energetic guy the authors have ever met.

To Durwood's wonderful family: wife, Carolyn; daughter, Maria; and son, Mickey. And to the entire Merrill family, from Durwood's father, Ebenezer Levi, to the eight grandchildren.

To Jim Donovan, our agent. Jim is rapidly becoming one of the leading agents in the Southwest, and didn't need much prodding when Jim Dent approached him with the book idea. Donovan, in fact, sold the book to Wolverton in about two days and, for that, the authors are especially grateful. He also added a nice touch with the editing pencil.

To Ken Griffey Jr. for writing the foreword and for spending about ninety minutes one dull afternoon telling hardball stories to the authors. We even learned a lot about Junior's golf game.

To Durwood's umpiring crew during the 1997 season: Rocky Roe, Davey Phillips, and Dale Scott. Rocky and Davey provided some keen insight, not only into Durwood's life, but also into the general lifestyle of umpires. Durwood calls this threesome "the best group I've ever been around."

To all of the umpires from both leagues, and especially Larry McCoy and Don Denkinger, for their great stories, and to the head man, Marty Springstead, who taught Durwood how to umpire and who remains his mentor. Also, to Dr. Gene Budig, the American League president, for supporting this project. To Dick Butler for bringing Durwood into the major leagues in 1977, and to Bobby Bragan for believing in him. Durwood also thanks past American League presidents Lee MacPhail and Dr. Bobby Brown.

To Steve Palermo, one of the greatest human beings to ever grace the game of baseball. Steve has been Durwood's great friend since they met in umpiring school in 1972. Steve provided numerous anecdotes and some riveting details about the summer night in 1991 when he was gunned down in the streets of Dallas.

To the numerous writers who provided help with their columns, stories, books, and suggestions: Randy Galloway, Jim Reeves, Denne Freeman, Gil LeBreton, Ken Daley, Johnny Paul, T. R. Sullivan, Frank Luksa, Gerry Callahan, Tom Verducci, Paul Hagen, Ken Sins, Tracy Ringolsby, Tim Kurkjian, John Eisenberg, Tim Crothers, Hal Bodley, David Fisher, Al Eshbeck, Jerome Holtzman, John C. Skipper, Phil Pepe, Robert Creamer, Eliot Asinof, Phil Rogers, and Peter Gammons. Also to the electronic wizards: Norm Hitzges, Dale Hansen, Robin Roberts, Bob Barry, Bob Barry Jr., Brad Sham, and Eric Nadel.

To Bill Eisenhauer in Dallas for providing light in a very dark computer hour. To Richard "Hoggy" Price, the Boss Hog in the umpires' room in Arlington and one of the great network guys in all of baseball. Durwood would also like to thank the umpires' room attendants across the American League.

To John Blake, Doug Melvin, Tom Smith, and Tom Schieffer of the Texas Rangers. For general support, the following group was unmatched: Pat Snuffer, Ben Elliott, Doug Marcella, Joe Holladay, Roddy O'Neal, Bill Bain, and Dr. Don Beck. The authors also had a lot of fun with the early diners at Jimmy D.'s in Hooks, Texas. They offered up-close and funny stories for the book.

As always, Jim Dent thanks his talented and overfed cat, Rolly, for the hundreds of hours he spent lying at the co-author's feet as he wrote on the computer, and for keeping the chair warm during coffee breaks.

Foreword

When I heard that Durwood Merrill was writing a book, I thought about the hilarious stories he'd told me through the years and I started laughing again. This would be better than *Oprah*, I thought. Durwood is a man of many words and most of them are funny.

The Durwood I've come to know around the ballparks is someone you always want to talk to. Having a bad day? Go see Durwood. He'll cheer you up. Through the years, I've gone far out of my way just to hear him crack a few one-liners. If he's at first base, and our dugout's over on the third base side, I'll angle all the way across the infield on my way to center field to catch some laughs.

When I broke into the major leagues in 1989, one of the first people my dad told me about was Durwood. I'm sure you've heard of my dad, Ken Griffey Sr. He's got three World Series rings and likes to remind me every day that I'm still scoreless in that department.

My dad met Durwood down in Puerto Rico during winter ball in the mid-1970s, and they shared a lot of laughs in the American League in the '80s. I was told in my rookie season that one of the first people I needed to get to know was Durwood. "Get ready to laugh," my dad told me.

Before we get to the punch lines, though, let me tell you about another side of Durwood that some people might not know about. Back in 1993, my wife, Melissa, and I were watching the Sunday morning sports news when Durwood's face popped up on the tube. Our respect for the garrulous Mr. Merrill would grow immensely from watching that report by ESPN. We learned just how many people he helped during the Christmas holidays. We really related to what he was doing. When it comes to helping other people, Durwood leads the major leagues in runs, hits, and tape-measure home runs.

There he was, walking through some run-down houses near his hometown of Hooks, Texas, delivering food, toys, clothes, and bicycles to the needy families. I know that television sometimes paints a rosy picture of things, but not this time. We could quickly tell that these people were in dire need of assistance. Some of the windows on the houses were boarded up, and some homes didn't even have electricity. As ESPN reporter Robin Roberts walked with Durwood through the impoverished street, she started to cry. It was that grim.

Watching Durwood on TV, Melissa pointed and said, "That's the umpire I really like. I really like him a lot more now." Melissa doesn't know a lot about baseball and that's okay. She never really has gotten into the game. But that day, she was able to make a human connection with baseball that I'd never seen before. For Durwood to play Santa Claus to all of those needy people touched both of our hearts. Every time she sees him on TV now, Melissa yells, "There's Durwood! There's Durwood!" That's really neat, I think.

What a dirty rotten shame if these folks had been shut out at Christmas. There would have been no Christmas, though, for those people without Durwood and the army of volunteers down in Texas. Since 1979, when Durwood learned that a family was virtually starving at Christmastime, he's been leading the Hooks Christian Service in a heavenly cause. These are men and women who give up several days during the Christmas holidays to buy and deliver the goods and the toys. Durwood's work is really year-round, collecting the money and acting as front man for the cause. A lot of people in major league baseball have heard about the charity work and have donated toys and money. For each of the last two Christmases, Durwood and his volunteers have come to the aid of almost two hundred very needy families there in Hooks.

It means a lot to me and my family to see Durwood making that kind of sacrifice. I know that as players and umpires, we need to get our rest during the off-season. That time is precious to me because I do a lot of charity work myself when I'm away from baseball. It seems that as one baseball season is ending, another one is starting. You finish up at some point in October, and you're back in spring training in February. So I especially respect people who'll take the time in the off-season to help others.

Melissa would later tell my dad about seeing Durwood on TV. Of course, he already knew the work that Durwood does, and he was able to tell her a few more stories. It seems we sat around the Griffey home and talked a lot about Durwood during that off-season. That's why I told Durwood that if he ever needs me to come down there and help him, I'll do what I can.

What really links me to Durwood is that we both do what we can for the needy kids that we encounter. I work with several charities around Seattle and my off-season home in Orlando. Nike and I donated $2,000 per home run a couple of years ago to the Girls and Boys Clubs. Luckily, I had fifty dingers that year.

Recently, I was watching one of the TV talk shows when an eleven-year-old boy named Dominique Mayo said I was his only real male role model. Dominique doesn't have a father. So, when the Mariners were playing at Yankee Stadium, I brought him and his mom to New York, and we had some fun at the All-Star Cafe and at The Stadium. I'm starting a Big Brothers program in Seattle, and I'll bring some teenagers to the Kingdome every day. We're doing our best in Seattle to get the inner-city kids into some good seats on the weekends. Kids are going to rule the world someday, so we might as well get them on the right track.

The two most important people in my life are my kids, Trey and Taryn, and I know how important it is that I get out and play ball with them. But, you know, there are a lot of kids who don't have parents to provide for them and to play with them.

Durwood and I both realize that baseball is not a life-or-death situation, and in the big picture, this game is just a small part of our lives. The important thing is to use baseball as our vehicle to help other people. If we do that, then we're really getting somewhere.

From day one, Durwood and I hit it off like a couple of guys who were just meant to be friends. I can't say that about all player-umpire relationships. In my eight years of major league baseball, I've never had any trouble with the umpires. Lately, though, we've been hearing that the umpires are trying to take over the game and that they're too arrogant and that some of them actually think they're bigger than baseball. It seems some umpires don't want to argue anymore. They just want to toss you out of the game. That's certainly not the case with Durwood.

I've seen guys get into arguments with Durwood and they'll end up laughing and forgetting what the whole thing was all about. I've never seen anyone who's able to stay mad at him. A lot of players call him ''Naked Gun'' after the movie that came out a few years ago. The umpire in that movie calls strikes and outs with two hands, just like our real-life Durwood.

If everybody in baseball had Durwood's attitude and ability to communicate, we'd all be having a heckuva lot more fun and we'd all be getting along. One thing that I've always looked forward to is the banter between Durwood and my manager, Lou Piniella. One day, Lou got so mad at Durwood that he pulled second base out of the ground and heaved it. The next day, my teammates and I set up a simulated javelin range with taped boundaries so Lou could practice his base throw.

Lou and Durwood might fight like cats and dogs. But the next day, you'll see them laughing and slapping each other on the back. Sometimes they act like a couple of slapstick comics. Now that Lou's a granddad, the players are always telling him to mellow out. That man really has a macho side that goes all the way back to his playing days with the Yankees. We'll sit around the dugout, and somebody will say, "Mellow out, Skip. You know that you've got a grandchild now. You're not supposed to be the big, bad Lou Piniella anymore." Lou just laughs.

One day in Seattle, though, I told Lou, "You know, I wouldn't mind seeing the old fiery Lou today." He looked at me and said, "Junior, hang around. You just might see it in this game." I just smiled and said, "Yeah, right."

About the third inning, Paul Sorrento hit what appeared to be a home run into the center field seats. One of the umpires ruled it a home run, and then Durwood came running in, yelling and raising his arms. Much to the unhappiness of the Mariners, he reversed the call. Durwood ruled that a fan had reached over the center field wall and snagged the ball with his glove. Actually, Durwood was right. But Lou didn't want to hear about it. He came charging out of the dugout like a raging bull and yelled, "You're not even supposed to be watching!"

"That's my job, Lou," Durwood deadpanned.

Pretty soon, Lou was stomping his cap and cussing and kicking dirt at Durwood. Only problem was that Lou kept missing Durwood with the dirt. Durwood looked over in the dugout, and there I was acting like an NFL referee, yelling, "No good! Wide right! No good!" That just made Durwood laugh even harder.

Lou finally kicked some dirt on Durwood's shoes, and Granddad got kicked out of the game. It was one of the funniest things that I've ever seen in baseball.

Back in 1990, I was still a naive nineteen-year-old trying to get to know the league, when I learned about Durwood's big strike zone. It was the ninth inning at old Arlington Stadium and we were losing. As a matter of fact, when I stepped to the plate, I represented the potential last out of the game for the Mariners.

Now, my dad and I have talked about the intricacies of hitting since I got into The Bigs in 1989. The phone will ring in the Mariners dugout and it's my dad. He'll say, "Hey, you're swinging at bad pitches.'' I get voice mail pages and he'll say, ''Stop turning so quick. That's why you're pulling the ball.'' I'll look up in the seats, and he'll be standing there demonstrating something that I'm doing wrong with my bat.

But he forgot to tell me about Durwood's big strike zone before it was too late.

With two strikes on me, the next pitch came in and I thought it was wide until Durwood yelled, ''Strike three!'' I turned around and said, ''Huh?'' And he yelled, ''Hall of Fame pitch!'' I sure as heck didn't know what he was talking about. Before I could argue, Durwood was jogging off the field.

When I got back to the hotel, the message light on my phone was on. My dad and I were teammates back then, but we didn't get a chance to talk after the game. So I gave him a call. ''Dad,'' I said, ''what in the world is a Hall of Fame pitch?''

My dad started laughing so hard, he was having trouble catching his breath. ''Did you say anything to Durwood?'' he said.

''No, I didn't,'' I said. ''But why are you laughing, Dad? I struck out.''

''Oh, don't worry,'' he said. ''Durwood's been calling that outside pitch for years. He calls it the Hall of Fame pitch because it puts some pitchers in Cooperstown before their time. He'll probably call it again on you.''

Durwood likes to call the Hall of Fame pitch, and to me, he's Hall of Fame funny. He's a man of many talents and one who really cares about a lot of people. For years, the man has been a book just waiting to happen. As my dad once said, get ready to laugh.

—Ken Griffey Jr.

YOU'RE OUT

OUT

AND YOU'RE UGLY, TOO!

Hick from the Sticks

FOR EIGHT DAYS AND SIX GAMES, I'd been buzzing around ballparks in Cleveland and Baltimore, umpiring a play-off series that had turned crazier than a henhouse rat. Four games had been decided by one run, and game three lasted so long that in the twelfth inning I thought about flagging down a hot dog vendor. After twenty-one years in the major leagues, I still can't recall a game won in extra innings on a botched squeeze play that'd be replayed more times than the Zapruder film.

As the Cleveland Indians were clinching the 1997 American League Championship Series, I took a long, slow walk from left field to the tunnel behind home plate. Most times, an umpire will haul his backside off the field after a series filled with controversy, heartbreak, and media overkill. When a trip to the World Series goes up in smoke, the home crowd tends to get a little cuckoo, and they like to throw everything that isn't bolted down. But I wanted to take my time and just kind of soak up the joy and sorrow from an ALCS too bizarre to ever forget.

I've witnessed a lot of crazy celebrations through the years and can't tell you how many times in the major leagues I've watched the championship team pile up on the infield grass and pound the dickens out of each other. Sometimes you wonder how many dislocated shoulders and sprained knees come out of those those public love-fests. When this series ended, though, even the underdog Indians didn't have the energy for that silly stuff. The players high-fived and hugged each other and that was the end of it.

For more than two decades, I've been living at the center of this madness we call The Bigs. I'm Durwood Merrill, a hick from the sticks, and most of my friends just call me Dur. I guess I'm lucky in that I've spent my working hours in ballparks all over America. I still remember my first trip to Yankee Stadium, when I looked around and asked somebody just how much hay you could stack in that place. In the 1940s, I grew up in the dust bowl of western Oklahoma, where about all we had were our dreams. My four brothers and I toiled in the cotton fields and learned the value of hard work. I remain the only major league umpire to be born in Oklahoma.

My life's travels had carried me all the way to the tiny East Texas town of Hooks when, in 1972, I caught the fever. I'd been coaching high school sports for about ten years and I could feel the walls closing in. I just decided to chuck it all and chase some rainbows. My family and friends thought I was about half loco when I took off for umpiring school down in Florida, but it was just one of those things. Every once in a while, you've got to say what the heck.

My home is still in Hooks, a town of about four thousand people, and my address is 3R St. Johns Road. The 3R, in case you were wondering, stands for the second house on the right. I'm sure you could send anything to Durwood Merrill C/O Hooks, Texas, and I'd get it. Or you could just drive down to Jimmy D.'s in the morning and catch me and rest of the boys drinking our coffee and knocking down some flapjacks.

I live on a thirty-acre ranch where we have twelve head of cattle, twelve donkeys, eight Canadian geese, two swans, six ducks, a pond filled with catfish, two dogs, and a few coyotes who sneak onto the property from time to time. The coyotes don't stay long because the donkeys like to gang up on them, grab them by the scruff of the neck, and bang them on the ground. The wrought iron sign above my swinging gate welcomes visitors to the "Field of Dreams."

I've seen a lot, done a lot, and met a heckuva lot of people over the years. I've known presidents and congressmen and some of the greatest athletes in the world. Right before the start of the 1991 baseball season, I got a phone call at my ranch in Hooks and the voice on the other end sounded a little peculiar.

"Mr. Merrill," the man said in a formal tone. "This is the White House calling. Now, Mr. Merrill, you may not be aware of this, but President George Bush is one of your biggest fans. I'm sure you're aware that President Bush is America's biggest baseball follower. Well, Mr. Merrill, the president will be in Arlington, Texas, tomorrow to throw out the ceremonial first pitch for the season opener of the Texas Rangers. And he'd like to borrow a piece of your equipment. Mr. Bush was wondering if he might wear your umpiring windbreaker with your number thirty-three on it."

Well, I'd heard enough from the man in the White House. As far as I knew, he was calling from the Nut House. I figured it was probably my next-door neighbor pulling another little practical joke on me. So I yelled into the phone, "Hang up, loser!" Then I hollered, "Give this little message to the president," and I slammed the receiver down so hard that I almost broke the phone.

I went about my business of packing for the start of the baseball season when the phone rang again about five minutes later. I picked it up and the man on the other end said, "Durwood, this is George W. Bush. Please don't hang up." Of course, I wasn't going to hang up on George W. For a moment, though, I thought my heart had stopped. "Durwood, you might not realize this," George W. continued, "but you just hung up on Marlin Fitzwater."

Yep, even I knew that Marlin Fitzwater was the president's media man. And, of course, I knew that George W. Bush was not only a minority owner of the Texas Rangers, he was the son of the president himself. In fact, I'd gotten to know George W. from my trips to Arlington Stadium and really liked the personable young man. What I didn't know was how to explain my lack of phone etiquette.

"Uh, George W.," I said, "I guess you figured by now that I've had some jokesters calling me lately. Tell the president I'm sorry. Normally, I don't make it a habit of hanging up on the White House."

Well, I guess the president was willing to forgive me because the next afternoon the door swung open in the umpires' room and in walked a couple of guys wearing dark suits and aviator sunglasses. They wore earplugs and carried walkie-talkies and had some pretty serious looks on their faces. They started sniffing around our little room in the bowels of Arlington Stadium, and they even searched through all of our bags. Now I can't say that I'd ever had the Secret Service rummaging through my equipment bag. But, at least, I knew we were all going to be safe from terrorist attacks on that first night of the baseball season.

A few minutes later, the president himself walked through the door, and, with a wide smile, he said, "Durwood, I can't tell you how long I've wanted to meet you. I've been a fan of yours from afar for a long time."

"Ditto for me, Mr. Prez," I said.

You'd have thought that two best friends had been reunited after thirty years. We laughed and joked and I began to think that maybe I was his favorite umpire after all. I knew that the president had been a first baseman back in his days at Yale, and that he'd been one big Boston Red Sox fan before he moved down to Texas and got his political career rolling. But I really had no idea that he knew as much about baseball as he did. He asked me about the nuances of certain pitchers and hitters, and even had some predictions about the season. I think he predicted that the Braves and the Twins would meet in the World Series and, if he did, the man was dead on the money.

Shoot, we got along so well that he invited me out to the armor-plated limousine that was sitting in the tunnel beneath the stadium. For about two hours, we talked about everything from politics to how to raise a family right. That day was especially gratifying because my son, Sergeant Mickey Merrill, had called to tell me and his mom that he was coming home from Desert Storm. Man, what a great feeling that was.

When I told the president how overjoyed we were about Mickey coming home, he just kind of looked away for a minute. Then I realized that a big ol' alligator tear was rolling down his cheek.

"Durwood," he said. "I'd like to sign a ball for the sergeant. Will you make sure that he gets it?"

"Doggone right, Mr. Prez," I said. Mickey, who's now coaching high school sports in Richardson, just outside of Dallas, still has the ball and, as you might expect, is pretty doggone proud of it.

A few minutes before the game started, I helped the president into my windbreaker with the number thirty-three on the right sleeve, and we were walking down the tunnel toward the field when I noticed that the two big Secret Service agents were shucking their suits and getting dressed in overalls. They had on big floppy hats and were carrying rakes. Their earpieces were still in place and they'd forgotten to take off their shades. So I tried not to laugh as I walked by.

Out on the field, as the president marched toward the mound and waved to the cheering crowd, I noticed that our two new groundskeepers were raking the soft dirt around home plate. I don't think anyone in the crowd noticed anything out of the ordinary. But standing along the third base line, I could see that both agents had Uzis protruding from their overalls. Those boys looked mighty weird with those big guns sticking out of their bibs. It was kind of like Jed Clampett and his brother had just joined the Secret Service.

The president had told me earlier that his greatest fear standing there on the mound would be bouncing the ball to home plate. I offered to warm him up before we went onto the field, but we never got around to it. The former Yalie had his old left-handed college mitt, and he could have kicked himself in the butt when he uncorked a one-hopper to the Rangers catcher. But he smiled like a good politician and managed to hide his embarrassment. But to this day, I would wager that President George Bush would rather have a long lunch with Ted Kennedy than to short-hop the ball to home plate in front of a sold-out ballpark.

I've seen George Bush a couple of times since he lost the White House to Bill Clinton, and I've become close friends with Governor George W. Bush, who became Texas's top man in 1995. The governor owned a share of the Rangers through January 1998, when the club was sold to a Dallas-based group.

The governor was at the Ball Park in Arlington in May of 1997 when I was working a series between the Rangers and Boston. I was standing at home plate, waiting for the lineup cards to be exchanged, when he started waving me over to his box seats just to the right of home plate. Rangers fans probably thought I'd lost my marbles when I ran over to the stands and started shaking hands with the governor and his family. I guess an umpire can get caught up in politics, too.

The 1997 season was a good one for me, and a great one for the Baltimore Orioles, who pretty much dominated the American League from opening day until the end of the season. The Yankees had made a couple of runs at Baltimore, but the Orioles led the American League East from wire to wire. New York got into the postseason as the wild card team before losing to the Indians in the divisional round. A lot was expected of the Orioles and they breezed by Seattle in their first-round series.

When you win ninety-eight games, and then out-hit your ALCS opponent by fifty-five points, fans normally expect you to wind up in the World Series. That's why the Orioles were feeling like a Kennedy who'd just lost a November election when they blew game six to Cleveland. You really couldn't blame the Orioles fans for just sitting there like all of the milk had been drained out of their Cheerios.

Right before the final game in Baltimore, I'd seen a banner that read, "There'll be no Indian summer." Another one said, "We stole your football team. Now we're going to steal the World Series." The Orioles backers, normally a laid-back bunch who spends more time talking on cell phones than cheering their ballclub, had turned downright loud and ugly.

In all of the postseason games I'd umpired, I can't remember two ballparks as loud as Oriole Park at Camden Yards and Cleveland's Jacobs Field. The umpires had to get in each other's faces just to talk, and I knew that my ears would be ringing for days. But when Cleveland's Tony Fernandez cracked a solo homer in the eleventh inning for a 1–0 lead, it was like a giant vacuum cleaner had sucked all of the sound and the madness right out of the place. In the end, the Orioles players just sat there slumped over in the dugout and their fans acted like they had no homes to return to. It was like they were waiting for the voice of God to say, "Hey, everybody, this is a big joke. Let's play one more inning."

When you put fourteen baserunners on, and you don't score in eleven innings, that's what happens. Cleveland pitcher Charles Nagy had teased the Birds like a topless woman standing atop the tote board on Kentucky Derby day. He allowed the lead-off hitter on base in five of the first eight innings. Then he yanked the wool right down over their eyes.

As I walked toward the tunnel behind home plate, I could see the word "denial" written all over Baltimore's dugout. They were just a sick bunch of puppies over there. Several more minutes would pass before reality sunk in and they'd trudge back to the clubhouse to meet the press. I was the last umpire off the field that evening and I almost got run over by the media army that had come charging down the tunnel and was now barreling toward both clubhouses. I couldn't believe that the doggone thing had finally ended, and that I'd be back on my ranch in Texas by noon the next day. As I headed down the concourse toward the umpires' dressing room, I felt about four tons of bricks crashing off both shoulders. The last eight days, and the last six games, had been the toughest stretch of umpiring that I'd ever been through in my life. Like the players and managers from both clubs, the six umpires who'd worked this series were totally spent.

Sure, I'd been in a lot of pressure cookers during my umpiring career, but working four- and five-hour games can shatter your nerves. My good friend John Hirschbeck was at third base for game six and he sauntered down the left field line after the eighth inning. Having worked every other spot on the field, I was now in the outfield. I could see the fatigue tugging at John's face as he said, "Dur, I really think I've hit the wall. I really don't know how much farther I can go."

For two straight days, John and I'd gotten more TV airtime than the Budweiser frogs. Our calls at home plate had come under more media scrutiny than the Clinton tapes. It'd gotten to the point where we'd walk into our hotel just a couple of blocks from Camden Yards and the fans would start pointing at us. The bellmen even knew our names. If this series hadn't ended after game six, we would've been taking the freight elevator back to our rooms like a couple of over-the-hill rock stars.

John and I could thank Tim McCarver for much of the misinformation that had turned us into neon signs. Tim played in the The Bigs for twenty-one seasons and he's been a TV talking dog since about 1981. The guy really should know something about baseball by now, and somebody needs to issue him a baseball rule book. Or, maybe, Tim could climb down out of the broadcast booth from time to time and get to know the game that he's trying to analyze. Tim, you see, hasn't come around much since Deion Sanders dumped an ice bucket on his head a few years ago.

Controversy grabbed baseball by the throat in game three, a four-hour-and-fifty-one-minute marathon which is the longest play-off game ever. It will also be remembered as the game that John Hirschbeck stood tall like a big oak tree and made one of the greatest calls at home plate in the history of baseball.

John had been a household name for more than a year, thanks to Baltimore second baseman Robbie Alomar turning him into a human spittoon one night in Toronto. But the real pressure of getting this call right was tethered to a foul-up at Yankee Stadium during the 1996 ALCS, when a twelve-year-old kid reached over the outfield railing and snagged a fly ball headed for Tony Tarasco's glove. Umpire Richie

Garcia, who was in right field, didn't see the fan interference and mistakenly ruled it a home run for the Yankees. The Orioles still claim that Garcia cost them a trip to the World Series, and there's little doubt that Richie, in spite of being a great umpire, will never live it down.

So when the dust had cleared from game three of the 1997 ALCS, and the Orioles had lost again, they naturally felt like pointing all fingers at the umpires. Only this time, baby, they were dead wrong. And so was Tim McCarver.

In truth, the game should have never gotten to the twelfth inning because the Indians led 1–0 in the bottom of the ninth and were ready to close the thing out, when center fielder Marquis Grissom lost a fly ball in the blue and orange sky that looked like a big Tahitian drink. Marquis said the ball, after clearing the light standards, just disappeared into some white smoke. Whatever, it landed twenty feet behind him and Baltimore's Jeff Reboulet easily scored from second to tie the game.

The Indians would blame me for a botched call at first base in the bottom of the ninth inning that would amount to nothing and was so borderline that even the TV replays couldn't help. I called catcher Sandy Alomar out to end the inning and again my man, McCarver, was saying in the booth, "Durwood Merrill called him out. But Sandy Alomar was safe."

Between innings, Indians manager Mike Hargrove, a guy I really like, came trotting out to first base. Things hadn't been going Mike's way and he snarled between clinched teeth, "Durwood, I just can't keep taking this. Everything's going against me. Everything, dammit!"

I knew what Mike was talking about. They'd blown a five-run lead in their first game in the divisional round against the Yankees. They'd lost the first game against Baltimore in the ALCS. He'd just watched helplessly as Marquis Grissom had been overcome by some strange voodoo in center field. Throwing his hands into the air, Hargrove blurted, "Durwood, I could've called that damm play from the dugout!"

"Now, hold on, Mike!" I snapped. "You and I are both from Texas and we both can spot a bullshitter from here to Amarillo. If you can call that one from the dugout, then let me go back over there with you." Knowing I was right, Mike turned on his heels and walked away. But I had something else on the tip of my tongue, and try as I might, I couldn't hold it. "By the way, Mike," I said. "You know, I didn't say anything when your center fielder blew a sure pop-up, now, did I?"

Between innings, first base coach Davey Nelson walked over to me and delivered what amounted to be a half apology. "Durwood, you've got to know just how frustrated we are over in that dugout," he said. "The breaks are going against us and Mike's going crazy." Davey paused and grinned. "By the way," he said. "About half the guys believe you got it right, and about half the guys believe you got it wrong. Me, I just don't know."

Some umpires will tell you that they really don't care if they get a call wrong. They believe that since they've got to make so many decisions every season, they're forgiven for a few bad ones. After all, even Golden Glove winners commit errors. Big Ken Kaiser once told me that he never worries about missing plays, and it's a good thing since he had a couple of tough calls in the 1997 World Series. Me, on the other hand, I normally shudder when I think I've really kicked one. I can't sleep that night and I don't feel good until I get back on the field the next day. My early years in umpiring, I might go back to the umpires' room and cry a little after missing a crucial call.

Umpires caught some flak in the postseason and some of it might have been justified. Ken Kaiser missed a call in game five of the World Series that might have turned the game around. Sure, I watched some of the National League Championship Series on TV and I know Eric Gregg took a lot of abuse for his strike zone in game five. I know that a lot of players, baseball writers, and broadcasters criticized Eric for ringing up strikes that seemed far off the plate. I'm not so sure that they were justified in ripping Eric because his strike zone has basically been the same for years. When an umpire establishes his strike zone, everybody in the league had better get ready to deal with it. You have to understand that no two strike zones are the same. If you have 32 umpires in the National League, and 32 in the American League, you're going to have 64 different strike zones. That's a fact of life in baseball bigger than corked bats and spitballs.

I know that the 1997 World Series brought to life the big disparity in the strike zones between the National and American League umpires. That's pretty funny when you consider that my esteemed brethren over in the N.L. have for decades had a larger strike zone than the umps from the A.L. This just didn't happen yesterday, you know. They say that A.L. umps have shoebox strike zone and that's pretty funny when you consider that I've got one of the bigger strike zones in either leagues. I must wear some pretty big shoes.

The 1997 season may have been the most controversial I can remember for the umpires. Thanks to the Robbie Alomar spitting incident, the umpires asked for a code of conduct from Major League Baseball and were basically rebuffed. That's why our union chief, Richie Phillips, drew a line in the sand before the start of the '97 postseason, telling the players and managers to stay off the umpires. He notified the both leagues that we'd eject anyone who got within an arm's length of us. The Baseball Lords tried to tell Richie that he was violating the collective bargaining agreement by unilaterally imposing conditions on players and managers. I don't think you ever really *tell* Richie anything. He's a fighter and a battler and a guy who is generally disliked all over baseball. But when it comes to taking care of umpiring business, there's never been anyone better. By golly, we need somebody to stand up for us in the face of this abuse we've been taking. Call him a bully, but his tactics are no worse than the ones used by some managers I'd known through the years.

Is there a war going on between the umpires and everyone else in baseball? I don't really think so. But don't push it because this this could escalate pretty quickly. Somebody among the Baseball Lords needs to step forward and mend this rift before it gets out of hand. The baseball power brokers like to drag their feet, so I don't think we'll have our code of conduct any time soon. It's time that we all start getting along.

After the controversial call in game three, I naturally cued up the VCR in the umpires' room to take a gander at my controversial piece of work. I ran it backward and forward and in slow-motion. I saw Cal Ripken field the high hop and make the looping throw, and I saw Sandy Alomar lumber down the first base line. In my mind, I could hear the thunder of the crowd. I showed it to my fellow umpires and we all concurred. It was simply too close to call.

Let me point out that I'm a big believer in instant replay for reversing certain umpiring calls. Just think if Richie Garcia had been able to use instant replay to reverse his big boo-boo in the '96 ALCS. The whole mess could've been cleaned up in about three minutes. With my call in Cleveland, though, I really don't think TV could have reversed it. Even from a lot of different angles, you just couldn't see the whole play on one camera. You couldn't get a really clear view of the ball hitting the mitt and the foot hitting the bag.

In the whole scheme of things, my little play at first base was the equivalent of one deck chair blowing off the *Titanic*. There were too many other factors to point a finger at. For instance, the Indians would get runners at second and third with nobody out in the eleventh inning without pushing home the winning run. You had the Grissom fly ball. You also had the Indians, leading 1–0, blowing a potential double play in the ninth inning that could have ended the game.

The clinching play finally came in the bottom of the twelfth with Grissom at third and Omar Vizquel at third base. Hargrove had foregone the squeeze bunt in the eleventh inning, which, I'm sure, had further fed his frustration. But I had a sneaking feeling that Mike wouldn't make the same mistake again. Then I heard Davey Nelson whispering something to his runner at first base.

A lot of times, the first base coach will tip an umpire to

the squeeze play at home so he won't be caught off guard. So I sneaked a glance at Nelson and he formed the two magic words with his mouth: "Squeeze play." I felt my heart accelerate as I moved two steps closer to home plate. In these situations, it's the job of the first and third base umpires to help the plate man with the call. I saw Grissom make his break and then I heard voices from the Baltimore dugout: "He's going! He's going!" Heeding the warning, catcher Lenny Webster tried to sneak a peek around Vizquel. Taking his eye off Randy Myers's pitch for one instant was a costly mistake. Vizquel squared to bunt and, as he poked at the low pitch, the ball cleared the bat by about two inches. Even from about ninety feet, I knew it wasn't a foul tip. Webster, who had lost sight of the ball for a split second, would feel it bounce off the heel of his glove. Then, he casually watched it roll in front of home plate. Grissom scored easily and John Hirschbeck's two quick signs made my heart soar. He signaled a strike on Vizquel, and then he signaled Grissom safe at home. John was dead right and the game was over.

Even though the Fat Lady had sung, I knew there was plenty of shouting still to be done. Davey Johnson came roaring out of the Baltimore dugout and frantically argued the call with Hirschbeck. Up in the booth, McCarver was saying, "Why did John Hirschbeck signal foul ball and then change his mind?" People who know baseball knew that John raised his right hand to signal a strike, not to call a foul tip. Naturally, he then followed with the safe sign for Grissom. John would say later to the media, "If it'd been foul, I would have thrown up my arms and stopped play." The Orioles would review the videotape far into the night and, like everyone else, they were left with three conclusions: John was right, McCarver was wrong, and the game was still over.

Standing on the field for almost five hours, any umpire will tell you that fatigue makes poor judges of us all. Marathon games are the curse of umpires because you just can't think as clearly after that much time on your feet and all that pressure on your head. That's why John's bang-bang play at the plate was even more impressive, and why our little um-pires' room was full of life after the game. It was good to see American League president Dr. Gene Budig, along with umpiring executive director Marty Springstead and his assistant, Phil Jansen, walk through the door after the game. They all had big smiles and Dr. Budig, while shaking hands all around the room, said, "You know, guys, the pressure didn't get to you. I can't tell you how proud I am of each and every one of you. It was one of the best umpired games I've ever seen."

As I looked around the room, I studied the eyes of my fellow umpires—Jimmy Joyce, Joe Brinkman, Mike Reilly, John Hirschbeck, and Larry McCoy. God, I thought about the years that I'd spent with each man on crews that had worked together in every American League park. I thought about the managers who'd cussed us and tried to cheat us and of all the players who went off like Roman candles after being caught looking at strike three. I thought about the hot little tangos with Billy Martin and Earl Weaver and the afternoon in Oakland when I thought I was going to have to toss the entire A's team out of the game. I also thought about the real joy of umpiring and the great relationships I've had with players like George Brett and Reggie Jackson and Ken Griffey Jr. I thought that, in spite of the headaches and the constant travel and homesick days on the road, I'd probably still have a smile on my face when I hung up the mask. Baseball is a crazy biz, but you've still got to love it.

McCoy had been on my first crew when I was a rookie back in 1977. He and Joe Brinkman helped raise me as an umpire when I was young and restless and just itching to establish myself in The Bigs. In those early years, I'd throw players and managers out of games for unnecessary breathing. This was about the time that Ron Luciano was retiring from umpiring and calling me his heir apparent. Talk about a mantle to carry around with you. Ronnie, who would write four books and sell truckloads of them, was not only a great showman, but he also might have been the biggest pain in the ass to ever wear the mask. The big suits in the

American League office never liked Ronnie and were pushing him toward the retirement door. So you can imagine what my bosses were thinking when they heard another Luciano was coming off the assembly line. Baseball execs would spend the next few years making sure I didn't get out of control.

Reilly came along the same year I was promoted from the minor leagues, and Hirschbeck joined us in 1984. John has rubbed some people the wrong way through the years because he's brash and he speaks his mind, especially in the heat of the moment. You'd better not cross John, or try to get in his face, because he'll teach you a few words that you haven't yet heard. But you've got to give John a lot of credit, especially for the work that he did in the 1997 ALCS. Everywhere he turned, John was hearing about the spitting incident with Robbie Alomar, and everybody was wondering if he'd ever try to get even. That's a lot of pressure for an umpire to carry around.

Jimmy Joyce was the youngest of the crew members and he came into the American League in 1989. Not only does he win a lot of style points for his work behind home plate, the guy's a real pro.

With everybody sitting around, just kind of relaxed, we had some time to reminisce and to tell some stories about the lives we'd been leading in this crazy game. I could see Dr. Budig's eyes getting bigger as the stories got funnier. McCoy remembered some fun we'd had back during my rookie year in 1977, when Larry was trying to lose a few pounds. This is how Larry remembered it: "Now, I told Durwood that I was trying to watch my weight because I'd been eating way too much in the off-season. I said, 'Durwood, if you see me eating too much, you just tell me to stop. And if I won't stop, then I want you to physically stop me, dang it. Do whatever you have to. Tie me up, whatever. But, by God, you've got to stop me from eating too much.'

"Well, we were in Minnesota and they brought the food in after the game. They brought in ribs and cole slaw and and potato salad. So I just sat down and started pigging out.

I finished everything they brought into the room. Then I wiped my mouth and said, 'Hey, rookie, you're really following instructions aren't you. I thought you were gonna help me out here.' So the next night, they brought in a big platter of chicken breasts and they were all perfectly Southern fried. I grabbed the biggest one on the platter and just started gobbling. The next thing I know, the room is turned upside down. The ceiling lights are where the floor used to be, and the floor's where the ceiling used to be. It then hit me that I'd been body-slammed by this big bear named Durwood. I looked up and Durwood's sitting on top of me with a chicken breast still in his hand. And he's still chomping down on it.''

That rookie season, I was awfully nervous about the first game that I'd umpire in the state of Texas. It would be the first and last time that my mother and father would watch me umpire a major league game together. Mom died a few years later. I must have had fifty family members and friends drive down to Arlington from my little hometown in Hooks, and there was enough pressure on me to fill up Yankee Stadium on the seventh game of the World Series. Larry picked up the story: ''That doggone Durwood got about thirty-five tickets that night and we still had to let another thirty-five of his friends walk through the umpires' room so they could get in the ballpark.

''That first inning, Durwood was having trouble with the strike zone. No, let me put it this way. I've never seen an umpire having more trouble with balls and strikes in my life. Dennis Leonard is on the hill for the Kansas City Royals and I'm umping second base. About halfway through the first inning, Dennis turns around to me and yells, 'Hey, Larry. That Durwood character is getting them mixed up. The ones out of the strike zone, he's calling strikes. And the ones over the plate, he's calling balls.' Now I'm just laughing my butt off and wondering how the hell we're going to get this thing fixed. Problem is, Leonard's pretty well got Durwood figured out and he's started throwing everything about six inches off the plate. And Durwood's calling them all strikes.

"Well, back then, the Rangers and the Royals were known for bench-clearing brawls about every other night. In the fourth inning, a real bugger breaks out. Fists are flying and guys are getting wrestled to the ground and there's a big dog pile right in the middle of the field. It takes about thirty minutes to break up the fights and we have to throw five or six players and both managers out of the game. By the time the whole dang thing is over, the umpires are totally sweated out and exhausted. We're huffing and puffing and all standing around the mound when Don Denkinger, who was working first base, looked at Durwood and said, 'I hope to hell you're over your nervous jitters.' Sure enough, Durwood started calling the good ones strikes, and the bad ones balls. The Big Fella just buzzed through the next five innings without a glitch. I do remember Dennis Leonard being so confused that they had to take him out of the game, though.''

Of course, everybody in the umpires' room is laughing so hard at Larry's story that their jaws and ribs were aching. And to think we'd just finished one of the toughest games we'll ever umpire in our lives and we should be lying on the floor in total exhaustion. The real fun part was seeing our big boss, Dr. Gene Budig, laughing along like one of the boys. Dr. Budig is an educated man who was the chancellor of Kansas University and recently had a building named in his honor. He's a highbrow kind of guy who came down to our room to offer some moral support, and ended up watching stand-up comedy.

Marty Springstead, the head of A.L. umpiring, looked around the room and said, "You boys can laugh and cut up now because tomorrow, Durwood's gonna be conducting church in here.''

How right he was. On the day that I work the plate, I'm no longer the jovial fun-loving Yogi Bear who everybody's gotten to know over the last couple of decades. I don't sleep well the night before I have the plate, and I'm grumpier than Jack Lemmon and Walter Matthau combined when I get up in the morning. I have no desire for food and that says a lot about somebody who's got an "All-World Omelette" that'd choke a gorilla named for him back in Texas.

From the moment I get up in the morning until the game is over, all I think about is working that plate and calling balls and strikes. I'm just like a hitter in that I visualize pitches and I try to calculate what's coming next. I ask myself, "What does Scott Erickson throw with a two-one count against a man in the middle of the order?" If one of the pitchers going that night has a nasty sinker, I'll focus on the bottom of my strike zone. If he's got the big curve, I'll think about where to draw the line on the outside corner of the plate. If I'm facing a knuckleballer, I go into the bathroom and get sick.

I got to the ballpark for game four several hours before the first pitch. I looked at the platter of chopped barbecued chicken and felt my appetite ball up and go straight into my throat. We were working a tension-packed 2–1 series led by Cleveland, and we were coming off a game that didn't just end; it'd erupted like a volcano. There'd be 45,000 screaming fans watching from Jacobs Field, and millions more on TV, and a good number of those people would still talking about what the doggone umpires had done to screw up game three. I dug through my travel kit for the Pepto-Bismol.

An hour or so before the first pitch, the umpires' valet delivered a couple of hot dogs, and I watched them and smelled them and savored them. Those hot dogs were the only things that had looked good enough to eat in almost twenty-four hours. I could've cried that I hadn't ordered them myself. Hirschbeck was the lucky man who'd gotten the weiners. I could just imagine him smothering them with mustard, relish, and onions, and having a big feast.

John's locker was right next to mine, and when I walked back into the dressing area, my eyes homed in on an entree of utter delight. Right there in my cubicle sat one of the hot dogs, and it was prettier than an East Texas chicken-fried steak smothered with white cream gravy.

Putting his hand on my shoulder, John asked, "Durwood, do you really think I'd have ordered me a hot dog without ordering you one?'' As I stuffed it down my throat, I mumbled, ''God bless you, John Hirschbeck.''

As the game approached, I really could feel the clock ticking in the pit of my stomach. All I have to do is check my pulse rate to know the difference between a game played in the postseason and one during the dog days of August. Umpires in October are just like players in the post-season because we're out there laying everything on the line. Ask any major league player about the play-offs and he'll tell you that he's finding energy in his body that he didn't know existed.

When an umpire says that he doesn't have fear in his heart, he's just whistling through the graveyard. The last thing you want to do in the postseason is to make a bad call that can turn a game around, because it could mean the end of the line for one of the teams. When an umpire is assigned to the postseason, you shudder at the thought of missing the call that could turn the entire series around. I was so antsy and irritable in the week leading to the ALCS that my son, Mickey, told my wife, Carolyn, that she should lock me in the back pasture with the twelve donkeys.

Some of my very close friends have missed calls in the postseason that still haunt their lives. Larry Barnett will never live down a controversial call at home plate in the 1975 Word Series. Don Denkinger still sees his botched call at first base in the 1985 World Series replayed over and over and over. St. Louis fans still blame Don for costing them the World Series against Kansas City. And the call that is still fresh on everyone's memory is Richie Garcia not seeing the kid leaning over the rail to steal a ball from Tony Tarasco. To their credit, all three of those umpires were able to move on with their careers, and are still considered three of the best in the business.

Me, I doubt I could ever forget missing a call in a play-off series. I've umpired a lot of games in October, and I thank my lucky stars that it's never happened. But it weighed heavily on my mind as I got ready to stroll into the eye of the hurricane in game four of the ALCS. With Scott Erickson on the hill for Baltimore and rookie sensation Jaret Wright going for Cleveland, I yelled "Play ball!"

My reputation at the plate is that I've got a big strike zone, and if you don't like it, I'll yell, "Get the damn bat off your shoulder. Fans don't pay big bucks to see you walk." Hitters from Baltimore and Cleveland know all about my strike zone, so they came to the plate with limber lumber. It was a lively tempo from the first inning and I knew that both starting pitchers were wading into troubled waters. Erickson had dominated the Indians by throwing a shutout in game one of the series, but now Cleveland was on him like stink on an oyster. Wright's great fastball was getting rocked, and I knew he wasn't going to live up to his press clippings.

The Indians were playing to their strength—hitting the long ball with runners on base. Sandy Alomar, who'd been struggling his last few times at the plate, went to a lighter bat and smoked a two-run shot. In the fifth inning, he was on second base when all hell broke loose. Catcher Lenny Webster let a ball scoot past him and then he made a weak flip to pitcher Arthur Rhodes, who was covering home. Dave Justice scored easily from third base and, as the ball rolled about ten feet to left of the plate, Alomar set his sights on home. Justice and Webster got tangled a few feet from the plate, and I could see Alomar and Cal Ripken Jr. in a footrace from third to home. Alomar knew that, since Webster was down, all he had to do was outrun Cal to the plate.

Smack-dab in the middle of this chaos was me. There were so many bodies strewn around home plate that you almost expected Marcus Allen to come flying over the pile for a touchdown. As Justice scored, I threw both arms in the air, looking like an overfed big bird trying to take flight. Since the ball was now lying on the ground, I started pointing to it, just as they had taught me in umpiring school. I know this must have seemed confusing to the broadcasters in the Fox booth because, once again, McCarver was motoring his mouth into an area he knew nothing about—umpiring.

Rhodes picked up the ball and flipped it toward Ripken, who was running alongside Alomar. Clearly, the runner was safe and, again, I was standing on my toes, arms flailing and signaling the runner safe. As the Fox cameras caught my act, the phone was ringing at my house back in Hooks. A friend called Carolyn and said, "You see, I knew that Durwood could dance after all." Since I'm the son of a Baptist preacher, I guess nobody thought I had those kinds of moves.

Not one person in the stands doubted I was right on the money in calling both runners safe. But manager Davey Johnson still thought he had a gripe because Cleveland's Justice had leaned on his catcher, Webster, who was unable to scramble to his feet and cover the plate. "Dammit, Durwood, my catcher was pinned down," Davey said.

Davey might have been right in calling for interference if Justice had deliberately sat on the catcher, or tried to hold him. But Justice was just trying to get the hell out of the way so Rhodes could toss the ball to Ripken. All of this became pretty clear in a *Sports Illustrated* picture that had Justice, Alomar, and Webster on the ground with Ripken fielding the ball that'd been tossed by Rhodes. Right there in traffic central was me, signaling Alomar safe with all of the vigor of a condor trapped in a swamp. For a guy who is no spring chicken, I thought I looked pretty much like Fred Astaire wrapped in plastic. Tim McCarver, of course, didn't think so.

As the chaotic play at home was replayed several times for the Fox viewers, he kept saying, "Why is Durwood Merrill pointing at the ball?" A little later, McCarver blurted, "Maybe Durwood's trying to tell the Orioles where the ball is." Then came the dumbest remark I've ever heard, even for McCarver. "Maybe Durwood Merrill is trying to tell himself where the ball is."

I guess I'm going to get a job as a bus driver so I can take Tim to school. He obviously didn't know that umpires are taught on the second day of umpiring school to do exactly what I did at home plate. If the ball is loose, the closest umpire is supposed to point so the others will know he's aware of where it is. Otherwise, one of the other umpires is going to come running in to help the home plate umpire find the ball. It's just that simple. My whole objective in pointing to the ball was to tell the other five umpires that I had everything under control, and that I knew exactly where the ball was.

Since Tim was a player himself, I know exactly what he was thinking. It's the mindset of players and managers to cheat whenever they get a chance. They believe it is the equivalent of their First Amendment right in baseball to cheat. I have a quote on my office wall back in Texas that reads "Cheating in baseball is just like hot dogs, french fries, and cold Cokes." The author of that quote, of course, is Billy Martin, and even though Billy is long gone, that kind of thinking still exists in our grand old game.

The Cleveland Indians didn't have to cheat that night because their bats were hot, and Sandy Alomar blasted an Armando Benitez fastball to the warning track in the ninth inning to drive in the winning run. The Indians had just completed one of the most hectic weekends in American League history by taking game four, 8–7. But there were still plenty of tension-packed moments ahead.

Thanks to a two-run dinger by Eric Davis, the Orioles won Monday night to cut their series deficit to 3–2. Now we were on the road back to Baltimore, where the fans were shot full of raw energy and their hopes were eight miles high. And why not? With their ace, Mike Mussina, back on the mound, Baltimore looked almost like a cinch to tie up the series and send this thing to game seven. Of course, they'd wasted a heroic effort by Mussina on Saturday when he struck out fifteen and didn't allow a run. But that was before some pretty crazy things happened and the Indians pulled off a win in the twelfth inning.

The deeper we went into the series, the worse the food looked, even in Baltimore where the crab cakes just melt in your mouth. One consistent thing about umpires is that we clean our plates. Most of us have been on serious exercise regimens the last decade and you'll find that a lot of the guys are in pretty good shape. But we've still got some guys who have to fight their weight every step of the way these days.

In this series, though, we were eating just to exist. The morning before game six, I went to breakfast with Mike Reilly. Since he had the plate that day, he decided to order a small chicken sandwich. As we were leaving the restaurant, he turned and said, "I ate my sandwich and it pretty well filled me up. But I don't think that I tasted one bite." For eight days, most of us had barely even tasted our food.

As the tension built, Hirschbeck, Joyce, and myself would sit in the back of the dressing room and act like we were shaving our heads for a trip to the electric chair. We were laughing on the outside, but I think we were all pretty tense on the inside.

Now, I really figured that Mussina would mow down the Indians in game six, and he was about as strong as you could be through the first eight innings. His fastball was still whistling in at ninety-three mph. When Davey Johnson decided to pull Mussina to start the ninth, I think it was the boo-boo of the whole series. In a scoreless game, I really can't think of a guy I'd rather have on the mound than Mussina, who's a bulldog. But the Baltimore relievers had been so dominant through the regular part of the season that I guess you couldn't blame Davey for going to the best closer in the American League, Randy Myers. The problem, though, was that that the Birds couldn't push a single run across and Myers, like most closers, just couldn't go more than two innings. So Davey had to turn to Armando Benitez in the eleventh and that's when Fernandez shocked Camden Yards into a deathly silence with his one-run shot.

While the Indians were expending their last ounce of energy on a postgame celebration, and the Orioles were trying to figure what had gone so wrong, the umpires were wrapped in a six-man bear hug in our little room beneath the complex. I've never seen a crew so happy, and so relieved, that a series had finally ended. We'd given blood, sweat, and tears to this series and we'd been berated, booed, and finally vindicated. As *Baltimore Sun* columnist John Eisenberg said, "Nobody in Baltimore was blaming the umpires this time. They had no reason to do that. You get 14 men on base, and you can't get them home, that pretty much tells the story.''

Again, Dr. Budig came to our little dressing room after the game and he was thrilled with what he'd seen. ''You just can't umpire any better than you guys did in this series,'' he said. I saw a tear trickle down the cheek of our umpiring boss, Marty Springstead. Mike Reilly kissed Joe Brinkman on the cheek.

Later, Dr. Budig took me to the side and said, ''Now, Durwood, I don't think I've ever seen a man as intense about his job who really enjoys it as much as you do. Keep that big smile on your face and stay humble.''

As you might expect, I really do like and appreciate Dr. Budig, although I can't say that feeling exists in the rank-and-file of American League umpires. I think that Dr. Budig is basically a caring man. I know that opinion would be challenged by a lot of my fellow umpires. But if you want my opinion, I really think that his heart is in the right place.

It took only about thirty minutes for the six of us to get dressed and to start the trek back to our hotel just two blocks away. I barely recognized a city that had been filled with electricity just an hour earlier. Camden Yards sounded like a freight train rumbling through town. But now, the place was dead. ''Where in the heck did everybody go?'' I asked Joe Brinkman. You'd see a few pockets of people headed up the sidewalk, but they talked in hushed voices.

Before the game, as we headed over to the ballpark, the city had been alive. People were dressed in orange and black and the office buildings were covered with computer paper spelling out ''O's.'' The lobby of the hotel had been jam-packed, but now it was empty and quiet. It was like a vicious storm had blown through, leaving nothing behind but puddles.

After going to our rooms to call the families back home, the umpires reconvened in the hotel lobby. For the first time in the series we were all going out to dinner together. And I can tell you that the food at Sabatino's in Baltimore that night never tasted better in my life.

I hit the streets at five the next morning and hailed a

taxicab for the ride to the airport. After all the hell and high water that had passed through that city, Baltimore was now in mourning. My cabdriver, Ron Reightler, was leading the wake. He kept shaking his head and saying, "How could this happen? I can't believe this just happened to my team."

"Sir," I said. "I don't know how it happened, either. But my day is done, and now it's time for me to go home."

Dumber than a
Steer . . .

OLD COACHES NEVER DIE. They start selling insurance or get promoted to high school principal. Or they ride off to the golf course. Me, I became an umpire in the major leagues. I heard it was a glamorous job. That was only a rumor.

I wouldn't exactly say I was old at age thirty-two. But I was a lot older than most of the young turks who decide to start chasing that umpiring dream. At the time, I was still listening to Buddy Holly. ZZ Top, I thought, was some kind of strange voodoo.

I like to call my wife, Carolyn, "Mama." Just about everybody around Hooks calls her that, too. We were watching the Saturday afternoon *Game of the Week* late in the 1971 season—it must have been September—and, as fate would have it, the address for an umpiring school appeared on the TV screen. Mama grabbed a pen and piece of paper and wrote it down.

Back then, the umpiring schools wanted to see a résumé. Nowadays, you plunk down your money and you go running off to six weeks of pure hell and denigration. So I sent a letter and my résumé off to the school. And I waited.

I'd reached a crossroads in my life and I knew it. I could feel the clock ticking. My mind was starting to wander. I knew I was burned out on coaching high school kids, even though we'd won a slew of championships at Hooks High School. My baseball teams won three straight state titles and finished second another time. Hooks had never won much in football until I came along in 1963, and even then, it took me a while to turn the thing around. When we went 2–8 my first year as head coach, I thought they were going to run me plumb out of town. But we tied for the district title in 1965 and won it outright the next year, and we averaged winning about seven games a year.

While I was the athletic director, our teams won sixteen straight district titles from football to basketball to golf to baseball to track. We swept district championships in every sport in 1966. I was a good motivator and a good coach. People around Hooks would tell you that. But there was something that I couldn't get off my mind. Umpiring.

Back then, I was a big St. Louis Cardinals fan. The Rangers hadn't moved to Texas from Washington. So we made a lot of long driving trips up the Arkansas two-laners into Missouri and St. Louis. We watched Stan Musial and Bob Gibson and those great teams of the '60s. What I really watched were the umpires. I was fascinated with the way the umpires positioned themselves and with their footwork. They were always in the right place at the right time. I told Mama that I thought I could become a big-time umpire if I could just get a little instruction. Coaching had given me this great love of sports. Now I wanted to take it a step further.

Coaching just didn't satisfy me anymore. My heart was someplace else. That's why I'd taken a principal's job, and why my mind was dead set on umpiring. It was like I was married to something and didn't know it.

About two months after I sent my letter to Bill Kinnamon's umpiring school, I got a letter from a guy named Barney Deary, the guy who ran their minor league program. I'd been accepted. They told me to report to St. Petersburg in late January. I thought I'd hit the jackpot. I was going off to a school where the lead instructor was Bill Kinnamon, a major league umpire from 1960 through 1969. Kinnamon was behind the plate in 1961 for Roger Maris's sixtieth and record-breaking sixty-first home run. I was sure he had a lot to teach me and a lot of stories to tell.

As I was preparing for umpiring school, I could sense some strange vibes from my closest friends around Hooks. They weren't saying it to my face. But some of them thought I'd gone off the deep end. Here was a man with a good job, a great wife, two wonderful kids, and I was driving off to Florida to start a new life. It was almost like I'd taken leave of my mind. Ol' Durwood, they were saying behind my back, was just bailing out on everything he'd built. I knew that my dad and my mama had some serious reservations. But they never said a word.

My first day in St. Petersburg quickly changed my romantic view of professional umpiring. They stuck me in a cubbyhole down below the bleachers of a Little League complex. It had no air-conditioning. It seemed hotter than Amarillo on Fourth of July. I'd wake up in the middle of the night in puddles of sweat on my bunk bed.

I learned quickly that umpiring school is a cross between going to marine boot camp and mucking horse stalls. The instructors yell at you for six straight weeks. They say there's a method to their madness. But I never could figure it out. My friend and fellow umpire Rocky Roe once said about umpiring school, "It's twenty guys sleeping on bunk beds, farting, wheezing, coughing, puking, and trying to survive the dog days without air-conditioning."

I really didn't know what to expect. I just know that I expected something better than what they had. We didn't have many luxuries. It was primitive living. If you wanted to make a call, there was a pay phone out there nailed to a pole.

The Umpire Hilton was built to house kids, not a bunch of grown men. There were no windows and virtually no ventilation. Some guys bought fans to help circulate the hot air.

They divided the barracks with reed-thin partitions, and we slept twelve men to a room on bunk beds. Since the beds were built for twelve-year-olds, we all looked pretty funny with our feet hanging off the end. We were so closely quartered, and the walls were so thin, that you could hear a guy snoring from far down the hall. Sometimes the snoring sounded like a chorus of overfed bullfrogs.

Right in the middle of the Umpire Hilton was a long stall with showers. I guess we looked like a herd of cows all soaped up.

Our alarm clock at seven in the morning was an old cook banging a big pot with a metal spoon. I jumped out of bed early every morning because I wanted a little privacy in the showers. I never missed breakfast, which was seven until eight-thirty. The guys with hangovers would sleep until the nine o'clock rules meetings.

From eleven until noon we would do calisthenics and we'd work on our out-safe and ball-strike signs. After a small lunch, we hit the field for a grueling afternoon. There were four Little League fields situated around one big park with major league dimensions.

Most of the instruction was from about one o'clock until four, when we would break off and umpire a high school or a junior college game on the main field. If you needed some personal instruction or some tutoring, the instructors would help you from six to seven.

The fields were alive every afternoon with the sounds of guys yelling and screaming and cussing. A lot of frustration was being vented. Guys like me were always face-to-face with some drill sergeant instructor with a voice like a foghorn. There was a high school right next door to our fields. About two in the afternoon, you'd see the principal walking over to the fence, waving his arms, telling us to knock it off or tone it down. That man probably didn't want his kids growing up to be umpires.

Most of us had been pretty good amateur umpires. So the instructors' first job is to tear you down piece by piece and then teach you their system. They wanted you to forget everything you'd already learned. You'd either do it their way or take the highway home. They teach you how to walk. They teach you how to put on your cap, how to put on your mask, and how to take off your mask. They teach you to call a strike, a ball, and an out. They even told us when to go to the bathroom. It kind of reminded me of high school coaching. Only this time, I was the one getting knocked around.

Job one is determining if you can handle stress. That is what separates the quitters from the keepers. You've got about six marine drill sergeants out there masquerading as instructors. They want to know if you'll cower like a beaten dog or if you'll handle the heat. They're looking for that chink in your psychological armor. They are constantly in your face, yelling and and cussing and spitting and spreading around a lot of bad breath. You might have one instructor playing the role of the hostile manager and another one pretending to be the hacked-off hitter. Before the dust settles, you've got to throw three or four instructors out of the game just to restore order. They want to know if you've got any backbone.

You'll have a close play at second base, and you'll call the runner safe. You turn around and one of the instructors, pretending to be the manager, is yelling and spitting in your face. "What the f—— do you think you're doing? There's no way he's safe, you stupid sumbitch!" You've got to react quickly. You can't back down or stutter. You've got to defend your call and stand your ground. At first, the instructors don't care if you've made the right call. They just want to know if you've got the guts to back it up.

It was obvious from the start that my chances of surviving, or even graduating, were no larger than a popcorn fart. With a hundred students, the odds didn't look too favorable. I was told that less than 5 percent of the students normally made it to the minor leagues, and 1 percent got to the majors. But I wasn't too good with odds anyway. I never frequented the horse tracks.

My age wasn't helping matters. Here I was, at least ten years older than most of the kids in camp. And I stuck out like an unraked bunker at The Masters. To make matters worse, I couldn't get anything right. The instructors were on my butt every minute of the day. They thought I was dumber than a steer at an orgy.

Umpiring school is where I met Steve Palermo, a skinny

and cocky kid who was a natural umpire. He was like a lightweight fighter from Boston. He was so thin that you almost expected the next strong gust of wind to blow him over. I was the roughneck football coach from a little town in East Texas. At first, I couldn't understand a word he was saying. And vice versa. Stevie was the best candidate in umpiring school. You couldn't intimidate him. He wouldn't have flinched if you'd set off a firecracker in his back pocket. This kid was unflappable. Every move was perfect and they could never back him into a corner. On the other hand, I missed just about every other call the first two weeks of camp. I'd look over and there would be this skinny kid just folded over, laughing at me. Funny thing is that it made me laugh, too. Stevie and I were instant friends.

About halfway through camp, I decided that I couldn't take it anymore. So I walked out to the pay phone nailed to a pole and called Mama back in Hooks and told her that I was finished and was headed home. "I can't do anything right," I said. "This is not what I thought it'd be, Mama. I think that I've had it."

"Fine," Mama said. "But how are you going to face these kids back here in Hooks? You've preached to these kids for ten years. You told the kids to stick it out when things got tough. And now you're going to quit after just two weeks. It's against all of your basic beliefs to quit. But if you want to come on home and face the shame, then come on!"

With head bowed and big fat tears rolling down my face, I mumbled, "You're right, Mama. We're going to see this thing until the end. I promise, Mama. I'm going to make it through one way or the other." When I hung up the phone, I felt lower than a toad on a flat rock. I told myself, "You can't even go home, rockhead. You've run plumb out of options." I had no choice. I was staying in Florida until the bitter end, or until the alligators ate me.

Now, I don't consider myself to be a baseball Einstein. But an idea popped into my head that may have saved my umpiring career. I walked down to the closest little dime store and bought a big sheet of poster board. Then I gathered some loose change. I drew a big baseball diamond on the poster board. For the base runners, I used pennies. For the umpires, I used dimes. And I would try to imagine every possible scenario in a baseball game. With runners at first and second, the ball would be hit into left field. Then I'd position the two umpires according to the play.

At night, when everyone else was going out to dinner or the bars, I'd stay in my hot little cubbyhole and work with my poster board. One night I was down on my hands and knees when Frank Pulli, a great umpire and one of our instructors, walked in. He chuckled and then he got down on the floor with me. He was on his hands and knees, just like me, and I think he admired what I was doing. I would work with my little board night after night until the wee hours. I would work until I was exhausted. It finally started coming together. I was getting better on the field.

My biggest hurdle was learning the two-umpire system. They taught us the two-man system because that's what we'd be using in the minor leagues. That is, if I made it. It just seemed that in the two-man system I had to be all over the field all the time. All the while, the instructors were chasing me around the field like a loose calf.

Big John McSherry may have been the most intimidating man I'd met to that point in my life. (Big John would die of a heart attack on Opening Day in 1996 at Cincinnati's Riverfront Stadium. He just tipped over face first and died right there on the ground behind home plate. That was one of my saddest days.)

Big John, in the spring of 1972, seemed larger than life to me. For a big guy, he moved just like a cat. He had the feet of a prizefighter. And he was a genius of an umpire. He could scan the field and tell you instantly that you'd just taken two steps the wrong way. John was also a big screamer. They'd send a runner sliding into second base and I'd call the guy out, and Big John would be standing there, hands on hips, just bellowing in my ear like a big cow. Since John was from New York, he was the Billy Martin of cutdowns and put-downs. That man could just unravel me.

Then, one day, the screaming toned down a little. Then a little bit more the next day. Instead of hollering at me all of the time, he was making fun of me. Pretty soon, I was carrying Big John's clipboard around, acting like his first assistant. I'd follow him around the field, and he'd call me his liaison officer—whatever the hell that meant.

Big John would laugh and say, "Ya'll know this boy from Texas. Well, his name is Durwood. Where he got that name, I don't know. But he's gonna make a pretty funny-looking umpire, don't you think?"

One day, the instructors had us choose up a team to play the local junior college team in an exhibition game. John made me the captain and the coach. John said, "Durwood, you'll either lead us to victory, or I'll run your butt around this field for three straight days." We won the game, and I think Big John liked me even more.

Day by day, I was doing better in the drills. My problem wasn't with judgment or even with making the right call. They say that you're either blessed with judgment or you're not. I guess I was a natural-born umpire. But I needed to improve my mechanics. By the fourth week, I was starting to feel better about how I was handling myself on the field. My scores on the written tests were getting better.

I kept staying in the barracks at night, studying all of the situations with my little poster board. While the young guns were out barhopping and chasing women, I was sleeping. My physical conditioning was improving. The instructors would run us around the field until our tongues hung out. The guys who'd been drinking the night before were puking it up all over the field. Me, I was hanging together just fine. I was running farther and faster than the boys ten years younger. Some of them were busting out—pulling hamstrings or quad muscles.

The final evaluation was coming up. We were cleaning up the mess hall for an end-of-camp banquet when Barney Deary's wife walked by. "Durwood," she said, "you'd better get ready to get out of teaching.'' I took the hint. Somehow, I thought I'd made it.

That night, they passed out three trophies, and I won the Sam Smith Award as the best hustler in camp. My confidence was growing. But I still didn't know if I'd passed the course. The next morning, I was called into a room where Deary and the umpiring instructors had assembled. Around the room were Nick Bremigan, Larry Napp, Jim McKean, Bill Deegan, Kinnamon, and Pulli. I was numb when I walked through the door. The room was dead silent. They all had stern expressions. My heart was sinking. I knew they were about to tell me one of three things: go home and forget umpiring, come back next year, or prepare for my first minor league assignment.

In a somber tone, Kinnamon said, ''Durwood, I think you should go back home.'' He paused and my heart was breaking. Then Bill smiled and added, ''And get ready to start your career in professional umpiring.''

I'd scored 97 on the final exam and finished third in my class. Six of us graduated and soon were all headed to our assignments in Class A ball. The others were Al Clark, Ed Montague, Dallas Parks, Mike Reilly, and Palermo. Several years later, and several miles down the road, they'd say it was the best umpiring class ever. Someday, we would all make it the major leagues. All I know is that in February of 1972, the major leagues still seemed farther away than the sun.

They sent me back to Hooks for a few days before I got my assignment. I was hoping I'd be sent to Class A ball in Florida. That's where the best students went. Instead, I was told to report to Scottsdale, Arizona, for spring training. My next stop would be Class A ball in the California League.

On the day I left, Mama packed me a lunch of fried chicken. She put it in a brown basket and wrapped a white napkin around it. I stood at the door and cried until my tear ducts could produce no more. Mama cried. Mickey and Maria cried. (Mickey was ten at the time and Maria was seven.)

Somehow, I think the kids thought I'd be back in a couple of days. As a coach, I'd traveled a lot. But I was always back pretty quick. Mama, well, she was pretty strong about me leaving. Now I understand her reason for the bright outlook. She knew that I needed to try umpiring—I would either succeed, or I would flop and somehow flush it from my system. But until I tried and gave it my best shot, she knew that my mind would wander back to umpiring. Instead of asking why, it was time for me to say why not. The moment of truth had finally arrived. Ol' Durwood needed to get on down that highway to wherever he was going.

It was time to float the boat.

I swore as I drove out of Hooks and headed west that I wouldn't look back. But as the miles passed, I kept asking, "What have you done? Where are you going? What in the devil has possessed you to do this?" I worried that God would get even with me for walking away from that perfect world back in Hooks. This whole experience was like driving off into the sunset and not knowing where the heck it was taking me. Driving across the vast flatlands, I reached the little West Texas town of Big Spring. I pulled off to the side of the road and started eating my fried chicken. And I started thinking: I'd been a successful coach. I'd been promoted to principal. Now I was sitting on the side of the road in West Texas, eating fried chicken by myself. The chicken tasted great. But the whole scene just didn't make sense.

I finally drove to El Paso, which sits on the Texas–New Mexico border. I think I slept about an hour that night. Life was weighing heavy on my heart when I drove out to the interstate that next morning. I must have sat at the stop sign for more than ten minutes. As I gripped the wheel tighter and tighter, my hands began to shake. I started crying again. Pretty soon, my whole body was shaking. I told myself that I could make one of two moves. I could turn right and go back to my great life in Texas. Or I could turn left and take off for the brave new world of professional umpiring. I screamed at the top of my lungs. Then I turned left.

*   *   *

Scottsdale, Arizona, was a funny-looking place. The first thing I noticed were miles and miles of beautiful homes with no grass in the yards. Not much would grow in the desert. I was used to a hot place, but at least we had grass back in East Texas, not rocks and cactus.

The first day, I was assigned a room at the Motel 6 by the minor league director. He gave me $40 the first week for meals. It was enough to make your stomach growl. Thank God for Ted Hendry. He was waiting for me like an angel there in Scottsdale. He'd been in umpiring a year, and he was a little older than the other boys, just like me. And he was in charge of handing out the assignments for the minor league umpires. Ted liked me from the start. Since we were about the same age, he decided to make me his project and I guess he was used to training house pets.

We'd sit around the Motel 6, and he'd tell war stories about umpiring in the minor leagues. He started preparing me for this tough life. I could identify with this man. He'd survived some battles, and now he was preparing me to do the same.

That first day, Ted said, "Durwood, you and I are going to work the Triple-A game between Albuquerque and Evansville." Feeling a little desperate, I looked at him in the eye and blurted, "Do you know who you're dealing with here, Ted? I've worked some Little League games back in Hooks and some high school games. I've worked two college games in my life. And now you want me to work a Triple-A game first rattle out of the box!"

"Durwood," he said, "it's time to get your feet wet."

Then came the bad news. Ted decided to put me behind the plate. About the fourth inning, the manager for the Evansville club came strolling out of the dugout. It was Del Crandall, the old major leaguer. Del sauntered up beside me said, "Son, how long you been in the game?" I said, "Mr. Crandall, about four innings." We both laughed. After a pause, I said, "Mr. Crandall, I don't know what I'm doing." He chuckled under his breath and said, "Well, son, you're having a little trouble. You're calling strikes ankle-high."

Believe it or not, we didn't get much instruction on calling balls and strikes in umpiring school. They gave us the basic parameters—from the letters to the knees—and then they sent us off to the wolves. No one stood behind me at umpiring school and said "Durwood, that strike you just called was a little high." I'd later learn that you really can't teach a man to call balls and strikes. You're blessed with the eye to call balls and strikes. Or you go home and get your old job back.

I spent a good amount of time picking people's brains about the strike zone. Getting that part of the job down would make me or break me. I didn't want to get sent back to Hooks.

This is how I started to learn the strike zone. If I called a strike high and everybody in the park yelled at me, I dropped my strike zone down. If I called a strike ankle-high and the bellowing started again, I'd raise my strike zone. It was like a baby touching a hot stove. You get burned and you learn pretty quick to stop doing that.

Other things that I learned about the strike zone: First, you need to relax behind the plate. Then you study the catcher's mitt. You set your eyes at the upper part of the strike zone. And if the catcher's mitt blocks your view, you know the ball is too high. If the catcher turns the mitt upside down, then you know the pitch is likely too low.

Then you study the catcher's knees. Those knees normally are aligned with both sides of the plate. If he catches the pitch outside of his knees, then it's likely to be a ball. Inside the knees and it's a strike. By using the knees and the mitt, you start to develop an imaginary frame that becomes your strike zone.

I will say this about spring training. They cut you some slack until you proved time after time that you couldn't figure it out. This was your time to learn by trial and error.

After a few weeks in Scottsdale, I couldn't wait to get to the California League, even though it was a string of one-horse towns and ballparks to match. They gathered all the umpires together for a little meeting just before the start of the season. Peering around the room, one of the veteran umps, Joe Baldino, said, "I see right now that most of these boys won't be around halfway through the season."

I was running on pure adrenaline for my first night behind the plate in the Cal League, as we learned to call it. Opening night was a game between Stockton and the San Jose Bees. I was full of piss and vinegar until I discovered that the umpires' dressing room in Stockton was full of cockroaches.

The manager for the San Jose Bees was Harry Momberg. Harry would get a lot of credit for developing George Brett as a hitter. Before that, though, he rode my butt all over the Cal League. I wore him like a cheap suit that first year in Class A ball.

That night, I called five or six batters out on strikes. Each time, the batter would turn around and say, "Hey, ump, it's only two strikes." I learned quickly that I wasn't in Scottsdale anymore. Just like Dorothy and Toto, I'd landed in a place that didn't look too familiar.

Harry turned out to be one of the orneriest managers in Oz. That first night, he walked past and said, "Durwood, I hope you didn't give up your day job in Texas for this." A few weeks later, he got so mad at me after a loss that he started chasing me off the field. He chased me all the way to our little dressing room right there underneath the ballpark. I slammed the door behind me and thought I was done with this wisecracker. But there was an inch-long crack between the door and the dirt floor. I looked down through the crack and there was Harry, lying on his back like a big ol' cockroach turned upside down. His eyes were bulging, and his face was red and contorted. He was flapping his arms and legs. Harry yelled and screamed through that crack for more than thirty minutes. And this is a grown man that I'm talking about.

You never forget the first manager you have to run out of a game. His name was Frank Funk, a former major league pitcher, who is today the pitching coach of the Colorado Rockies. Frank had a few great fireballing years in his younger days with the Cleveland Indians. Frank also has a titanic temper. He got so mad at a bullpen catcher one night that he threw the kid's glove in the toilet. They say he once stabbed one of his teammates (Daddy Leon Wagner) in the leg.

Managing the Fresno Giants in 1972, Frank had on his staff one of the first Japanese pitchers to ever come over to the States. We were in Reno one afternoon, and his Japanese pitcher showed me a little trick that I'd never seen in baseball. He faked a throw to third and then spun and faked a throw to first. When he didn't release the ball to first, I called a balk. I just figured that after all of those leg kicks and gyrations, he should throw it to somebody. I was wrong. The pitcher had taken his foot off the rubber, meaning he was now considered an infielder and no longer obligated to throw.

Well, I blew it and Frank Funk knew it. He called me every sorry name you've ever heard. So I threw him out in about six seconds. Walking away, Frank said, "I hope you got another job you can go back to." I said, "Now, Frank, there are plenty of jobs that pay more than this. And just maybe I'll take your advice." Then I threw his butt out of the game.

After a few weeks of this abuse, I was beginning to feel a little homesick. My feelings were hurt. I was hoping that everyone would like me. But they didn't. At least I still had my partner, Bill Malone, an ex–Los Angeles deputy sheriff. Bill left police work after nearly catching a bullet. He said the near miss had jangled his nerves. It was his second year in the Cal League, and the managers didn't pick on him too bad. Malone was like a big rock I could lean on. Until that sad day in San Jose when he came down with pneumonia.

The league sent me Joe Baldino, the guy who predicted at our first meeting that most of the young umpires would not make it halfway through the season. Granted, Joe had been around the block. But he hadn't learned much. Joe had one strange habit. He was constantly trying to save his expense money. He'd buy dozens of three-day-old doughnuts and carry them around in a sack. We'd go into a restaurant, and I'd order a regular meal. Joe would order a glass of milk and eat six or eight of those old doughnuts.

I was about to drop off to sleep one night in the hotel room when he started rolling around in his bed, screaming about pain in his stomach. I rushed him to the hospital. Guess what the doctor told him? To stop eating the stupid doughnuts. We went to Denny's and he ate a regular meal. The next day, Joe packed up the Malibu and hit the road. He said his nerves were shot. He just drove off into the sunset. My partners were falling faster than Leon Spinks.

Down in Bakersfield, they assigned me a new umpire named Gary Lieberman. We had a tough game one Sunday afternoon when he lost a fly ball in the setting sun. Gary came running into the infield, yelling, "I've lost it. I've lost it." I thought, Well, just fine. At least he could have kept his mouth shut. It was pretty clear that since he couldn't find the ball, it was somewhere on the other side of the fence. (The outfielders would tell us the next day that it flew over the fence by forty feet.)

When Gary started yelling, both managers came running out of the dugout. We ended up tossing five or six players and both managers. The crowd threw everything at us that wasn't bolted down. We had so many people wanting to argue that we told the players to take a number. But this much I knew in my heart. Nobody on either bench could tell me exactly where the ball had landed. We're talking about a fierce glare coming off that setting sun. (From that day on, games would be delayed from the time the sun reached a certain point on the horizon until it finally set.)

I was willing to stand my ground and keep throwing them out until there was silence. Ducky LeJohn, the manager of the Bakersfield Dodgers, kept jumping up and down, screaming in my face. I said, "Ducky, you don't know where the darn ball landed, either." I knew Ducky was bluffing. I'd done the same thing in my days as a high school coach. I was reading Ducky like a book.

Thank God the game finally ended, so we could get back to the umpires' room. That was until I came face-to-face with the biggest black widow spider you've ever seen. So we're sitting in this cramped little room, dejected about the game and hanging our heads. Gary finally said, "Durwood, I'm really sorry. I know that I embarrassed both of us out there today."

The fight had taken its toll on my partner. Then I heard something go *click,* and I bolted to my feet. I yelled, "Gary, I think that we've been locked in!" Sure enough they'd locked this big heavy door and there was no way we were going to knock it down. We screamed and hollered until our lungs almost popped. We got to spend the night in this musty little room with a black widow spider just waiting to attack. I didn't sleep a wink.

At six o'clock the next morning, somebody finally came around and let us out. After we got back to the hotel, Gary looked at me and said, "Durwood, I'm not putting up with this." And he got in his car and just drove away. I'd lost three partners in four weeks.

The deeper I waded into this nightmare called the Cal League, the more I thought about what Jim McKean had said to me back in umpiring school. He was very candid when he talked to me about my age. (Little did McKean or anybody know that my real age was thirty-two. I'd listed my age on my application as thirty, thinking they might not accept an umpire who was thirty-two. So no one knew my real age.)

McKean knew that my bosses in the minor league system wouldn't have much patience with me. That's why they sent me to the hell-forsaken Cal League. They'd either weed me out quickly, or they'd know in a year if they had an umpire who could handle the bullcrap.

What they didn't know was that I was determined to make it to the major leagues, come hell or black widow spiders. They could lock me in the dressing room in Bakersfield, but they couldn't lock me out of my dream. I really think that my age worked in my favor. It was the biggest reason I stuck it out. If I hadn't had some maturity, or if I hadn't been hardened by some years in high school coaching, I might have headed home to Mama.

One small-town crowd that almost got to me was in Visalia, a blip on the map about halfway between Fresno and Bakersfield. I was fighting the home team and the hometown fans to boot. My brother, Larry, had gotten a weekend pass from Army Special Forces training, and he was in the stands. Larry had been training in the Mojave Desert for several weeks. After the game, this old cowboy was giving me the business from the other side of the fence. His head was so ugly, it would have worn out two bodies. He must have worked for the Del Monte Cannery. He kept threatening to cut me to pieces.

Little did the cowboy know that my badass brother was standing right behind him. Here was a man who'd been trained to bite your throat out. Here was a man who'd just walked out of the desert in a bad mood. So Larry got a little tired of the ol' cowboy cursing his brother every step of the way. I heard something go *ka-pow*! I looked up into the stands, and Larry was standing over my tormentor. He'd knocked him out cold. Too bad I didn't have Larry around every night in those mean little ballparks.

Because umpires were quitting left and right, the Cal League finally had to send me a softball umpire who lasted all of thirteen days. Then they sent me Steve Cox, who, before the Cal League ruined him, was a damned good umpire. We were in Visalia and the cannery boys were out in force again. They came from the Del Monte Cannery and from the Libby's Cannery, and they came to let out some frustration. Nobody was safe from these boys. Heck, they'd slice their own manager to pieces.

Visalia was at home against the Lodi Orioles, and I had a close call at second base. The Visalia runner just cross body-blocked Bobby Baylor, the Lodi shortstop. He sent Baylor reeling into center field. So I called the runner out for interference.

No sooner had I turned around than the Visalia manager was in my face. It was Joe Frazier, one of the toughest suckers I've ever met. He was nine miles of soft concrete. Joe started cursing and spitting chewing tobacco all over my face and my shirt. Joe had verbally spread enough horse manure on the field to draw flies all the way from Portland.

Joe didn't much care for my name. So he called me Darewood. "Why don't you just go on back to Texas and get out of umpiring, Darewood," Joe said. "Because you ain't got no business in this game."

I had no choice. I had to throw Joe and all of his nasty habits right out of the game. As Joe walked off the field, I thought the cannery boys were going to come right over the backstop and chop me into French-style green beans. They were frothing and slobbering and calling me everything but my name. I think the cannery boys must have invented the word "redneck."

After the game, Steve and I waited until the crowd had completely cleared out before walking to his car in the parking lot. The boys indeed had done some handiwork with their knives. They'd slashed all four of the tires, and the rims were resting on the dusty ol' parking lot.

Now, there was no way you were going to run me out of the Cal League. But I was worried about Steve. He took it pretty well at first. We called a wrecker and had the car towed back into town. While the service station attendant patched our tires, Steve and I tried to patch our battered psyches. Steve would stick it out the rest of the year. But it would be his last in professional umpiring.

At that point of my career, I felt the whole world leaning on me. But nobody—not even the cantankerous Joe Frazier— was going run me out of umpiring. I knew Joe Frazier. I could read his mail. Here was a man totally frustrated with his profession. He'd been passed over for a promotion to Double-A ball even though his team had won the league title the year before. My first night in Visalia, they'd honored Joe for winning the championship. They had a little ceremony behind home plate and gave him a wallet with $500 in it. They also gave him a La-Z-Boy recliner.

Wouldn't you know that Joe's pitcher would get roughed

up the first couple of innings that night? Modesto jumped off to a 7–0 lead, and they were knocking Joe's pitcher all over the park. But Joe didn't even go to the mound for a conference. Getting itchy, the cannery boys jumped on Joe. "Hey, Meathead, why don't you get out of the damned recliner and go get your pitcher."

Joe finally went to the mound. On his way back, he stopped and yelled through the fence, "I didn't want the damned recliner in the first place!"

As the season moved along, Joe started yelling less and less at me. He even called me Durwood a few times. I appreciated that. One night in Visalia, I answered a knock on our dressing room and there stood Joe.

"Durwood, can I come in?" he said. "I got a couple of things to show you."

"Sure, Joe, come on in."

"Durwood, you're really starting to develop as an umpire. But there's one thing you need to work on. You're still messing up on the half-swing."

The half-swing, also called the checked swing, is one of the hardest things in baseball for an umpire to call. That's why you see so many plate umpires asking for help on the call from the base umpires. Joe's rules on the half-swing were simple. If the batter rolls over his wrists or if the barrel of the bat goes past the plate, it's a strike. Otherwise, it's a ball.

Those guidelines have since been swept out with the morning trash. You know why? Because an umpire standing close to third base, more than ninety feet away, can't see if the batter rolls over his wrists or if the barrel of the bat clears the plate.

Anyway, Joe put a stool right in the middle of the umpires' room and used it as home plate. Then he went to work on his interpretations of the half-swing.

Here is the real deal on the half-swing. The umpire must determine if the batter has "offered" a swing at the ball. Did the batter intend to swing? Or were his intentions clearly to check that swing?

That night, with Joe Frazier watching like a hawk, Visalia's big right fielder, Benny Ayala, strode to the plate. There were two outs in the bottom of the ninth with Visalia trailing by a run.

The baseball gods couldn't have planned it any better, or any worse. With two strikes, Benny tried to check his swing. But he didn't. I called strike three and the game was over.

Joe came tearing out of the dugout, calling me Darewood again.

"You're the dumbest sumbitch I've ever seen," he said. "You're even dumber than most Texans. There's no way that Benny broke his wrist on that half-swing."

I said, "Sorry, Joe, but the game's over. I guess your lesson didn't take."

In spite of all of the abuse, I never thought about quitting. But I was dying for even the smallest sign that I was doing something right. Lou Climshock, the sawed-off manager of the Reno Indians, walked past me one day and, with a big smile, said, "Durwood, you're having a good year. You know, you've been voted by the managers as the second-best umpire in the league." I couldn't believe my ears. Pride was swelling in my chest. I was beaming.

"Really, Lou!" I said almost gleefully. "Who was voted first?"

With that devilish look, he winked and said, "Durwood, the other seven umpires tied for first place."

Here I was getting killed on the field by those half-cocked so-called managers, eating fast-food garbage on the road, and walking miles to a Laundromat just to wash my clothes and uniform.

I'd heard plenty of barnyard language in my days as both a college and high school player and later as a coach. Football can be pretty rough on your vocabulary. But never had I heard the blue language that would greet me in the Cal League. I never could understand why another man would want to call you horse manure. But I had enough horse manure caked on me in the Cal League to fertilize half the state of Kentucky.

They'd warned us in umpiring school about what we might hear on the field. But nothing could have prepared me for this. As it turned out, being called horsesh—— was mild. Another term they really like in baseball is cough sufferer. Of course, I'm substituting cough sufferer for a word that sounds just like it. Then there is mother forker. (I think you get my drift on this one.) I never could figure why grown baseball players would be so obsessed with another man's mother.

I ask this question all the time during my off-season banquet speeches: Where do they teach this kind of foul language? Where do you get a college degree in calling another man a cough sufferer?

Other umpires have their own magical words for tossing guys out of the game. Bill Klem, who worked in the National League from 1905 to 1941, is generally considered the greatest umpire of all time. He worked behind the plate for five no-hitters. He hated to be called "Catfish." If he saw a player or manager even mouth the word, Bill gave them the heave-ho.

Sure, I know that baseball is a frustrating sport. The top-paid guys in the game are the .300 hitters. That means that a really good batter will fail seven times out of ten at the plate. Players are naturally going to be mad at themselves, and mad at umpires, and mad at fans, and mad at the world, and mad at the Gatorade bucket.

Every time you step onto the diamond, you'll encounter players in a slump. There will be guys out there who just can't buy a hit. So you're going to be working among a class of verbal degenerates. But there are times when you just can't take it anymore.

I'll tell you what'll get you tossed out in a hurry. If you personally insult me or my family, you're gone. Then there are the magical words—like horse manure, mother forker, and cough sufferer. Throw in a f—— you and you're outta here, brother-in-law.

When I was a young umpire in the major leagues, Marty Springstead, my second crew chief, gave me a great piece of advice. Marty's been the American League's supervisor of umpires since 1987. He said, "Durwood, when one team is chewing on you, the other side is going to be watching. They want to see what the other team is getting away with. If you let one team get away with something, the other side will try it next. Pretty soon the entire league will be trying you. Pretty soon you've got to draw that line in the sand."

As a young umpire learning to stand my ground, I learned to look at both benches and say, "Do you want any more?" And pretty soon, they're all saying, "Look at the crazy roughneck son of a gun. God, he's crazy. We'd better not mess with that guy anymore." Later in the game, a guy will come to the plate and say, "Durwood, we like you. But you're the craziest bastard we've ever seen." By then, I know I've got them.

I can honestly say that I hated just about every town in the Cal League. But Lodi was the worst. There's an old Creedence song about the sorry place that goes "Oh Lord, stuck in Lodi again." One Sunday afternoon, I had to toss about seven or eight players and both managers. The next day, I opened the door to the umpire's room, and all of my gear came floating out. Somebody had stopped up the shower drain and turned the faucet on full blast.

Only two of the original eight umpires survived the season. The other was my umpiring school classmate Ed Montague. The only reason Ed stuck around was because he got to spend about half the season replacing an injured umpire in the Triple-A Pacific Coast League. So, as it worked out, two rookie umpires got to work the five-game California League championship series.

The playoffs ended at eleven o'clock on a Friday night. I jumped in that Volvo and headed back to Texas. I drove all Friday night, all Saturday night, and finally got back to East Texas on Sunday. I was devouring No-Doz and washing them down with quarts of milk. I became so disoriented that I landed in Tyler, which is on the other side of Hooks. I told the the gas station attendant that I was from Hooks and I couldn't find my way home. He must have thought I was a real druggie. When I finally got home, they had to put me in the hospital for two days because of exhaustion.

When Mama went to file our income tax, she handed our CPA my W-2 form from umpiring. He laughed out loud. "You need to tell your husband to get a real job," he said. I'd made $1,800 that first year. Mama fired that CPA on the spot. I think it was the only time Mama ever completely lost her cool.

The happiest day of my life was the day I got the call from Mr. Bobby Bragan, the president of the Double-A Texas League. I was being promoted, which meant I didn't have to go back to the Cal League. That was actually a greater thrill than being promoted to the major leagues.

This is not to say that the Texas League didn't provide its share of thrills and spills. (Wouldn't you know that Joe Frazier would be promoted into the Texas League that year.) We were in Little Rock when I ran into trouble with Travellers manager Jack Kroll. In the first game of the doubleheader, Jack got mad about a call I made on a trapped ball. His outfielder, Hector Cruz, made a diving stab at it, but he didn't make the catch.

Jack came running out and began spewing more than his share of magical words. "Durwood," he said, "why don't you go f—— yourself."

Between games, I filled out my game report on Kroll and his foul mouth. You have to remember that I was the naive son of a Baptist preacher. Even though I was in my mid-thirties, I was like a babe in the woods in some respects. So I had a hard time putting on paper exactly what Jack Kroll had said. I wrote, "I decided to run Jack out of the game, Mr. Bragan, because Jack told me to do something that is physically impossible."

Before the start of the second game, Jack Kroll came to the plate with the lineup card, and I figured he might be ready to apologize. Instead, he snarled at me and said, "I've said it before and I'll say it again. Go f—— yourself, Durwood."

I couldn't believe my ears. I was tossing Jack Kroll for the second time in one day.

After the game, I sat down and wrote my second report on Jack Kroll. "Mr. Bragan," I began, "Jack Kroll said it again! So I had to run him out of the second game, too."

I'd been through a lot my first couple of years of professional umpiring. But nothing really scared me until I got to Amarillo, Texas, that first season in the Texas League. My partner that night was a skinny guy from Philadelphia named Bob Nelson, who was about five-foot-eight. And we'd had a rough night on the Texas Panhandle. It had been a real rodeo. We'd tossed out several players and both managers, and the crowd was getting restless. (There was once a minor league umpire named Harry "Steamboat" Johnson who claimed that some cowboys pulled their guns in the bleachers and blew a home run ball to smithereens. It wasn't that bad in Amarillo. But it was doggone close.)

Gold Sox Park was a peculiar place because the right and left field lines started sloping toward the outfield fence just past first base. The field was built with a hill in the outfield so it would drain better.

You've never seen rain until you've been to Amarillo. Because it's pancake flat, the Texas Panhandle attracts some of the most vicious storms you've ever seen. Storms roll down from the Rocky Mountains, and there's nothing blocking their path. After a hard rain, Gold Sox Park was known to flood in about five minutes.

Thanks to the drainage slope, you couldn't see the outfield lines as they approached the fence. We had trouble that night calling fair and foul balls. The cowpokes were pissed off the whole game. (I was waiting for the shooting to start.)

One other thing I remember about Gold Sox Park. The cattle yards were right across the street. The stench and the swarm of flies were almost unbearable.

As we dressed after the game, the door burst open and twelve people rushed in. The ringleader was a rough-looking woman who proceeded to tell us just what the eleven men were going to do to us. "We'll beat you to hell and back for that game you called tonight. We'll tar and feather you and run you out of town.'' She was standing next to a dusty ol' cowboy who was about six-foot-four.

I finally stood up and walked over to the cowboy. I looked him right in the eye and I began, ''Here we are, me and my partner, both minor league umpires, just trying to do the best we can. And you're in here to harm us. We've done nothing wrong except work this ball game. You're probably going to hurt us, but before I go down, I'm going to take you with me. You're going down with me because you're letting your dadgum wife lead this mob. You can put it on my tombstone that I went down this night in Amarillo. But also put it on my tombstone that I took this sorry old cowboy with me!''

That man grabbed his wife and spun her around. They hit that door in a heartbeat. And when she went out the door, everybody else followed.

The cowboys in Amarillo may have been tougher than a ten-cent steak. But the travel in the Texas League could be even more brutal. Two umpires had to travel in a car from one end of the state to the other. Once, my partner and I had to cover almost twelve hundred miles from El Paso to Memphis in a twenty-four-hour period to make our next game. There were times when I was so tired that I didn't think I could make it to the next Denny's. But I will say this. I do love my Denny's. It always seems to be at the next exit, and it always seems to be open. You just throw down another patty melt and try to make it to the next little town, where you can be sure they'll have another Denny's.

Ted Barrett, an outstanding young major league umpire, was telling me about his travails in the Texas League. They wanted him and his partner to drive all the way from El Paso to Jackson, Mississippi, in less than twenty-four hours. They'd have to drive all night with any hope of making it. He called league commissioner Carl Sawatski to complain. And you know what Sawatski told him? He said, ''Teddy, you're the one who chose to lead this dog's life. Now go out there and lead it!''

The Texas League was a very lonely time. But I guess it

was all part of the growing up and the life-hardening experience of umpiring. There were some long trips when I wondered if anyone in the world was thinking about me. I'd just be traveling down some of the country two-laners, feeling very detached from the world. But I knew it was a road I had to travel if I was going to make it to the major leagues.

By my fourth year in umpiring, I'd made it to Triple-A ball. I was on the cusp of the major leagues. I was moving along faster than 90 percent of the umpires in pro baseball. Normally, it takes about eight years to make it to the majors.

Back in the mid-1970s, Double-A baseball was a lot more fun to umpire than Triple-A. The major league teams were dumping their old spares into Triple-A ball instead of releasing them. That meant you had a bunch of hacked-off over-the-hill sluggos who'd already bounced around the one-horse towns on a worn-out Greyhound bus and were damn tired of it. Some of these guys had been in the big leagues for years and were used to the comforts. They were generally irritable and impossible to handle. I guess they were feeling just like me.

One of those players on the down escalator was Denny McLain, the last pitcher in major league baseball with a thirty-win season. Here was a man who had been to the top. In 1968, at age twenty-four, he won thirty-one games for the Detroit Tigers. He'd become the first pitcher to eclipse the thirty-win mark since the legendary Dizzy Dean in 1934. He had a few more impressive statistics in 1968: twenty-eight complete games, only six losses, 280 strikeouts, and an ERA of 1.96.

When I met Denny, he was knocking around the Texas League, with Shreveport, riding on buses and, amazingly, eating at Denny's.

I'll tell you this about a downtrodden Denny McLain. Even though each and every pitch had deserted him, he was a nice guy. After a game, he'd walked up to the umpires and say, "You guys really called a good one." He signed autographs. He smiled. He entertained. You would've never thought this man was in free fall.

In Evansville, I encountered a curly-haired kid who was definitely a rising star, although you couldn't tell it by looking at him. One afternoon in Evansville, it rained so hard that you couldn't see the outfield fence. We were sitting in the dugout when I spotted one of their pitchers, a twenty-year-old goofball, helping the grounds crew roll out the tarpaulin. He was soaked and knee-deep in mud. And, yes, he was in full uniform. This kid was floppy-armed and goofy-gaited. He talked to baseballs and patted the mound. A year later, during his rookie year with the Detroit Tigers, they would name him after a character on Sesame Street. He was Mark "the Bird" Fidrych.

As a rookie with Detroit, he would win nineteen games and post an ERA of 2.34. He was voted Rookie of the Year. But when I met Fidrych, he was knocking around the Evansville bullpen trying to make it as a reliever. My biggest memory, though, will be sitting in the dugout, listening to his teammates and his manager, Fred Hatfield, just howl at the kid helping the grounds crew. He was an entertainer from the start.

Wouldn't you know that Triple-A ball was where I was reunited with Steve Palermo, my little buddy from umpiring school? Steve's temper was worse than mine. After three years in the minor leagues, we were like a wild-horse tag team that didn't take lip from the pope. We weren't going to be pushed around.

Fred Hatfield was what we called a "chirper." He was always chirping at the umpires from the dugout. But he knew just when to cut it off before we tossed him out of the game. Hatfield ventured out of the dugout one night and approached me at first base. That was a mistake. I was in a foul mood. Steve walked over from third base, and he was standing close by. It's what we call "lurking."

So I drew a long line in the dirt with my shoe. I said, "Fred, if you cross this line, I'll toss you out of the game." Then I drew another line perpendicular to the first one. Then

I drew two more lines, and I had him boxed in. I said, "Go ahead, Fred, cross one of those lines."

Steve admired my little artwork and said, "Fred, what is the problem with you?"

In a whimper Fred said, "Durwood won't let me out of this box."

Steve said, "Now, Fred, will you be a good boy if we let you out of this box?" Fred agreed to behave. For about two innings. I finally had to deep-six him.

They sent us to Evansville later in the season for a game against Indianapolis. We had so much trouble with the Evansville team that we sent everybody except Hatfield and his trainer to the clubhouse. We just got tired of listening to their nonsense. Hatfield had to summon each batter from the clubhouse. We let them know who was boss in Evansville. That story gained a lot of notoriety around the American Association.

Later in the season, Dick Butler, the American League supervisor of umpires, sent an assistant named John Stephens to see Stevie and me. He'd heard about some of our exploits. John sat us down and said, "Mr. Butler is interested in ya'll for the American League. They want ya'll. But God, you can't go into the big leagues acting like you did in Evansville! Guys, you can't throw everybody out of the game. You guys are turning this thing into championship wrestling or something."

I held my tongue. But this was what I wanted to tell Mr. Dick Butler: I wanted to tell him that I'd been locked overnight in the umpires' room in Bakersfield with a black widow spider, that they'd slashed our tires in Visalia, that they'd flooded our room in Lodi, and that they'd run off four of my partners in the Cal League. I wanted to tell him that I'd needed a man from the Army Special Forces, who was doubling as my brother, to save my butt one night from an angry mob.

I wanted to tell him about the dirty dozen that wanted to lynch us in Amarillo. I wanted him to know that Jack Kroll once suggested that I do something physically impossible to myself. After an umpiring career that has spanned twenty-one years, I can put all of those crazy episodes into perspective. I know now what Mr. Dick Butler would have told me. He would have looked me squarely in the eye and said, "Durwood, I think you're ready for the big leagues."

Rising from the
Oklahoma Dust Bowl

EASTER SUNDAY of 1944 was a hot one in western Oklahoma. The southern wind was kicking up yellow dust that morning as the Merrill family piled into the light blue '38 Ford and drove to the Valley View Baptist Church. We were used to powerful straight-line gales in that part of the country. But we weren't prepared for what was headed our way that day.

The Merrill clan, as you might call us, lived on a string of farms between Cloud Chief and Cowden, tiny towns you've never heard of. Those cotton fields were just east of the Texas Panhandle. Folks used to say that if we didn't keep things bolted down, a strong easterly wind would blow us smack-dab into Texas.

We farmed our food. We grew cotton, raised hogs, and basically made our living off the flat dusty land. We were hardworking people and we believed in God, baseball, and the American way. The Merrill kids spent a good part of Easter afternoon hunting colored eggs all over the countryside.

I was six years old. I had two older brothers, Gailon Eben and Arvis Lee, and a younger brother, Larry. Ted Elden had yet to be born. We wore our overalls and new Buster Brown brogans to church. We were well-scrubbed kids who didn't talk during church and sang our hearts out from the Baptist hymnal. "Amazing Grace" was one of my favorites.

My dad, Ebenezer Levi Merrill, was a man with a calling.

Even though he was born a farmer and had spent his life tending to the cotton fields, the pulpit was where he wanted to be. After all, according to Scripture, Ebenezer was the stone of help.

He was fighting the temptation to chuck the farm life and enter the ministry on a full-time basis. But he had a wife and four boys and bills to pay. Eben, as they called him, had obligations that the ministry couldn't cover, and a farm mortgage the Lord couldn't pay. That, however, didn't keep him from dreaming.

My mother, Opal Lee, was a patient woman. We farmed everything that we ate. So there was full-time work in canning the sausage and the vegetables, shucking the peas, and preparing the food. We didn't have a deep freezer or an icebox, so everything had to be canned for winter. She canned the chow-cow, corn, apples and the cherries.

Opal Lee said she had a premonition that one of her children would someday perform onstage. Maybe she meant it as a metaphor. Maybe she knew that baseball would be like a stage for me someday.

Late in the day, the black clouds began boiling up from the south. The boys continued to play around my granddad's house, which sat on the farm next to ours. My granddad was Herbert Bell Merrill, and we called him H. B. My grandmother was Ella.

Western Oklahoma was flat like a waffle iron. Trees were scarce in that part of the country. They used to say that if your dog left home in western Oklahoma, he wasn't officially lost for three days. You could really see that far in all directions. Shoot, you could see our dog, Tige, chasing a cat in the next county. We named him after the little dog in the Buster Brown commercials.

Surveying the wicked-looking sky, my dad said to Mom, ''I don't think that we'll be going to church tonight.'' I knew something was terribly wrong. We went to church every time they opened the doors. A change in the Sunday evening prayer plans was like forgoing the planting season. You almost needed a death in the family to skip church.

The wind was howling as my dad drove us back to our farmhouse. Dusk was an hour away. But the sky was growing darker by the minute. Dust plumes were rising from the cotton fields. The air was turning a brownish gray, and you could feel the chill of the weather front as it approached from the southwest. Tumbleweeds bounded along the ground at ever-quickening speeds. I was scared. I secretly studied my dad's expression for any sign of emotion. His eyes were focused, but something weighed heavily on his mind.

As he hustled us into the house, I knew that trouble was brewing on the Oklahoma plains. Dad led us to the southwest corner, where we all sat on the floor. He walked onto the front porch to survey the storm that had moved within a few miles of the farm. Rushing back into the house, Dad said to my mother, "There's a tornado to the south. But I think it's going around us. I'll keep an eye on it."

We lived in an area that was then considered tornado alley. But I was too young to know what a tornado was. Nobody talked about twisters around the Merrill home. I guess they were too scary to discuss.

I knew we had a storm cellar in our backyard. It was about fifty feet from the east door. I kept wondering why we weren't making a run for it.

This is what my dad saw as he stood on the front porch on that eerie Easter afternoon: "I thought at first that it was going to loop around the farm," he said. "Then it turned around and started coming straight for us. It was midnight black by now. You couldn't see your hand in front of your face. But I could see the tornado through the lightning flashes. It extended from the sky to the ground and was the biggest doggone twister I'd ever seen. It must've been a half-mile wide. The monster was boiling up dust and sucking up fence posts and heading straight for us. It was just a vicious-looking thing. I thought about running everybody to the storm cellar.

"Right before the tornado got to the house, everything went silent. The wind stopped blowing. It was like the storm had just died. I knew we were in big trouble. This was what they called the calm before the big storm and was chilling."

My dad ran back into the house and hollered, "Hit the east door." That meant that we were making a run for the storm cellar. Dad and Gailon, who was fourteen, lit into the east door with their shoulders. But they couldn't budge it. The calm had been shattered by the fierce winds. We were stuck in the house.

I could hear the heavy raindrops on the roof. The wind was rocking the house. My brother Arvis started reciting the Lord's Prayer: "Our father who art in heaven . . ." Then came the horrible sound. It was like a freight train going sixty miles an hour and headed straight for us. The fear was almost paralyzing. The walls started expanding and contracting. It was as if the house had taken on human life and was breathing. The ceiling was crashing piece by piece to the floor. My dad stood over his family and put both hands on the walls. He was trying to hold the house off his wife and four kids. The tornado was literally sucking all the air out of the house. A Coleman lantern that was hanging from the ceiling fell with a crash.

Then came the explosion.

I landed in the front yard next to my mother, who was holding Larry. He was less than a year old. I was about fifty feet from the house and rolling. Looking up, I could see our cedar tree being sucked into the vortex of the tornado. The tree was spinning upward and away, kind of like Dorothy's house in *The Wizard of Oz*.

I could hear my mother crying next to me. My dad flew more than 120 feet in the air and crashed into a barbed-wire fence. If not for the fence, he might have flown clean out of Ouachita County. He broke his collarbone.

Gailon said he flew several feet in the air and, inexplicably, landed on the roof of the house. When the house blew up, Galen was catapulted like a rocket into the black sky. This is how he describes it: "I went high into the air and remember the sensation of flying. It was total pitch dark, and I was in the air for a while. I landed on my back, and the air gushed out of me. I couldn't get any wind back in my body. That tornado had pulled all of the oxygen out of the air and I was suffocating.

"When my breath came back, I grabbed an old quilt and put it over my head to protect myself from the hail. I could hear Daddy whistling. I'd just learned to whistle. But I managed to whistle back."

As I raised my head, I was struck by a horrific sight. Our house was gone. This vicious beast had swept it into the air and now was carrying most of the house across the county, along with everything else it had swallowed. All that was left was the concrete foundation and a crumpled wall. I rolled along the ground and tried to protect my head from the enormous hailstones that were pelting the ground. The sky had turned purple, and I wondered for several seconds if this was hell or Oklahoma.

I saw my dad stumbling toward us, holding his shoulder. He ran toward my one-year-old brother, who was bleeding from the head. A flying object had struck little Larry across the forehead and had peeled his scalp back. His head had been ripped open in a V shape. There were leaves and sticks stuck in his scalp, and he was bleeding everywhere. Mother screamed and stuck Larry underneath the crumpled wall to protect him from the wind and the hail.

Arvis flew about a hundred feet from the house, and Dad whistled for him. When the family was back together, we took refuge in the only thing we had left—the storm cellar.

Have you ever wondered just how smart animals are? Well, as we climbed into the storm cellar, we found our two greyhounds and our two cats already there. They had crawled into the cellar long before the tornado hit.

We were all alive. But the damage to property and livestock was devastating. My dad's car had been turned over and crushed. Three pigs were carried more than a mile by the twister and then dropped back to earth. We found their bodies down by the creek. Horses and cows were scattered all over the county. They had been lifted into the air and then deposited like so many pieces of kindling. It would take days to find all the dead animals. More than a hundred chickens just disappeared into the black sky. Amazingly, a few returned to earth about a mile away and survived. We found them living quite happily on one of the neighbors' farms.

If tornadoes were measured then as they are today, that sucker would have been considered an F-5, which is the largest on anybody's scale. It was the most violent storm that anyone in that part of the country could ever remember. The twister had stayed on the ground for more than twenty miles. It had chewed up small towns, farmhouses, tractors, trees, cars, barns, and cotton gins. Places like Corn and Colony were in total disarray.

We know that tornadoes are a bizarre act of nature. The damage was testament to that. A table that weighed more than a hundred pounds was carried a half mile away. But a picture frame next to that table never moved. Pieces of straw from a bale of hay were sticking from a telephone pole. Down the road, at another farmhouse, a two-by-four had been shredded into thousands of pieces by a screen door. The screen remained intact.

Mother's stove, which weighed about two hundred pounds, flew more than a mile and was wrapped around a tree. More than fifty years later, it's still there, still hugging the same tree.

Her keepsake chest was found more than three miles away, still intact.

Because the tornado struck a rural area, many lives were spared. Storm shelters saved many people. If this cold-blooded killer had struck Oklahoma City, hundreds, possibly thousands, of people, would have lost their lives.

One of our neighbors, Lizzy Walker, was milking a cow when the tornado came rumbling through. Someone tried to coax her into their storm cellar. But Lizzy was what we considered a fatalist. She always said, "If God wants to take me, he will." Sure enough, the tornado swept her up and carried her two farms over, where she fell to earth and died instantly.

It took the Merrill men an hour to find a car that would run. Little Larry needed medical attention. Cars had been tossed around like balled-up pieces of notebook paper. Others were pancaked like junked cars in a scrap yard. One of the neighbor's cars that had a dead battery and hadn't started for more than a month cranked on the first try. My dad jumped in the car and headed for the hospital with Larry. However, he soon discovered that the main bridge over the creek had been washed out. He had to drive the car more than a mile over a muddy hill. The tires spun and that car fishtailed all the way up. But they made it to the main road. Doctors put twenty-five stitches in Larry's head, and Dad brought him home that night.

All of the Merrill farmhouses were gone. It just seemed impossible that one day you could be living happily in a rambling five-room house and the next day all would be lost. It made you ache inside.

The Red Cross arrived the next day and constructed a large tent next to Granddad's house. That was where the Merrill families lived for the next month, as the men rebuilt the houses. At night, when the wind rustled through that tent, I trembled. My grandmother let me sleep in their storm cellar during a lot of those windy nights when I was haunted by nightmares.

I'm sure that I suffered some psychological effects from that horribly frightening day. I would start to cry when clouds gathered in the sky. Mom would tell Gailon to take me to the storm cellar. Gailon would sleep on one of the iron cots to comfort me.

I am still scared to death of tornadoes. I keep a weather radio next to the bed at our house in Hooks. On those stormy nights when the national weather bureau has issued a tornado watch, I sometimes walk the floor all night. A few years ago, when I was on a road trip in Oakland, a tornado roared through our property in Hooks and passed within about 150 feet of the house. It demolished our barn. Just thinking about it puts my heart right back in my throat. I'll never forget Easter Sunday of 1944. Never.

*   *   *

Before winter arrived and the winds came whipping down the plains, the Merrill brothers performed an annual ritual. We ran the hogs up to granddad's place for the hog killing. It was time to prepare our food for the cold months.

To kill a hog, you'd put the barrel of the .22-caliber rifle right between its eyes, pull the trigger, cut the throat, and it was over. The Merrill boys got to do the shooting. So, at the age of six, my granddad decided it was time for me to learn the tradition.

Naturally, I was a little nervous. I aimed the little rifle right at the big hog's head. *Ka-boom!* I pulled the trigger and shot the poor thing right through the snout. That dern hog went nutso. All I did was blow his snout half off and draw a lot of blood. He started tearing up the hog pen. It took both of my older brothers and my dad about thirty minutes to finish that oinker off. Many years would pass before I got to shoot another hog.

Our address was Cloud Chief, a former Indian reservation. In the 1930s, the U.S. government traded some land in northern Oklahoma for the reservation around Cloud Chief. So the Choctaw Indians surrendered the cotton fields and moved into Osage County. It was about two days later when they struck oil. That basin in Osage County was rich with meandering rivers of oil and they're still cashing checks from those gushers.

Meanwhile, the cotton farmers moved into land around Cowden and Cloud Chief. Every summer, they would pray that the rains would come. If the water was plentiful and the rains cut deeply into the hard ground, we had a bumper crop. Those years, all the kids got bicycles and basketballs and BB guns and blue jeans for Christmas. But in the lean years, when the stubborn droughts held on, the boys shared one bike for Christmas and Grandma made us shirts out of flour sacks.

Come hell, tornadoes, or the droughts of summer, the Merrill family was bound and determined to survive in Oklahoma. Our fathers were going to farm the same land that their fathers and grandfathers had farmed. They were stubborn that way.

The tornado didn't kill me. But a white-faced bull belonging to our neighbor, Dennis Barbee, almost did a couple of years later. I was wearing an orange jumpsuit and was playing in one of the fields and not paying much attention to anything. Little did I know that about twenty-five feet away, a twelve-hundred-pound bull was about to charge me and my orange suit. That ol' bull was a mean SOB. He had four-foot horns and a penchant for smashing everything in the fields. I was a sitting duck.

Luckily, my brother Gailon was paying attention. He was a three-sport letterman and the best athlete in the county. He broad-jumped, long-jumped, and pole-vaulted on the school track team. Recognizing that the snorting bull was about to stomp me into the ground, he jumped the fence, swept me up from behind, and took off running. That bull was about ten feet behind us and gaining ground.

With me in tow, Gailon hurdled a three-strand barbed-wire fence that was three and a half feet tall. That fence was electrically charged, meaning it delivered a pretty good jolt to anyone or anything that touched it. Mr. Bull had been lit up by that fence before. So he stopped dead in his tracks. Meanwhile, Gailon sprinted more than two hundred yards before he realized we were out of danger.

My life had been saved twice.

Our school was in nearby Cowden, and it seemed more like home than Cloud Chief. Cowden, in its heyday, had a population of fifty (not including dogs, cats, hogs, and other four-legged livestock). There was a country grocery store and a blacksmith shop and the cotton gin. You couldn't find Cowden in any road atlas in America. In fact, it has since been boarded up and forgotten. Except by the Merrill families.

We had no running water, and our electricity had to be battery-powered. We had a man who delivered both ice and water. The water was stored in a concrete cistern out in the yard. When the water ran low, we would lower one of my brothers with ropes into the bottom of the cistern, and he would clean it out with bleach.

Up until 1946, the county didn't provide us with electricity. So we had a wind charger. It would charge up during the day, and at night, we'd use it to the power the lights and the radios. It seemed a radio was always tuned to a sporting event. In the summer, it was the St. Louis Cardinals and Harry Caray doing the play-by-play. We loved Stan Musial and Marty "Slats" Marion.

In the fall, we listened to the Oklahoma Sooners, who were coached by the great Bud Wilkinson. After football, we followed Henry Iba and his string of great teams at Oklahoma A&M, later to become Oklahoma State. Curt Gowdy, who was starting his broadcasting career, did play-by-play on the A&M games.

Basketball was big around the Merrill farm. Since we didn't have a goal in the backyard, I cut the bottom out of a metal milk bucket and hung it on the chicken coop. Hour after hour, I'd be out back, shooting an old croquet ball through that bucket.

My formative years were also filled with hoe handles and cotton sacks. During the fall, as the first blue norther blasted us from Kansas and Colorado, it was time to pull cotton. I'll always remember exactly where I was on October 3, 1951.

Gailon, Arvis, and I were out on my grandfather's farmland, which covered about 250 acres. It was one of those days when you hustled hard and your hands bled. We didn't pick the cotton out of the burr. We pulled the whole burr. Grandpa was paying us $2 for every hundred pounds of cotton we pulled. That would pay for a lot of blue jeans and a lot of Saturday afternoon cowboy movies.

Our hands and our bodies might have been working in the cotton fields that day. But our hearts and our minds were in the Polo Grounds in New York. The Dodgers and the Giants were playing the third and final game of a play-off series to decide the National League pennant.

Now, we knew that Granddad wasn't going to let us listen to much of the game. There was work to be done. Granddad was driving around the fields in his 1948 Chevrolet, a four-door that seemed bigger than a cotton gin. He'd drive up and down the rows of cotton with the ball game blaring on his car radio. When the boys took water breaks, he'd let us stand there and listen to three or four minutes of the game.

If you really hustled with your sack of cotton, Granddad would let you hear more and more of the radio broadcast as the game progressed. In the ninth inning, with the Dodgers leading the Giants 4–2, Granddad honked his horn and told us all to gather around the old Chevy. I guess he sensed that something exciting and historic was about to happen.

Red Barber was doing the play-by-play with Russ Hodges as the color man. We were listening so intently that you couldn't hear us breathe. We had tough old cotton sacks slung over our shoulders and dirt on our faces. We would've made Norman Rockwell proud.

The Giants had runners at first and second. Ralph Branca replaced starter Don Newcombe. The Dodgers had the option of not pitching to Bobby Thomson, but Willie Mays was waiting on deck.

Branca served up the pitch, and Thomson hit the "shot heard 'round the world." And I will never forget hearing Russ Hodges and that crazy euphoric call: "The Giants win the pennant! The Giants win the pennant!"

A few minutes later, the brothers were back to pulling cotton. But our heads were still spinning with images of Thomson rounding the bases and jumping into the arms of his teammates at home plate. "The Giants win the pennant! The Giants win the pennant!" I had chills down my spine the rest of the afternoon. The Merrill boys broke all records that day for cotton pulling in Granddad's fields.

Baseball touched us in several different ways. At the old picture show, we saw baseball highlights on the movie reels. Occasionally, we would load up and take the long road trip into St. Louis to see the Cardinals play.

Or the game of baseball might just come walking into those cotton fields, kind of like Joe Jackson strolling through the corn stalks in Iowa.

Dale Mitchell was a big man, about six-three and 210 pounds. He was among the American League's top three hitters in 1948 and 1952. He played in the World Series for the Indians in 1948 and 1954. Trivia buffs may remember him as the Brooklyn Dodger who made the final out in Don Larsen's perfect game in the 1956 World Series.

Dale was also my cousin by marriage.

During the off-season, the big man would come back to Oklahoma and live in nearby Cloud Chief. Every time he drove back into town in that big Cadillac, we felt a piece of major league baseball coming with him. To the hick kids, that car looked like a mile-long train pulling into the station. You would've thought that God had returned to the dusty plains.

He brought baseballs and bats. He sat around and told us stories about the Indians and the Dodgers and about playing in the World Series. Mostly, I guess, he brought dreams to the kids. It was magical that you could reach out and touch a major league ballplayer. At night, when we got down on our knees, we asked the Lord if we could someday be like Dale.

Sadly, I never got to see Dale play in person. I do remember listening to the 1948 and 1954 World Series like they were yesterday. He was one of the best contact hitters of his time, and a man who could run like the wind.

The Indians tried to convert Dale from a hitter to a slugger. Hank Greenberg, the Cleveland general manager, once told Dale, ''Home run hitters drive Cadillacs. Guys who hit singles and doubles drive Fords.'' I guess Greenberg never checked the players' parking lot. If so, he'd have seen Dale's Cadillac.

If it hadn't been for Dale Mitchell, I don't think we would have had organized baseball in Cowden–Cloud Chief. Kids just didn't get much time off from their summer chores. When I was ten, summer baseball came to the count for the first time. The games were played in the late afternoons, and the daddies would just shut down the machines for two or three hours. It was the only time of the week when farming was put on hold. Some of the farmers would pull their tractors or their trucks right to the third base line. They would sit there on the machinery and watch the games.

We would play teams from Alfalfa and Corn and Burns Flat. You might see an old farmer wearing overalls driving his tractor several miles down the highway just to watch his team play. When the games ended, the farm equipment was fired back up and everybody returned to work.

Dale sent a dozen bats and a dozen balls from Cleveland and it was about all of the baseball equipment we had. When the cover on a ball started getting worn, we'd tape it up. When we broke one of the bats, we'd take it home and nail it back together. A nailed-up bat is never going to be quite the same. But it was all we had.

Dad believed in sports, and he believed you should work as hard on the playing fields as you did in the cotton fields. I'd come home from a game, and he'd say, "Durwood, you need to work on your free throws."

I think Gailon became a great athlete partly because Dad cared so much. Gailon should have gone far in pro baseball. But his high school coach overworked him and ruined his arm.

Gailon was the best rock-thrower I'd ever seen. Grandma would say, "Gailon, go outside and get me a fryer." Gailon didn't need to shoo that chicken into a box or snag it with a wire. He'd just chunk one rock and that chicken would be deader than a Thanksgiving turkey.

Ebenezer Levi was slightly under six foot and as stout as Mr. Barbee's bull. He could yank up a plow with one hand. The man had come from generations of farmers. He could be as tough as the land and he had an aura about him. He told you to do something once and it was done. His rules were very clear.

Dad also was a well-read man and a student of the Bible. To this day, as he approaches ninety, he can quote Scripture and give you the number of the page. He read something every night, whether it was the *Daily Oklahoman*, the Bible, or *Popular Mechanics*.

His calling was not to be a hell-and-brimstone preacher. It was to educate and to share his views of the faith. He studies prophecy. He knows a great deal about the nation of Israel and its plight.   That's why we knew the day would come when he would trade the plow for the pulpit. He could no longer hold in strict abeyance a cotton crop that had been up and down for years. He made the decision to leave the farm for the seminary in Dallas. That was 1952.

As I reflect back on my Oklahoma days, I can see a man who was much like me as I grew older. Dad felt the same anxieties about pulling up stakes and moving forward. He had a family to support, and it was hard knowing that his heart was no longer in farming. For years, he fought the temptation. But it was time to answer his heart and to answer that calling.

Mom and Dad and four brothers loaded up the car and headed south. Gailon had taken a job in the small Texas Panhandle town of Borger. We hadn't seen or talked to him in a few months. Back then, you didn't just pick up the phone and call somebody 150 miles away.

Two days later, a homesick Gailon pulled up in front of our farmhouse. All he found was little Tige. Gailon sat down in the floor and cried and cried. He couldn't figure out where we'd gone, why we hadn't told him, and why we hadn't taken Tige. He didn't know that our uncle was planning to take Tige into his care.

Granddad had to break the news to Gailon. To this day, Gailon says he's still heartsick from the day he found the farm cold and deserted. He believed the Merrills would forever be farmers. Boy, was that about to change.

Moving from western Oklahoma to a burgeoning city was like going from the watermelon patch to Neiman Marcus. By day, Dad was a painter at the Ford assembly plant. By night, he was a student of the ministry. Me, I was just trying to get off the watermelon truck. I didn't have a prayer.

They sent me to Forest Avenue Junior High School, which was close to the Cotton Bowl. It was so big that I couldn't even find my way to class. So I'd sit in a phone booth, hiding from the world. I couldn't summon the courage to ask for directions to class.

I was different from everybody in that schoolhouse. I wore overalls and those Buster Brown brogans and a shirt made out of a flour sack. I walked like a hick, talked like a hick, and had a burr haircut. Those big-city kids thought I'd wandered in from the hills. They were partly right. Only I came from the plains of Oklahoma where they had no hills.

All the boys were ducktail haircuts in the 1950s. I had no hair at all. Dad just whacked it off once a week with the clippers. There wasn't such a thing as a flattop in our family. Those kids in junior high would bend over laughing just watching me walk down the hall.

I was lucky right off the bat that I met a guy named Johnny Burchett, a big redneck boy who didn't take lip from anybody. He was the toughest kid in school. He was a member of the Grove Rats, which was kind of like a gang back then. Johnny would open his locker, and there would be a bicycle chain with a handle on it. I thought he looked ten feet tall.

He'd come to school all marked up from the previous night's fights. His knuckles would be scraped and he'd say, "Oh, we had a rumble last night." Back then, kids in gangs didn't carry guns and knives like they do today. They just beat the hell out of each other with chains and their two bare fists.

Baseball was my salvation. They found out pretty quickly that ol' country could hit the ball. I had hits in four straight games and went twelve for twelve in that stretch. I rarely made an error at shortstop. Pretty soon, I got my wish and they moved me to catcher. I thought I was destined to be the next Yogi Berra. Those city slickers realized they needed me around. It was a great feeling.

I was just getting comfortable in Dallas. My burr haircut and my overalls were long gone. I had a ducktail and slick clothes. But Dad, who'd been doing some part-time ministry work, got a call from the Austin Chapel Missionary Baptist Church in tiny DeKalb (pronounced Da-Kab). We were moving to a little town in East Texas close to both the Arkansas and Oklahoma borders. The Merrills were going back to the country. I'd been a city boy for only a year.

My personal transition became much easier when I met a girl named Carolyn Carter, the church pianist. Discovering the game of football also made life more exciting in that quiet little town.

I'd wanted to play football since I was a little kid in the Oklahoma cotton fields. I loved listening to the Oklahoma games on radio.

At DeKalb High School, they learned pretty quickly that the new boy in town had a great desire to play football. But it became quickly apparent that he didn't know a touchdown from a first down. I couldn't even hit the blocking sled. And I sure as heck didn't know how to put on a uniform.

That first day, they gave us thigh pads and knee pads and told us to stick them in our pants. At the top of the thigh pad is a point. That point is supposed to be on the outside. If that point winds up on the inside, well, it's pointing right into your genitals. Ouch.

That first day, my thigh pads were pointing the wrong direction. The student manager grabbed me as I walked through the front door and said, "Durwood, you big dummy, you're gonna wind up with a lot of pain." The coach couldn't understand why I was always late to practice. I was back in the field house fixing my pads.

I thought, at first, that it was a stroke of bad luck that DeKalb had a brand-new coach. Talk about confusing the issue. He didn't know me and I didn't know football. That first day, he was searching for a new quarterback. So he told me to throw a few passes. Heck, I didn't know you were supposed to grip the laces. I threw the ball end over end like a kickoff. Coach told me to stand over with the linemen and to be quiet.

I didn't know how to block or tackle. I couldn't run very fast. But I had a couple of intangibles that coach was looking for: heart and blind determination. I didn't know when to quit. Most of the time, I'd keep charging right through the referee's whistle.

I normally finished at the back of the pack when we ran wind sprints during practice. Yet on Friday nights, when we played our games, I was all over the field. Lining up at defensive end, a lot of times I was in the backfield before the running back could get started. I was a wild banshee and a classic overachiever. I played football like I pulled cotton— with gritted teeth.

Pretty soon, coach gave me a shot in the offensive backfield. I was so slow that I reached top speed on the second step out of my stance. But I had an attitude about running the football. I was a hard man to bring down. Soon I was becoming a student of the game. I'd sit in church and diagram plays. I came to learn everybody's assignment on the field. I was just consumed with football. During my idle time, I'd be in the coach's office, watching films with my best friend, Mike Pinkham, who was our quarterback.

Cecil Pirkey, our coach, would become the second most influential man in my life behind my dad. He was an all-American at East Texas State and played with the Philadelphia Eagles. Simply, he was a fine groomer of young men. He'd tell you that you had some talent, and you believed him.

Practice is boring to most players. But I loved to practice and I hated to leave the field. You could give me a dirty uniform and a wet jockstrap, and I'd still give you everything in practice. By no means was I a great player, but I just loved to practice and play the game.

One of the best athletes in Texas lived just down the road in Mount Vernon. With me guarding him most of the night, he scored thirty-eight points against us in basketball. We still managed to lose by only two points.

Our dream was to beat this guy in football. He was just a great quarterback. We had Mount Vernon down by four points with two minutes to play when, in the rain and the mud, they shifted from the T formation and moved their quarterback into the shotgun formation. Throwing a wet and sloppy football all over the field, he moved his team eighty yards. They scored in the final seconds to beat us. I knew that Dandy Don Meredith was going to be something special.

It was a miracle that I improved as much as I did in football. Some people had made a big mistake by telling me I wasn't good enough to play for the Bears. That just fired me up like a hot Roman candle from the Texas Panhandle. When you tell ol' Durwood he can't do something, I normally find a way to prove you wrong.

Down at the Dairy Queen, they were even saying that I might be good enough to play some college ball.

At church, I had my eye on the little eighth-grade pianist. On that first Sunday when they introduced the Merrill family to the congregation, I knew she had her eye on me. We kept our eyes on each other much of the day at school. Since we were two years apart, it would have been sinful to date. Besides, kids really didn't date back then. You didn't pick a girl up at her house and run all over town and take her back at one in the morning. You were lucky if you got to meet your girlfriend for a couple of hours at the Saturday afternoon movies.

So we used church for our courtship. Both families went to church on Wednesday night, Sunday morning, and Sunday night. My mom and dad sang in a Southern gospel quartet with her dad, G. L. Carter, and DeKalb mayor Noble Bates. They practiced Saturday nights at the Carter house. While Carolyn played the piano for the quartet, I sat in the living room and watched TV. When we got the chance, we gawked at each other across the house.

When Carolyn got into high school, her folks bought a 1951 Ford Crown Victoria. Her mother would send her to the store, and Carolyn would take a detour down farm-to-market road 1840 to Austin Chapel, where the Merrill family lived in the parsonage next to the church. That little visit didn't last too long. Her mother knew what she was up to.

On Saturday afternoons at the State Theatre in DeKalb, Carolyn and I loved our Flash Gordon serials. And our favorites in the Western movies were Roy Rogers, Randolph

Scott, and Hopalong Cassidy. We rarely missed Tarzan.

Along with movies and church, we also had DeKalb Bear football games on Friday night. Talk about making the social scene. Carolyn was elected runner-up to the homecoming queen a couple of times, and I was selected our team's most valuable player. Carolyn and I just knew that we were made for each other.

Most of the big four-year colleges thought I needed a little more seasoning before I stepped into the big time. So Texarkana Junior College, about forty miles from DeKalb, was the place I decided to continue my football career. College might not have been in the cards for me without a football scholarship.

When I left Texarkana J.C. two years later, we'd won a national championship and lost a grand total of two games. One of those losses was to the Arkansas Razorbacks freshman team that boasted one of the most gifted athletes of any era, Lance Alworth. They beat us by a touchdown. That win, I'm sure, helped launch Lance to the Pro Football Hall of Fame.

I did a little cutting up in junior college. But not much. Five of us went to the barbershop before we played the nation's top-ranked ju-co team, the Tyler Apaches.

Texarkana's Grim Stadium was packed. We ran onto the field with our helmets on. But right before the pregame prayer, I pulled off my lid and revealed my fashionable new hairstyle—a mohawk. My mom and dad almost passed out in the stands.

Mom looked at Carolyn, and Carolyn looked at mom, and in unison they said, "Oh my God." Dad had to walk down to the concession stand to compose himself.

Tyler needed a two-point conversion late in the game to beat us. Playing defensive end, I sensed a bootleg. Their quarterback faked the handoff and then rolled in the opposite direction. He ran right into my waiting arms. I'd made one of the biggest plays in a win over the nation's top team. But I was no hero at home.

I was allowed to eat dinner with the family that night. But I wasn't invited to church the next morning. Until my hair grew back, I didn't attend church with Ebenezer Levi in the pulpit.

The courtship with Carolyn continued. She came to my home football games. We rode around from time to time in her Ford Crown Victoria. And in my sophomore year, we decided to get married the day before Thanksgiving.

Carolyn said, "Now, Durwood, I know that football is still the top priority. But I think we can squeeze in a wedding during the season."

Squeeze we did. On Thanksgiving, the fourth-ranked Texarkana J. C. Bulldogs were scheduled to play for the third-ranked team from Wingate, North Carolina. So we set the wedding for seven o'clock on the evening before Thanksgiving.

The walk-through practice on Wednesday ran a little long, and our coach, Duncan Thompson, decided to give us one of his Knute Rockne speeches afterward. I loved the speech. But I was checking my watch and wondering if I was going to make it to the chapel on time.

It was about forty miles from our practice field to the church, and I knew we were going to be late. Two of my teammates, Wesley Duncan and Larry Green, rode with me. We got there about 7:20, and my dad, who was performing the ceremony, was pacing on the porch. The organist just kept playing. The church was packed, and I'm sure a lot of the guests were wondering if I was going to show.

Carolyn, however, was as cool as a cucumber. She knew that football was my vehicle through college. She knew that I had to practice with the team and that I would somehow make it. The ceremony started about twenty minutes late. I remember my dad telling me right before the wedding that marriage was "making a lifetime commitment." I never thought it would be anything else.

That night, we drove her dad's shiny new Buick to the Sands Motel in Texarkana. We watched the Macy's Thanksgiving Day parade on TV the next morning, and that afternoon the Bulldogs beat the boys from North Carolina 42–7. We finished number two in the country that year, right behind perennial powerhouse Fresno State, the winner of the Little Rose Bowl.

Not many people outside of Texas have heard of East Texas State (now called Texas A&M–Commerce). But that little school turned out players like Dwight White, the great defensive end for the Steelers, and Harvey Martin, the sack leader for the Dallas Cowboys. Wade Wilson, an ETSU quarterback, played fifteen seasons for the Cowboys and Vikings.

In the 1950s, we were just one cut below the NCAA big-time programs. We would be the equivalent of today's 1-AA schools. During my years on the roster, we were regularly in the NAIA top ten. We could have beaten some of the Southwest Conference teams.

From that team, John Gilliam went on to play for Kansas City, and Dee Mackey had some great years for the New York Jets and Baltimore Colts.

After I finished my junior college career in Texarkana, East Texas State came calling. I decided to take their scholarship and finish up my eligibility there. I walked into the student union that first day, and somebody was tapping me on the shoulder. I turned around and it was Johnny Burchett, one of the Grove Rats. "Johnny," I said, "you saved my life. They were going to kill me." Johnny just kind of snickered and walked away. I never saw him again.

Truth is, I was just a run-of-the-mill player at ETSU. I was on all of the kicking teams, and in some ways, I was like Bill Bates, who just finished up his fifteenth year with the Dallas Cowboys. They say that mediocre players make the best coaches. I certainly fit that formula for success.

I was well-liked and a team player. My teammates were sure pleased that I didn't drink. After games, they'd order up several kegs of beer, and they'd go out in the woods and build a big bonfire. They'd take me along to make sure that when they got drunk, they didn't fall into the fire. When they went to the Dallas bars, which were about sixty miles away, they'd call me for a ride home after they drank too much. I guess that made me even more of a team player.

Here was the tough part. My new wife, Carolyn, didn't go to Commerce with me. She continued to live with her parents there in DeKalb and took a job at the Red River Army Depot in Hooks. I'd make the two-hour drive home after our Saturday games. Then I was up at four o'clock Monday morning, heading back to college. Leaving Carolyn behind like that every week was awfully hard. We both cried a little those Monday mornings. But we both knew that we'd have a great future, especially if I graduated from college.

We got a big break. I finished up at ETSU and headed off for my first coaching assignment—back home with the DeKalb Bears. It just seemed that my life had already come full circle.

Out at Home

MY WIFE, CAROLYN, KEEPS a placard on our kitchen wall in Hooks that reads "We interrupt this marriage to bring you the baseball season." To live in the Merrill household all of these years is to know the truth behind that little message.

Leaving my small-town life and going into professional umpiring, I knew that things would never be the same. A lot of my friends thought I was crazier than a cuckoo clock at midnight. I'd been living the good life in Hooks, teaching and coaching, and I'd been promoted to principal. Mama and I'd been building this life of ours brick by brick from the days when football paid my way through college. Our lives had moved slowly but surely and always straight ahead, and we'd never looked back during more than ten years of raising our family. Then came the interruption.

After sending off my résumé to the Umpiring Development School, I decided to place a call to Mr. Bobby Bragan down in Fort Worth to get his input. I'd met Mr. Bragan a few years earlier and I thought he might help me get into umpiring. He'd played for the Brooklyn Dodgers and the Phillies and he'd managed seven years in the major leagues. He was the president of the Double-A Texas League when I called. Bobby is still what you'd consider a baseball ambassador, and for decades he's lived by the same motto: You can't hit the ball with the bat on your shoulder.

"Mr. Bragan," I began, "please understand. But I've

kind of lost my edge for the school business. I've had this dream of getting into umpiring, and I was just hoping—'' The softest southern drawl you'd ever heard stopped me in midsentence. Howard Cosell once said that Bobby was Elmer Gantry in uniform. His words were like molasses dripping into a jar.

"Say no more, my boy," Bobby said. "It's time to get on with your task. You call up Mr. Barney Deary down there in Florida and get yourself enrolled in umpiring school. I promise that I'll get you to the Texas League just as fast as I can. But, Durwood, you've got to act fast. Get to Florida and start taking your hacks."

Now, if Mr. Bobby Bragan had told me I was too old to start an umpiring career, I would've hung up the phone and gone back to work in the Hooks School District for the rest of my life. I'd decided that I wasn't even going to get a second opinion because, with so many years in the baseball business, I knew Mr. Bragan would give me the straight poop.

As I thought about my life ahead, I also reflected on the great things that had happened there in Hooks with all of the wonderful kids. I'd excelled at being the athletic director and the head football coach, and we'd pretty well filled up our glass case in the high school foyer with district championship trophies. I'd met a lot of successful people like Barry Switzer, the head coach at Oklahoma, along with Texas coach Darrell Royal and Arkansas coach Frank Broyles. I'm not saying that coaching wasn't what I'd envisioned. To the contrary, it'd been challenging and pretty doggone fun to stand there on the sideline on a Friday night with the high school band playing and the game on the line.

Had I become a hopeless dreamer, or was there really hope that I could pull this crazy little game plan off? I knew that a lot of my friends were whispering behind my back. None of them ever sat me down and told me that I might be making a mistake. But I could tell by the vibes that there were some doubters in my inner circle.

To this day, I still haven't asked my dad what he thought

about me just dropping everything at home and heading out around the country for about eight months every year. When I told him that I was going down to Florida to start a new life, it got awfully quiet on the other end of the phone. In my heart, I know he wanted to tell me to get my head out of the clouds and to stay there in Hooks with my wife and kids. But my dad walked off the farm one day when everybody in Washita County thought he was going to be a farmer for the rest of his life. And I guess he thought I was owed at least one trip around the bases to see if my rainbow was waiting there at home plate.

As I could have predicted, all of these visions were badly blurred on the day that I packed those bags and headed off for umpiring school. When I finally was faced with the reality of leaving my wife and kids behind, it just shook me right down to the bone marrow. My son, Mickey, was ten, and my daughter, Maria, was seven when I walked out the door. You couldn't have knocked that knot out of my throat with a sledgehammer. A man instinctively knows that he shouldn't leave his kids that long during their formative years. Sociologists have taught us for decades that the absence of a father normally leads to a dysfunctional family life. When I left home for baseball umpiring, my kids thought Daddy would be home in a few days. They just figured that I was off on another coaching trip and that when the game was over, my car would come rolling back the street in front of our house. Little did anyone really know where this adventure would take me.

It seems that I didn't come home for twenty years.

When I took off that day, I didn't think about the fact that umpires don't have home stands like the players and managers, and we don't get to sleep in our own beds about half the season. We do nothing but airports and road trips. Granted, our working conditions have improved in the 1990s, thanks to the growth of a strong union. But in my kids' formative years, Big Daddy was gone during spring training and the entire season with the exception of three days off at the All-Star break. I'd come home at the end of the baseball season, look at one of my two kids, and say, "Who's this?"

Umpires will tell you that the baseball season really is harder on the mamas and the kids than it is on us. You'd better have a family with thick skin and a willingness to make their own decisions. Life is going to be hell around the household if they don't have those qualities. I wouldn't have made it to the major leagues and stuck around for all of these years if I didn't have a great family.

During my four seasons in the minor leagues and those early years in The Bigs, umpires got about as many days off as the *New York Times*. I begged for trips back to Hooks to see Mickey and Maria graduate from high school and was denied both times. My bosses wouldn't give me a day off to fly home for Maria's wedding. I missed Mickey playing in the state baseball tournament. Those things you never can get back, so in some respects, my kids did a lot of growing up without me.

Whenever I asked my boss, Dick Butler, for time off for a special occasion, he'd either scowl and give me a flat no, or he'd just tune me out. I remember asking him about going back to Texas for Mickey's high school graduation, and he said, "What do you need to do, Durwood? Help him across the stage? Can't he pick up the diploma by himself?"

Mickey Dale Merrill was born to play baseball. Heck, I named him after the great Mickey Mantle and Dale Mitchell, a .312 lifetime hitter with the Cleveland Indians and Brooklyn Dodgers in the 1940s and early 1950s. Dale also happened to be my cousin. Mickey became an outstanding high school catcher. He was a big kid with soft hands and a great arm, and he really could hit the long ball. He was the kind of kid who listened intently and was one of the most coachable players you've ever seen. I mean, he was all "yes sir" and "no sir" and did everything for the team.

But I didn't see more than a handful of Mickey's high school games. I was never there to give him little tips on how to handle pitchers or how to punch the ball into right field. I wasn't there when he struck out and needed a pat on the back and a little understanding. Because I was a high-profile man from a small town, Mickey had some extra pressure to carry around at school and on the ball fields. I could have helped him deal with it if I just could have been there.

He was good enough to play three years at Southern Arkansas University and, to my thinking, talented enough to have considered a pro career. But I know why Mickey didn't pursue a pro career after giving it a lot of thought. I'm not sure he'll admit this even today. But the fact that I was away from home so much was really unsettling for him. He saw the life I was living, and I don't think he wanted to follow in his dad's footsteps. It might have been different if I'd been around more.

Today, I think he's proud of his dad and what I've accomplished in baseball. Mickey lives with his wife and family in Richardson, Texas, where he coaches sports and teaches school. He's got three kids. I know that Mickey is really happy these days that I come home more often, because we get to spend more time together. Maybe I'm making up for lost time, but it sure is fun.

My daughter, Maria, will flatly tell you that she missed her daddy during her formative years. I firmly believe that my absence had a greater impact on my daughter than it did on my son. At least Mickey had sports to occupy him. Back then, Maria thought I should have been able to come home when I wanted to. She thought I could just pack my bags and catch the next plane home from wherever when the family needed me. She'd ask Mama, "Why doesn't Daddy come home every once in a while?" When I didn't show up for her high school plays, I really believe the resentment began to build.

Maria distinguished herself in high school theater, and I know what she must have been feeling and thinking inside: "If I make it to Austin for the state finals, then maybe my daddy will show up and watch me." I didn't. Leaving my assigned games was tougher than she thought. Maybe I should have done a better job of explaining, or maybe I should have just packed a bag and told my bosses that I was leaving for a few days to go see my little girl perform on-stage.

When I was a rookie in the major leagues in 1977, Mama called one day from home to tell me that Maria was sick and needed surgery. I couldn't even get a pass from the American League to go home. So I was working the plate at Cleveland Municipal Stadium and having just a horrible night calling balls and strikes. I had the Orioles and the Indians all over my butt by the third inning. Focusing on pitches was next to impossible because my heart and my mind were back in Texas with my little girl.

Marty Springstead was working third base that night, and about the fourth inning, with both benches firing insults and magical words at me, Marty walked down the line and hol-lered, "Hey, Durwood! Just get it off your mind. There's nothing you can do about your daughter right now. Just get your head back into the game."

I took his advice and did a pretty good job of calling balls and strikes the rest of the way. I had to force myself to become distanced from the situation back in Hooks, and in some respects, I had to develop a second personality to put my troubles aside. But after the game, I went back to the hotel room and cried, even though the surgery had gone well and Maria was going to be okay.

Fortunately, the wounds have healed between me and my daughter. Why? Because Maria has been open and honest in talking about her childhood feelings and telling me about her pain. We've been able to work through it because we've talked. We're very close now, and I feel good about that. She has five children, and it's been a wonderful experience being with her entire family all these years.

Conversely, Mickey and I really haven't talked a lot about all the time I was gone when he was a kid and really needed me. I wonder about that sometimes.

Mama has been a trouper since the day I packed up the car and headed off to my first year in the Cal League. She knew there was something out there calling me and I needed to follow my heart. Instead of holding me back, she threw her full support behind everything that I did.

In effect, Mama for many years had to play the role of both parents. If the washing machine needed fixing or if the icebox was broken, she had to take care of it. These days, she can write a check or use a credit card, and the problem is instantly solved. But back in the early days, when I was off umpiring in some lonely Podunk minor league town or down in Puerto Rico, the Merrill family didn't have much money in the bank. If something broke down in those years, Mama had to do some creative financing.

Not only was Mama running the family, she had a full-time job at the army depot and she had five people working under her. Thank God for her job because otherwise we wouldn't have kept our heads above water in the tough times, especially that first year in the Cal League when I made $1,800. The fact that she could work and handle the family took a lot of pressure off the marriage. There were a few lean years before I got into The Bigs when she was the real breadwinner.

At times, when I've been out there on the road, I've had trouble overcoming my guilt because I know my kids have needed me and Carolyn has needed a husband around the house. During their growing-up years, kids just need their daddy. That's why our union for years has been making a priority of negotiating for days off during the season, and why umpires now can go home for graduations and weddings and state baseball play-offs. One of the really big changes has been the addition of substitute umpires who can replace the regular guys on short notice.

I still think about the early years when I asked for days off to be with my family on special occasions and was told by Mr. Butler, "You're lucky to be in the major leagues. Hell, you could be back in Oklahoma City umping in the bush leagues." Mr. Butler was a bachelor and didn't understand how important it was to have a family life, and, in one respect, he was just doing his job. We're all grateful today that our boss, Marty Springstead, was an umpire for twenty years and realizes that men need to go home to their families. Hopefully, our young umpires will never have to experience the brutal stuff we once faced.

Being on the road for so many days of the year, working in front of millions and millions of people, and dealing with so many egos can airbrush your view of the real world. I've always felt that people who do the road circus called pro sports see life a little differently than your average Kmart shopper.

I've really seen some ballplayers in my time who floated out there into the stratosphere and never came back. The showbiz mentality of baseball will do that to you, and God knows I've even seen it grab a few umpires by the throat. You just get so distanced from washing your own socks that you start thinking your feet don't stink. The baseball carnival starts to seem like real life. Pretty soon, you let your hair grow out and you stop wearing socks altogether, just like hardballers.

For years, I thought baseball was a bigger home-wrecker than a secretary in a miniskirt. Every day, you'd walk into a ballpark and hear that so-and-so had just moved out on the missus and he was planning on flying down to Rio during the off-season to practice his fastball on the topless beaches. All you have to do is check out the comp seats at any ballpark and you'll see the players aren't leaving will-call tickets for Uncle Eddie. Divorce, of course, has no exclusive hold on the ballplayers. It's taken its toll on the managers and the broadcasters and the team trainers and, yes, even the umpires. Just being away from home all that time will make a man forgetful.

I'm not saying that anyone should feel sorry for people in the baseball business. I know that the divorce rate is running rampant all over, especially in urban America. The point I'm trying to make is this: Given the nature of our lives and the stress we encounter, the baseball profession can be hard on the home life. I'm one of the lucky ones because I've had a solid family at home all these years.

Umpires normally don't talk openly about their problems, especially the ones back at home. The code of the profession is that you just don't delve into another umpire's personal life unless he initiates the conversation. The same principle applies to bad calls during a game. I'm not going to tell one of my crew members that he made a bad call unless he asks my opinion.

You're with your crew more than half the year, and you want to give each man his own space, especially when it comes to private matters. Besides, if we sat around and talked about all the things cooking at home, there wouldn't be time to play the games.

The late Jerry Neudecker was a twenty-year umpire, who, like the rest of us, barely recognized the house and the neighborhood at the end of the season. He umpired from 1965 through 1985, and I think Jerry probably had to stop at the corner gas station to find the road home in October. In the mid-1970s, Jerry knew his only time at home during the season would be the three-day All-Star break. Such was the sad state of affairs with most umpires back then. Our bosses knew that sending a man on the road all those months in succession wasn't good for his marriage, but they still wouldn't give us the days off.

So Jerry flew home for the All-Star break, and his wife picked him up at the airport. Of course, Jerry hadn't been back in a long time, and he was feeling like a stranger in his own house. But, as he walked through the front door, he thought everything was as normal as it could be. His wife was cooking him breakfast when the doorbell rang. Jerry got up from his chair and casually walked across the house and opened the door. And there stood the deputy sheriff, who pulled divorce papers out of his pocket and served Jerry right there on his own front porch.

Jerry wept when he told me the story, and he said he cried in court when the divorce became final. Given the nature of his occupation, and the fact that he was on the road almost two-thirds of the year, I wonder if there was anything Jerry could have done to save his marriage short of retiring from baseball. That's just a decision a lot of umpires have to make: either give up the marriage or give up the game. Divorce is a way of life in our profession, and I've seen a lot of good people go through some very sad times.

Marty Springstead might be the best person I've known on this job. Shoot, they promoted him to executive director of the American League umpires in 1986. He was like a big brother to me when I got into the major leagues and started working as a rookie on his crew in 1977. Marty gave me great advice on umpiring and life that I've followed and lived by for decades. But even Marty couldn't hold his marriage together during all those hard years on the road.

This life we lead in major league baseball is an exciting one that I wouldn't trade for anything that I know of. You don't have to work in an office from nine to five, you avoid rush hour traffic most of the time, and you get to meet some pretty doggone interesting people. But's it's also a fast-lane business that can lead to heartbreak if you're not careful. As I moved deeper and deeper into this jungle, I began to learn about the minefields. I came face-to-face with the reality that even the most innocent mistakes can cost you dearly.

A Tragic Call

I'LL NEVER FORGET MEETING Steve Palermo. It was during the dog days of umpiring school. We were as different as a Nolan Ryan fastball and a Phil Niekro knuckler. He was from Boston and I was a hick from the sticks.

Stevie nicknamed me "Spanky" after the kid in the TV show. He thought I was the big overgrown leader of "our gang." The gang included Al Clark and Ed Montague and a few other soon-to-be umpires. Everybody kind of followed me around back in those days because of my southern-fried wit that kept them laughing. I guess I helped ease the tension of camp. I named Steve "Bones" because he was skinnier than a Louisville Slugger.

I instantly liked Steve because he was a fireball and he didn't mind saying what was on his mind. When I made one of my many mistakes back in umpiring school, he'd laughed until there was no more air in his body. That might have set off another umpire. Me, I just laughed along with him. They say that laughter cuts trouble down to a size that you can talk to. Boy, howdy, was that ever true about my little buddy.

When the laughter stopped, though, Stevie could rage with the best of them. As we say in Texas, Stevie liked to open up a can of whip-ass from time to time. I haven't seen many tempers like his. One night at Fenway Park, Stevie and Bobby Valentine, who was managing the Rangers, almost broke up the umpire's room. It always seemed that Italians made Stevie the maddest. That's funny when you consider my pal is full-blooded Italian.

Stevie and I made a heck of a team, especially when we umpired together in Puerto Rico in the off-season of 1975. Which is another way of saying that we went to war together.

Umpiring in Puerto Rico during winter ball was like wrestling in the main event at the World Wrestling Federation. We were taking somebody to the mat every night and always testing the odds. Everybody on the island was mad at us, and about half of the crazy rascals carried handguns. At least, it seemed that way. You might have twenty thousand fans and ten thousand handguns in the same ballpark. We needed bulletproof vests, I guess.

The ballparks looked like prisons to me. They kept the so-called fans off the field by ringing the field in strands and strands of barbed wire. Every night was almost like a prison riot with fights in the stands and people pulling for their teams and baseball heroes. I kept telling my bosses back in the States to send lawyers, guns, and money.

Why were we there? I didn't even need to ask. We were there because Dick Butler, the supervisor of American League umpires, wanted us there. He said it would toughen us up. Butler kind of viewed Puerto Rico as a finishing school for umpires on their way to the major leagues. He's lucky it didn't finish us off. He also knew that the brand of baseball was better than what we'd seen in Triple-A ball. This experience was very helpful, but also stressful. I must admit, though, that sometimes I wondered if we were going to survive it.

Because we were from the States, umpires stood out like crawfish at a calf-fry. The Puerto Ricans knew the American umpires would come down much harder on their heroes. They never thought that we should throw one of their beloved players out of the game. When you factored all of the guns they were carrying, and the gambling that was going on involving these games, the umpires had plenty of reasons to be on edge.

Before taking off for winter ball in 1972, Joe Brinkman

had heard all the horror stories. He knew there were gun-toting crazies walking the streets. So he wasn't completely surprised when he got a letter a couple of days before his arrival. One of the radical groups down there was threatening to assassinate Joe. Since he was a low-paid umpire without a lot of money in his savings account, Joe decided to roll the dice and go on down anyway.

Coming out of a restaurant one night, Joe and his crew encountered what they thought was a militia loose in the street. They dived onto the sidewalk and hid their heads. They were waiting for the shooting to begin. After several minutes, they heard no shots. Local citizens just walked around the four silly-looking Americans lying on the sidewalk. Summoning the courage to crawl on their hands and knees, the men finally realized that their tormentor was a statue of a revolutionary rifleman on horseback. He was carrying the only unloaded gun in town.

Tommy Lasorda has never been afraid of anything, including umpires. God knows how many times I've tossed him out of meaningless spring training games. But Tommy ran into an umpire in the Caribbean that got his attention. I wish I'd been there.

Because he was an animated character, both as a player and manager, Tommy was a popular little jokester in the Caribbean. Pitching in winter ball in the 1950s, he was warned not to mess with a legendary Cuban plate umpire named Maistri. Of course, that didn't stop Tommy. Maistri called Tommy's first two pitches balls, even though they were straight down the heart of the plate. Tommy started walking toward the umpire. Maistri started walking toward him. About halfway to the mound, Maistri opened his jacket pocket to reveal a large pistol. Tommy said, "You know, Maistri, you're the best damned umpire I've ever seen." Maistri nodded in agreement.

I was sitting in the dugout with Steve Palermo one night during a long rain delay. The owner of the Santurce team came by and waved a gun at us and said, "I don't like the way you call my game." Actually, I think he was madder at

Palermo than me. The wild-eyed nutcase bellowed, "You show up at my game tomorrow night and I start shooting!" And Steve winked and said, "Well, then, señor, you'd better bring your pistol."

Steve and I were both young and cocky, and we were on the verge of making it to the major leagues. We knew that Puerto Rico was our last stop before we got the heck out of Triple-A ball and made it to the big time. And we weren't putting up with any lip from a bunch of half-baked thugs. As long as Stevie and I were together, nothing scared us. The other umpires on the island were Mike Reilly, Greg Kosc, Dale Ford, Ted Hendry, and Stevie. This group of umpires in 1975 wasn't going to be intimidated by anyone, especially by the stars like Orlando Cepeda, Sandy Alomar Sr., Willie Montanez, and Ellie Rodriguez. We treated them like professional ballplayers and, if they crossed the line, we removed them. This didn't set too well with the fans and some of the owners. But at least the Puerto Rican president was willing to stand up for us.

When you're down on the island, fighting those crazy people, you start acting a little crazy yourself. I was in my mid-thirties and not once in my life had I ever grown my hair out. So Palermo and I decided that it was time to liberate ourselves. We just let it grow and grow and grow, and it was down to our shoulders that winter. We looked like something straight out of a Grateful Dead concert.

One afternoon we were out on the beach, having a big time. Our condominium was right there on the ocean, and we loved the sand and sun. I had a big bottle of peroxide. Because I'm a stocky guy with big arms and big shoulders, we told everybody on the beach that I was a pro wrestler. Stevie, we said, was my manager.

My hair is sandy-colored anyway, and it was getting lighter by the day, bleaching out in the sun. But Steve's hair was black, like most Italians. When he put peroxide on his hair, it turned bright orange. He looked like a guy walking around with a basketball stuck to his head.

As my hair turned completely blond, everybody started

calling me Gorgeous George after the world-famous championship wrestler. We were acting just like the other fruitcakes down on the island until Dick Butler showed up at one of our games.

Now, we never expected Mr. Butler to come walking into the ballpark there at Bayamón. We didn't even know he was on the island. We thought he was back in the States, working on umpiring schedules. But Dick walked into the press box that night and started asking, "Where is Merrill and Palermo?" One of the writers said, "Well, that's Merrill behind the plate and that's Palermo on the bases." Looking plumb nauseated, Dick blurted, "That's impossible! That's not my guys!"

"Oh, yeah that's them," the writer said. "Trust me. That's your boys."

Dick Butler didn't talk to us for several days. But he finally did forgive us. He realized we were acting just like the rest of the Caribbean crazies down there.

For years, a picture of me and Steve with blond and orange hair was plastered on the wall at Umpire's Developmental School. It really was a portrait of two men just trying to survive winter ball. All we wanted to do was get out of the ballpark alive every night.

The first thing you learn from winter ball in the Caribbean is that you can't take any lip. Back down once and they'll crawl all over you. I had to take drastic measures. One of the managers would jump my butt, and I'd say something like, "Get the hell away from before I rip your lungs out." That seemed to get the message across.

I had so many rum bottles thrown at me that I could tell the difference between Bacardi and Captain Morgan just by the sound. Bacardi had a long-neck bottle, and Captain Morgan had almost no neck at all. They made a different whistling sound as they flew by my ear. The Bacardi bottles traveled farther and faster because the launcher could get a better grip with that long neck.

The longer you umpired in Puerto Rico, the better you became at judging how far those rum bottles could be thrown. You tried to work as far off the foul line as you could. I never got hit by a rum bottle. But I got pelted with enough oranges to open a fruit stand. If you made a tough call against the home team, you could expect oranges, pineapples, rum bottles, programs, shirts, bricks, and a few pieces of cement to come flying out of the stands. There were times we had to call out the police to restore peace and get the game going again.

When you first walk into the ballparks in Puerto Rico, they seem like friendly places. The atmosphere is festive. Salsa bands are playing, and people are dancing in the aisles and on the dugouts. The fans dress in their team's colors, and they seem ready for celebration. In Bayamón, a woman sprays the home team's players with holy water.

Then a couple of goons start pulling pistols and all hell breaks loose. Dale Ford and Nick Bremigan were working an Opening Day game when two fans pulled their pistols and started shooting at each other. In just a matter of minutes, the two wounded men were carried away on stretchers. The game continued as if nothing had happened.

Ford, who was doing his first tour of duty in Puerto Rico, walked over to Bremigan, who seemed quite calm in spite of the flying bullets. "Nick, how often does this happen?" Ford asked. "Don't worry," Bremigan replied. "They've got an ordinance down here about shooting toward a sporting event."

I did my best to try to soothe the fans. I'd walk over close to the stands and I'd throw Chiclets gum into the first few rows. I'd yell, "Here, have some Chiclets." It helped keep the fans off me.

Palmero used to call me "the Chiclets Man." He'd say, "Yeah, I'm over here, dodging rum bottles and Durwood's over there throwing gum into the stands. Tell me this makes sense."

Rick Dempsey was one of the feisty spark plugs of major league baseball. I think being in Puerto Rico just fired him up even more. The Orioles catchers just wouldn't take any lip from anybody. Playing for Caguas, Dempsey got irritated one night when big Jimmy Johnson, pitching for Bayamón, hit a batter. Dempsey started riding Johnson from the bench.

You knew what was going to happen when Dempsey got up to bat. Johnson drilled him in the rib cage. Johnson stands six-foot-three and weighs about 240 pounds. Dempsey was about five-ten and 180 pounds. But the size difference didn't stop Dempsey from charging the mound.

Since I was behind home plate, it was my job to get between them, even though I didn't want to. When Dempsey yelled, "Durwood, duck!" it really didn't make any sense. But I ducked anyway. Dempsey came right over the top of me and managed to land a rabbit punch squarely to Johnson's jaw. That was his only lucky shot of the fight. I managed to get out of his way, and Johnson started flailing away. Even though Dempsey stood his ground, Johnson was mad and he landed a lot of solid shots.

After our last game in Puerto Rico, we had armed guards drive us to the San Juan airport for a late-night flight back to the States. As we walked into the airport, one of the guards yelled, "Hey, señores, if we ever want you back on this island again, we will call you. In the meantime, señores, don't call us!" We never did!

I believe that God wanted me to be in Arlington, Texas, when Steve Palermo's umpiring career came crashing to a tragic halt on July 7, 1991. I'd switched crews to replace Larry Young, who'd gone on vacation. I stayed behind in Arlington to join Mike Reilly, Richie Garcia, and Stevie.

It was late on a Saturday night, and Stevie had been working third base. He was dead tired, just having come to Texas from Seattle. He'd worked home plate the night before. In spite of his near-exhaustion, Stevie was going out after the game come hell or half of Texas. He had a good friend, Corky Campisi, who was the co-owner of Campisi's Egyptian Restaurant over in Dallas. (Arlington is halfway between downtown Dallas and downtown Fort Worth.) Campisi's is a hot little Italian joint where the dinner line extends far down the sidewalk on Saturday nights. It's where Jack Ruby had his last meal before shooting Lee Harvey Oswald. Some strange and suspicious things have happened there the last thirty-five years or so.

Stevie and Corky Campisi had met several years ago during a game in Arlington. They'd become fast friends. They were further bonded by their Italian blood. (At least Stevie didn't want to beat him up.)

Stevie asked me to come along to Campisi's that night. But I was dead tired, too. And since I was staying with my daughter, Maria, just west of Fort Worth, I decided to pass on the invitation. But I made sure that Stevie didn't go alone. I convinced Richie Garcia to go along because I knew that Stevie was operating on fumes. The other umpires told me that Steve had been in a funk the last couple of weeks and that my being there had helped his morale. He'd been going through some tough mood swings. So I was feeling guilty about turning him down. We'd always protected each other, going all the way back twenty years to umpiring school. Stevie had this shrill ear-piercing whistle. Whenever he needed me, he'd whistle.

I really believe that Stevie thought something bad was going to happen that night. If we'd been in another city, I would have been there. But I was staying about forty miles from Dallas.

Steve kind of treated me like a father figure. And just like a father, I could sense that something wasn't right with him.

It was a little past eleven o'clock when Richie and Stevie arrived at Campisi's in Dallas. They ate and swapped stories and had a good time. Richie was getting tired and decided to take a cab back to the hotel a little after midnight. But Stevie and Corky and a former SMU football player named Terrance Mann were just getting revved up.

About twelve-thirty, one of the employees was closing the blinds at the front of the restaurant when he saw that two of the waitresses were being mugged in the median of Mockingbird Lane. Waitresses at Campisi's make big tips, and they carry a lot of cash. The restaurant does a cash-only business. The four thugs had the waitresses down on the ground and were trying to take off with their purses.

Told about the attack, Steve, Terrance, and Corky bolted through the front door. I'm sure the four hoodlums were startled to see three men running their way. Mann was a big ol' defensive tackle at SMU, checking in at about six-foot-six and 275 pounds. He probably scared the living bejeebers out of those guys.

Two of the waitress-bashing bandits jumped in the car that was being occupied by the getaway driver. They sped away, leaving one of their buddies on foot. The straggler started sprinting west down Mockingbird Lane. At that point, maybe Stevie, Corky, and Terrance should have called the Dallas police and considered their fine work to be done. They'd accomplished their goal—saving the waitresses from the bandits. Stevie and Terrance took off on foot, chasing the robber down Mockingbird. They were like raging animals loose on the street. Corky and Jimmy Upton, one of the restaurant employees, hopped in a Jeep and joined the chase.

This will give you an idea of just how intent they were on getting their man. They chased him about a mile down to Central Expressway. Instead of running across the Mockingbird Lane bridge, the robber sprinted down the steep fifty-foot concrete embankment and started crossing four lanes of Central Expressway. He was crazier than a henhouse rat. If you've ever driven in Dallas, you know that Central Expressway is one of the most dangerous roads in America. Locals drive it like the Daytona 500. They should have all been killed. Stevie and Terrance followed the man on foot across the expressway and up the embankment on the other side.

Picking up the chase again down Mockingbird Lane, Stevie and Terrance finally cornered their man in the Mrs. Baird's Bakery parking lot. That's where it should have ended. As they held him down, Jimmy Upton ran into the 7-Eleven to call the cops. The cops said they would be there in three to five minutes.

They arrived too late.

A car screeched to a halt a few feet away from where Steve and Terrance were holding their man down. It was the same three men who had bolted from Campisi's. Out of the blue, a gunman walked around from the passenger side of the car and raised a .25-caliber pistol. Stevie started yelling, "He's got a gun! Everybody get down!"

The gunman hit Terrance three times—in the chin, the side, and the arm. The fourth shot hit a wall behind the bakery. The fifth was aimed for Steve Palermo. This is how he remembered it:

"Naturally, I turned my back because I didn't wanted to get hit in the face. I knew by now that there was a pretty good chance that I was going to get shot.

"The bullet hit me in the right side at belt level and went through my spinal cord. It exited through my back. I immediately knew that I was in trouble when I hit the ground because I couldn't feel my legs. My two legs felt like big pieces of laundry. They were just mush. I lay there on that parking lot, looking at the stars and that hot Dallas sky. I kept pounding the hell out of my legs with my right hand. I could feel my hand. But my legs were totally numb. It was like the lower half of my body had been removed. It was just an ugly, terrible scene, and there wasn't a damn thing I could do about it.

"I could feel the life draining right out of me. It was like somebody had poured hot water through the top of my head and it was draining all the way down through my body. It was really like having an out-of-body experience."

With Terrance and Stevie lying on that parking lot, the foursome sped away before the cops could arrive. But a few blocks away, in the suburban town of Highland Park, they were stopped on a routine traffic violation. The car had a broken taillight. The gunman had planned to shoot the Highland Park cop, but his gun jammed. The four men were arrested and booked for attempted murder.

At around four o'clock that morning, the call came to my daughter's house. Somebody from Baylor Hospital in Dallas was telling me that a man named Steve Palermo had been shot several times and that he was in critical condition. I kept asking myself, "How is that possible?" Nobody, I thought, was capable of gunning down the Steve Palermo I knew. That would be like shooting Superman. This crazy Italian was bulletproof. You can't hurt Bones, I thought.

"What?" I said into the phone. "There must be a big mistake here."

I instantly went into denial. The next few hours were a blur. Somebody drove me to the hospital. I do remember getting there and standing over my best friend, who was lying there paralyzed from the waist down. I remember thinking that I might find him dead. Emotions shot through me like lightning bolts. I couldn't comprehend what I was seeing or hearing.

"Spanky," he whispered, "I felt all of the life draining right out of me. They kept shooting and shooting. I thought about my wife. I thought about my mother. I really thought it was over, Spanky."

There, as I stood over the finest umpire I'd ever known, I started to cry. For the first time in his life, Stevie Palermo had a look of fear on his face. It was chilling.

Sometimes when I see my great friend, I have to walk away. I don't want him to see my tears. You see, Steve Palmermo was supposed to be umpiring in the major leagues long after Spanky was gone. He was young and vibrant and alive. He was the best natural umpire I've ever seen. There was no better balls-and-strikes umpire in either league. Kids at umpiring school should be required to watch films of this man in action. It was a great gift that he gave to baseball.

I know that Stevie, who lives in Kansas City, still has bad days. But when we go into Royals Stadium for a series, and he walks into the umpire's room before the game, everything still lights up. It's almost as if he never went away. Even though he's on crutches, and even though Steve Palermo likely will never walk onto the field again to accept the lineup cards, the glow is still there. They may have taken his legs. They may have robbed him of some physical strength. But the man inside Stevie Palermo is still strong. The fire still burns. You can still see the light in his eyes. That helps keep me going. I guess ol' Bones will never know the strength he gives to me, and the strength he has given to others.

Yes, I'm a little bitter about what happened to my great friend. I'm trying not to affix blame. But if I'd been there, Stevie Palermo would have never taken off running down Mockingbird Lane in the wee hours of that morning. Corky Campisi, or somebody, should have tackled him. After saving the waitresses, they should have gone back into the restaurant, mixed a couple of drinks, and called the police. There was too much danger on the street for those guys to be running around like vigilantes. They had done their job in getting the thugs off the waitresses. Enough is enough.

But that wasn't enough for Stevie. You know why? Because Steve Palermo wasn't going to stand for what had happened on the street in Dallas that night. I learned that about the man in 1972 when we went to umpiring school together. I saw the pride grow inside the man with every passing season. That's the way he was raised. In Stevie's world, there was good and evil and nothing in between. You had no middle ground with Steve Palermo. That is the umpire's type A personality. Somebody had to pay for what they had done to those waitresses. Steve Palermo was simply trying to make things right on his own terms.

The night after Stevie was shot, I was behind the plate and Nolan Ryan was pitching at old Arlington Stadium against the California Angels. An hour before the game, Nolan called me in the umpire's room and said, "Old-timer, I think I might have one more [no-hitter] in me." Nolan had thrown six no-hitters, and his fastball and curveball were about as good as they'd ever been. Everybody knows that I've got a big strike zone. But that night at Arlington Stadium, it must have seemed bigger than the state of Texas. The Angels chewed on me from the dugout all night. Doug Rader, their manager, was out of the dugout just about every inning. About the sixth inning, Dave Parker turned around and said, "Durwood, you're gonna put him [Ryan] in the Hall of Fame before his time." I shot back, "Dammit, Dave, get the bat off your shoulder and hit the damn ball."

They didn't realize just how distracted I was by the events of the previous night. I may have been standing behind home plate. But my mind was somewhere in left field.

History was almost made that evening in Arlington. Thanks to the Ryan Express (his fastball) and my ever-inflating strike zone, Nolan took a perfect game into the ninth inning. Dave Winfield broke it up with a single up the middle. After Winfield's single, the Angels started teeing off. Nolan wound up losing everything, including the game. Ryan would pitch his seventh no-hitter, but it didn't come that night in Arlington.

In the clubhouse, the Angels players complained to the writers that I was giving Nolan special treatment. Well, so what. Heck, they didn't realize that the whole darn game was one big blur. They didn't know I couldn't get Steve Palermo lying in a hospital bed off my mind. They didn't know that I was barely cognizant of the world that I was living in.

That night, I was again staying with my daughter, Maria. I was stopped by a Lake Worth policeman on the way back to her house. I was in total panic when I realized I had left my wallet back at the ballpark. The only identification in my possession was my American League pass that gets me into the games. I had no driver's license. Shoot, I didn't even have a Sam's Club card.

I told the police officer that I was an American League umpire, that my best friend had just been shot and was in the hospital, partially paralyzed. I told him that I'd just dealt with a gorilla named Nolan Ryan for nine innings, and that the California Angels had been all over my ass. And I said, "Mr. Police Officer, now I've been stopped by you. I haven't had a good day." That cop smiled at me and said, "I can't give you a ticket. You just go on home."

Indictments for attempted murder came down in a matter of hours on the four men arrested in the shooting of Steve Palermo and Terrance Mann. The indictments were reportedly delivered even faster than the one on Lee Harvey Oswald for assassinating President John F. Kennedy.

The men went to trial in Dallas in November, just four months after the shooting. The trial was hard on everyone and especially Steve, who was in a wheelchair. It ended at five-thirty on a Friday afternoon. Steve and his wife, Debbie, flew out of Dallas–Fort Worth Airport about an hour later.

When they got home to Kansas City around nine-thirty, their phone was ringing. The shooter had been found guilty and sentenced to seventy-five years in prison. The other three men received sentences of between twenty-five and thirty-five years.

Life was beginning anew for Steve. He would meet the grueling physical therapy head-on. The Palermo pride went to work. Doctors at Baylor Hospital, where he did most of his rehab, told Steve that he wouldn't walk again. In a matter of months, he proved them wrong.

"Durwood," he told me, "those doctors are no longer in the business of making those kinds of predictions about me."

In about six months, Stevie was walking with arm braces. Today, he uses a cane and an ankle brace. He hasn't made a lot of progress in the last three years. But he clings to the hope that someday he'll be back on the baseball diamond. Knowing Steve Palermo as I do, you might just see him back on the field someday. Steve says, "You have to be realistic but also idealistic. The idealist inside me will get me back onto the field."

I can still see Steve Palermo bent over, laughing at my goof-ups in umpiring school. I can still see him setting up strong behind the plate, calling balls and strikes like no one before him. I can see him standing toe-to-toe with Billy Martin and Earl Weaver. I can still hear him whistle.

Baseball remains Stevie's passion, even though he feels like a man on the outside looking in. The action, the lights, and the ball speeding to the plate at 95 mph made his heart race faster. From the start, I knew the game was flowing in his veins. Then, one night, a bullet ended it all. Somebody took away the game that Steve Palermo truly loved.

Now he spends his time as a color analyst on about twenty New York Yankees television broadcasts for the Madison Square Garden network. He does a lot of charity appearances for the physically disabled. And he works as an assistant to the commissioner for Major League Baseball. One of his assignments was proposing some rules to speed up the game. The proposals are great. All we need to do now is speed up the owners and get these rules into place.

Terrance Mann continues to live in Dallas, where he suffers from numbness in his chin and lower jaw. He is a drug and alcohol counselor.

Four years to the day after the shooting, they had a reunion at Campisi's Restaurant. Steve, Terrance, Corky, and Debbie were there. It was the night before the All-Star game at the new ballpark in Arlington.

After they had dinner, around eleven-thirty, the foursome went down to the parking lot at Mrs. Baird's Bakery. They stood on the corner and remembered what happened on July 7, 1991. They talked about the four bullets that changed all of their lives and they cried.

The great irony is that two Dallas police squad cars pulled up as they stood there. One of the cops said, "Is everything all right here?"

Steve said, "Yes sir, we're all okay. We're just standing here, trying to chase away a few demons."

If I could change one thing in my lifetime, it would be the brutal shooting that hot July night in Dallas. It was a bitter pill to swallow. But at least Steve Palermo has some peace in his life. And he seems to have those demons on the run.

Good Guys Wear Blue

WHEN I GOT TO THE MAJOR LEAGUES, I still thought veal piccata was a screwed-up chicken-fried steak. I wore boots and jeans all of the time. In fact, I probably still look like Ernest Tubb walking through LaGuardia Airport. They don't say, "Get that man a cab." They yell, "Get that man a fresh horse and a round for the house."

After twenty-one years in The Bigs, I still love being an umpire. You know why? Because umpires are real people. Umpires love to argue and debate until the cows come home. We'd all make great radio talk-show hosts. That's why I still love listening to Don Imus in the morning and Rush Limbaugh in the afternoon. Those guys never back down. I can imagine doing my own talk show: "Let's go to Dan on a car phone. And, Dan, by the way, you're dead wrong!"

We don't change our minds with the next gust of wind. With us, there's black and there's white and there's nothing in between. You're either out or safe. Oh, I know people say that we're a lot of hot air, but you'll never catch an umpire walking around without an opinion or two stuck in his back pocket. We've always got something to say.

Me, I don't live the fancy life. I normally stay at a hotel connected to a Denny's. I eat a lot of Grand Slam breakfasts. Unlike a good many men in baseball, I don't drink or smoke, and I only cuss when cussed at. I don't fluff-dry my hair. I just wash it and push it straight down.

But on the field, I like to act up a little. My hat flies off sometimes. I like to punch out runners with a big, wide sweeping motion. My old boss, Dick Butler, used to say with great pain in his voice, "Durwood, can't you at least keep your hat on?" And I'd say, "What does it really matter, Mr. Butler? If I get the play right and my shirt flies off, leave me the heck alone."

Teddy Barrett, one of the young umps who's starting to spend a lot of time in The Bigs, tells me I've got a cult following down in the minors. "Those boys are always asking about you," said Ted, who splits time between the majors and the Triple-A Pacific League. "I think some of them are starting to act like you." (Better not tell my bosses in the American League office that.)

Because we're outgoing people, umpires usually make fast friends. This isn't to say we all get along. There have been loud arguments and some near fights. But we're bonded by the same experiences. We've been mentally beaten down like dogs in umpiring schools and the bush leagues. We've stuck together through brutal arguments and bench-clearing brawls. We've laughed and sometimes cried together. Some of us have had guns pointed at us in Caribbean winter ball.

Survival is sometimes tough in this business. I've had one of my best friends shot down in the streets, and I saw another one take his final breath on an emergency-room table.

Most umpires are type A personalities. We are hard-driven with high stress levels. Most umpires I know are competitive, even though you won't find our names in the box scores. Our egos are big, but not helium-fed like the ones that belong to players and managers. We aren't the main act. We are the judges and the cops of baseball. We're bonded together because we wear the same uniform. And because we've been yelled at, screamed at, and called everything from gutter rot to horse manure, we stick together.

Ron Luciano once said that an umpire who sticks around for ten years should be immortalized. A man who umpires for twenty years should be institutionalized.

Have you ever watched umpires real close down on the field? Well, there's a little ritual we go through after a tough call. If one of my fellow umps has made the right decision on a tough call, you'll see me patting my right thigh with my right hand. We aren't allowed to openly applaud each other. So that's our way of clapping for a man who's made the right call on a tough play.

I'll tell you this about umpires. When the time comes to play ball, you won't find a more honest foursome anywhere. You can't say that about politicians, doctors, lawyers, and certainly not golfers. That kind of honesty doesn't exist anywhere else.

Did you know there's never been a scandal among major league umpires? You can't say that about men from other professions. They've had their encounters with gambling sharks. Some have taken bribes. But not umpires.

Eight Chicago White Sox players agreed to fix the 1919 World Series for eighty thousand lousy bucks. They were defending world champions. But the gamblers of the day, were able to get to them, and it totally screwed up the series against the Cincinnati Reds. It also screwed up the lives of those players, who were banned from baseball for life. Shoeless Joe Jackson, one of the greatest players of all time, was among them.

One of the central figures of The Fix was Sport Sullivan, a big-time gambler from Boston. He was asked during testimony why the gamblers hadn't tried to bribe the umpires. After all, major league baseball used only two umpires in that day, even during the nine-game World Series.

"The price was way too high," Sport said.

"What do you mean, the price was too high?" the district attorney asked.

"The umpires were staying on the seventeenth floor of the hotel. If we'd gone up there, they probably would have dropped us off the ledge."

I will say that our honesty is impeccable. But, no, our umpiring is not always perfect. We'd like for it to be. But it's not. People in the baseball business expect an umpire to be perfect when we start off, and then they expect us to get better. They're expecting way too much.

I've kicked my share of calls. Fortunately, they didn't occur during a big postseason game, or on national television. But I've made mistakes, just like the rest of my peers.

I was having a bad game one night when Detroit manager Sparky Anderson came running out of the dugout. Sparky has a pretty even temperament. But on this night, he was mad. He started chewing on me, and I said, "I know, I know." He said, "What do you mean, you know?"

I said, "Look, Sparky, I'm not going to get no better." Sparky shook his head, smiled, and said, "Well, I guess I'm not going to get no better, either." With that, he turned and ran back to the dugout.

One of my favorite umpires was Marty Springstead, now the supervisor of American League umpires. He was my second crew chief. Marty had kicked a couple of calls one night, and Earl Weaver was riding his butt. Weaver ran out on the field and started chewing Marty pretty good. "Look," Marty said, "do you really think that I'm doing that man in the other dugout any better service than I'm doing for you?"

Weaver just chuckled and said, "Hell, no." And he ran back to the Orioles dugout.

What breaks my heart is when when one of my umpiring brethren is forever blacklisted because of a botched call. If you boot a call in a big game, your life will never be the same. Just bank on it. You can make a million right calls and still be haunted by that wrong call in the big game. It's a helluva weight to carry around with you.

Just ask Don Denkinger, a man I worked with several years and an umpire whose integrity is beyond reproach. Don just completed his thirtieth year of service in the American League. He worked his first World Series (1974) three years before I became a full-time major league ump. The man has worked five no-hitters. The man should be a giant in the industry.

Instead, Don is mostly remembered for blowing a call that single-handedly turned the 1985 World Series in the favor of the Kansas City Royals. It's a damn good thing that Don is an American League ump. He wouldn't have been able to work in St. Louis again. I doubt he even schedules connecting flights through St. Louis.

The St. Louis press called Don the biggest crook to hit town since Jesse James when, in truth, he should be in the Umpires' Hall of Fame. What really happened is that Don kicked one call—one in a million that he's made. So what? Cardinals catcher Darrell Porter and first baseman Jack Clark both had misplays in that same inning. If Jack Clark catches an easy pop-up in foul territory, Don Denkinger still could have dinner every once in a while at Tony's restaurant in St. Louis.

Here was the scene: The Cardinals and the Royals were in game six of the World Series with St. Louis holding a three-to-two edge in games. The Cardinals led 1–0 going into the ninth inning. Jorge Orta led off by hitting a ground ball to Clark, who flipped the ball to pitcher Todd Worrell for what appeared to be a routine first out.

But Don ruled that Orta was safe. That was a big booboo. He was clearly out.

Don has told me many times that he got trapped in a bad spot. Like many umpires, Don makes his calls at first base on sound. He was watching Orta's feet while waiting for the sound of the ball in the glove. Only one problem. The stadium was too loud for Don to hear the ball slap leather.

After some animated arguing, the Cardinals quickly fell apart. Clark let a pop fly fall. Steve Balboni then singled to right. Both runners were able to advance when Porter let a pitch get by him on a passed ball. Dane Iorg then drove in both the tying and the winning runs.

After the game, Don walked into the umpires' room to find then commissioner Pete Uebberoth waiting for him. His heart must have been sinking.

"Did I get the call right?" Don asked.

"No," the commissioner said flatly.

The nightmare continued in game seven. Don was behind the plate. Kansas City scored six runs in a crazy fifth inning, and Don had to eject Cardinals manager Whitey Herzog and hot-tempered pitcher Joaquin Andujar, who was making a rare and unexpected relief appearance. Whitey let Don have it.

"You cough sufferer," Herzog said. "If you hadn't f——ed up the call yesterday, we wouldn't be in this position." Kansas City won game seven 11–0.

Don has been to hell and back since that call. I once introduced a friend to Don. As they shook hands, my buddy said, "Oh, yeah, you're the guy who made that call back in St. Louis." He instantly regretted saying it. But it was almost a knee-jerk reaction because he'd heard about the St. Louis episode so many times.

Just like a natural disaster, Don made large headlines. He got so many death threats that the police had to block off his street in Waterloo, Iowa. All because a St. Louis disc jockey got ahold of Don's home address and phone number and broadcast the information all over the Midwest. Don and his family were inundated with death threats.

Can you imagine threatening to kill a man and his family because he kicked one call? And then having to surround his house with cops? They acted like Don Denkinger was lower than a mud varmint, when he's really one of the best in the business.

When tempers finally cooled, Whitey Herzog said that Don was one of the best umpires in the business. But the damage was already done. Don and famous bank robbers are still mentioned in the same breath in St. Louis.

Richie Garcia has been living the same tormented life. Ask any manager or baseball insider and they'll tell you that Richie is one of our best, not one of the blindest. He's very confident. Richie and I were once rated by the *Sporting News* as the two most outrageous umpires in all of baseball. Richie likes to hustle a play, just like me. But Richie will never outlive a call he made in October of 1996 in the American League Championship Series between Baltimore and New York.

Instead of calling fan interference, Richie awarded the Yankees a home run even though a twelve-year-old fan who was skipping school reached over the center field wall and snagged the ball. Richie totally kicked the call. Here is what he really did wrong: Richie was working right field. (Six umpires are assigned to each postseason game.) Because he is such a great hustler, Richie was running hard toward center field when he should have been trying to focus on the play. I know what he was thinking. He was waiting to see if the Baltimore right fielder Tony Torosco caught the ball. Richie tried to focus on the glove. When the ball didn't fall into the fielder's glove, common sense told him that the ball was over the wall. Surely, it had to be a home run, he thought. He didn't see the kid in the stands catch the ball.

Richie started getting nervous between innings when he noticed that American League president Gene Budig and our boss, Marty Springstead, had left their box seats. He knew that Budig and Springstead had gone to the press box to watch the TV replay. They didn't come back for a long time.

Sometimes it's possible for an umpire to get help from one of his crew members on a home run. But, in this situation, there was a runner at first so the first base umpire was focused on his job. The plate umpire had to see through the runner and first base coach, so his view was blocked. Nobody could help Richie out. He had to go down with this call. Richie said, at the time, that he thought he got it right. There are times when I've overturned a fellow umpire's call on a home run. It's a tough thing to do because you know you're going to end up throwing somebody out of the game.

Did you know that in 1876 the rules stated: ''Should the umpire be unable to see whether a catch has been fairly made or not, he shall be at liberty to appeal to the bystanders, and to render his decision according to the fairest testimony at hand''? Richie could have used that rule in 1996. Needless to say, that rule is far out of date.

The saddest part is this: When Richie Garcia got back to the umpire's room after the game and watched the replay on TV, he sat down and cried. Fellow umpires Rocky Roe and Dan Morrison also had tears in their eyes. The whole episode just shattered Richie, a man who takes great pride in his work. I'm still sad that it happened. God knows it could have been changed.

I just cringe when I hear people say that Richie intentionally kicked the call to get even with Baltimore for the Alomar spitting incident. That is crazy. That is unfair. That idea would have never crossed his mind. Would the man have sat down and cried if he meant to miss the call?

Most botched calls are born from crazy circumstances. They mostly occur when players are trying to ad-lib after an error. They'll boot a ball and all of the sudden everything is out of whack. An umpire with a bad angle is an umpire in trouble. In both cases with Don and Richie, things just got out of whack.

When does an umpire usually find out that he's blown a call? When we gather in our little room after a game. One of the umpires might ask his colleague, "Did I blow it?" He'll always get an honest answer. If no one is sure about the call, we might cue up the videotape in the VCR and take a look at it.

If the umpires have had a tough game, it's usually very quiet in our little room. There isn't much chatter at all. Do umpires hurt after they miss a call? Heck yes. And I won't get over that bad call until I get a chance to make another one. Remember. You're only as good as your last call.

Bill Klem, a National League umpire from 1905 through 1941, captured all of our feelings when he said, "I never missed one in my heart."

Heck yes, it's hard being ripped in the newspapers for a bad call. It's tough listening to the talk shows when they're tearing you apart. I think that Marty Springstead gave me the best piece of advice when he said you've just got to get on your horse and ride away from a bad game. I like to believe that nobody will remember a bad call in five days. (Unless you're Don Denkinger or Richie Garcia.) I still like to say that by Christmas morning I'm going to forget my bad ones.

*   *   *

As I've said, umpires are among the greatest people in the world. But that doesn't mean that we all get along. We've had our squabbles. There have been some knock-down drag-out arguments. There have been some serious philosophical clashes.

That's where the umpiring supervisors come in. We have two of the best in Marty Springstead and Dr. Phil Jansen. Their main job is to put compatible umpires together. They know how to get the maximum effort out of every umpire. I suppose they have to be a cheerleader, disciplinarian, minister, and boss at the same time. This is hard for Marty and Phil to do because umpires live in so many regions of the country and men, by nature, don't always get along. One of the greatest accomplishments of Umpire Legal Counsel Richie Phillips has been to negotiate umpires some time off so we can stay refreshed during the season.

Big Ken Kaiser dances to his own tune and you're not going to change him. The umpires will be sitting around before a game, trying to establish a game plan for certain scenarios, and Ken won't always pay attention. Some umpires say he's got his own agenda. That's a pretty good evaluation because he's not always a team player. On some crews that really causes some dissension.

The problem with Ken may be his size. He doesn't run much. He would be the first to say, "Do I look like a sprinter?" So you won't see him streaking toward a play to make the call. He sits back and tries to get a view of it. Because he doesn't hustle, it creates some coordination problems with the other umpires. That doesn't mean that he doesn't have the ability to make good calls. He's just out of sync with the rest of us.

I worked with Jerry Neudecker during some of his twenty-one-year career. (He was the American League assistant supervisor of umpires from 1985 through 1991.) When Jerry was the crew chief, he believed that he could tell you when to eat, when to be at the ballpark, and when to shower. He was gruff and had that army sergeant's voice, and it didn't go over well with some of the umpires. After a game, he didn't mind telling you that you were two steps out of position.

That's why things are so different today. You might have four different umpires flying four different airlines arriving at four different times and then eating at four different restaurants. We might take four different cabs to the game. At the stadium, it's the job of the crew chief to coordinate the crew. But he doesn't boss the crew.

If you do run into the crew chief at the airport, and he says, "Did you get my bag?" you just laugh and say, "Yeah, there it goes again around the baggage carousel. Go get it yourself."

I've been a substitute crew chief many times over the last twenty-one years. I know the most important thing is to keep everybody happy. If you do that, things will run more smoothly. These days, the crew chief lets the Indians do their own thing.

Another umpire I didn't get along with was Russ Goetz, who was difficult. He was in the major leagues from 1968 through 1983 and definitely subscribed to the old school rules. This is what bugged me about Russ. If you were out there hustling, trying to get an angle on a play, he always thought you were "false hustling." He thought you were showing him up. Baloney. Good thing we didn't spend more time together.

I never worked with Nester Shylock. But that didn't keep me from disagreeing with him. His ego was always his first priority. He loved telling people that he was the greatest umpire ever. The problem with Nester is that he was always competing with the umpires on his own crew. That's not right. As an umpire, you're just a spoke in the wheel. In the old days, the umps liked to blow their horns and say, "Look at me." Nester should have pulled for his fellow umpires.

When I got to the major leagues in 1977, I remember Dick Butler saying he tried to avoid "philosophical clashes" by putting the southern boys together and the northern boys together. That doesn't really happen anymore. Today, we all give each other enough space to get along. We don't see each other as much as we used to.

In years past, there was a lot more jealousy and conniving behind the back. Guys were competing for those postseason umpiring spots because they wanted the money. That all changed with our 1989 collective bargaining agreement. Today, we split up the play-off pie. You might get $20,000 to work the postseason games, and $15,000 to go home. After taxes, it might make sense just to go on home and not worry about umping the play-offs.

You've read my opinions about some fellow umpires, both past and present. So how do the other guys feel about Durwood?

I think most umpires would say that I keep things loose. If I hear a guy cutting up, I certainly will laugh. I still take the approach that baseball is a game. I don't think the profession ought to destroy you. I believe that you can't think about umpiring every second of the day. That's what destroys a lot of men in my profession; they get too carried away with themselves.

There are times when I'm very serious about the game. If it's my turn behind home plate, I like to take some quiet time before the game. I'll concentrate on the pitchers and even meditate on what might occur during the game.

But I'm not going to grit my teeth. I'm not going to give myself a heart attack over one little ball game. I still live by one very basic philosophy: There is going to be life after umpiring.

Umpires are always fighting back. You can talk about incidents between players and umpires. You can talk about the John Hirschbeck–Roberto Alomar spitting brouhaha of 1996. You can talk about Tony Phillips having it out with John Shulock, or Ray Knight getting suspended for three games in 1997 for his dirt-kicking base-throwing outburst with Jerry Layne. God, you could fill books with the dirty shameful things that Billy Martin did to the men in blue. Umpires have a long history of taking abuse. (I often wonder if there should be a shelter for abused umpires.)

Baseball is the only sport where you can assault one of the umpires and get away with it. I don't need to mention the abuse we took from the likes of Earl Weaver.

People ask me a lot if we should use instant replay to umpire games. My answer is "Heck yes!" I'd love to see one of our half-cocked managers come roaring out of the dugout and kick dirt on a TV monitor.

Still, umpires don't carry grudges—unlike a lot of other people in baseball. Don't get me wrong. As a group, we weren't happy with the way the Alomar spitting incident went down during the 1996 season: the fact that he didn't serve his suspension in the play-offs and that Baltimore owner Peter Angelos picked up the tab on his fine. That irritated the heck out of the umpires, and it's the biggest reason we didn't put up with any lip during the 1997 season.

But when we walk on the field, we don't think about the Alomars or of the high-strung managers who've hammered us through the years. We're there to call a ball game as fairly as we can. When those four umpires walk onto the field, we're going to give those two teams the best game we've got in us. Umpires don't have a memory when it comes to being spit on or cussed at. I've been bumped and called names and been told to do unnatural acts to myself all of my career. I forget all of that bullcrap when I walk on the field.

Oh, I've mellowed in my twenty-one years as an American League umpire. If a team gets on my butt, I'll walk over to their dugout, spread my arms out like a big bird, and say, "What the hell is this? Kick Durwood's butt night? Well, here. Start kicking." I'll get a pretty good laugh.

That wasn't the case when I came into the league in the late 1970s. Back then, I always felt that a good fight would purify your blood. My blood always seemed to get thicker after I hadn't fought for a while. I'd run over to the dugout and say, "Okay, boys who wants to be first? Who wants to fight me! Do you guys want any more?"

When I got into one of my moods, I might say anything

to a manager. Earl Weaver might walk by and say, "Durwood, how ya' feeling today." And I would snap back, "What do you care? Are you a doctor? You'll be screaming at me on the first pitch."

Now, that's a roughneck umpire talking. A roughneck umpire is one who is set on go all the time. A roughneck umpire takes no crap from nobody.

Not one fan or sportswriter in America can honestly say that umpires are homers—meaning we favor the home team. The Cleveland Indians, for example, know they can walk into Yankee Stadium or Fenway Park and get the same shot from the umpires that they'd receive at Jacobs Field, their home park. I'm not so sure that's the case in other sports. I know that in football the home field advantage can be worth between three and six points. Why? Home cooking from the refs. It may be worse in basketball. Basketball referees take a rash of abuse from fans who practically sit on top of the court. That's not the case in major league baseball. The visiting team and home team play on a level field in our game.

I'm still amazed at the talents of some of my fellow umpires. You don't realize how good Larry Barnett is until you watch him work day after day. Drew Coble is one of my favorites. I just wonder if I look that good. Jim Evans is a genius when it comes to the rule book. If baseball ever wanted to have a Supreme Court, Evans should be the lone sitting judge.

We could use a Jim Evans to rewrite our rule book, which is full of contradictions. The problem with the rule book is that you can't get everyone to agree on anything when it comes to interpretations.

If Jim was the lone sitting judge, I guess I'd be the good cop out on the street, thinking on my feet and making quick decisions. That is what I do best. I don't think I could sit in a room and mull over the meaning of the rules. I don't want to think about the ifs, ands, and buts. But I can go out on that diamond and make good decisions that make good sense. I guess you can call me the commonsense umpire.

*   *   *

I like the feeling when my nerves are on edge right before a game. It's the message that I'm ready to go. There's nothing wrong with having a little fear in your gut. If you can handle that fear.

The Detroit Tigers were playing their home opener April 7, 1984, and Jack Morris, the winningest pitcher of the decade, was close to the peak of his career. He was facing the White Sox. It was a sunny and cool day at Comiskey Park, and Big Jack carried a no-hitter into the ninth inning. Detroit led 4–0.

The bunting was out. The stadium was full. The game was on national TV. Ol' Durwood was behind home plate.

With two outs, and the count at two and two, I was faced with one of the toughest calls of my umpiring career. I drew a mental picture of what I'd do if the hitter decided not to swing at the next pitch. Sure enough, the pitch was low. I could have punched him out and been the hero of the day. Tiger Stadium would have exploded at the moment with the first no-hitter of a very young season. I would have been part of that history.

Everybody in baseball knows that I've got a big strike zone. Morris's two-two pitch was over the plate, but it was still low. I called it ball three.

I thought about the final pitch of Don Larsen's perfect game of the 1956 World Series. It was game five. Dale Mitchell was the pinch hitter for the Dodgers. The National League's Babe Pinelli, who was about to retire, was umpiring his final game behind the plate.

Mitchell took ball one and then strike one. He swung and missed strike two and then fouled one into the left field stands. Larsen's ninety-seventh pitch of the game was over the plate. But it was high. Way high. Go back and check the tape. Up until that game, there had been 307 World Series games without a no-hitter. A perfect game was unthinkable. So the only thought on Pinelli's mind was getting the game in the books and getting the hell out of Yankee Stadium. I'm sure he was thinking about making history and getting his name in the newspaper. He rang Mitchell up with strike three. Yogi Berra jumped into Larsen's arms, and bedlam broke loose at Yankee Stadium. It remains the single greatest memory in World Series history. Babe Pinelli retired with a big ol' smile on his face.

So, you ask, what would have Durwood done in that situation? I've thought about it a lot. I would have called the pitch ball two and let the chips fall where they may. Sure, the tension would have seemed unbearable at Yankee Stadium. The fans would have booed the heck out of me. It would have opened the door for Mitchell, a .312 lifetime hitter, to break up the perfect game. And the press might have crucified me. But that's the risk you take when you put on the mask. If Mitchell had singled and wrecked the perfect game, the umpires would've had to fight their way out of the Bronx.

Back to my dilemma in Chicago. Because I moved the count to three-two, Morris's no-hitter was still in jeopardy. But it went into the books on the next pitch. The hitter swung and missed, and Big Jack had the first No-No of 1984.

I quickly disappeared into the umpires' room. I'd stood my ground. (The ground did seem like it was shaking at the time, and so was I.) My fellow umpires spent the rest of the evening wondering out loud why I hadn't ended the game a pitch earlier and gotten them the heck out of there.

We walked out of Comiskey Park without incident. A two-out single on a three-two count and we might have needed a police escort.

I got caught in more cross fire in 1982 when Rickey Henderson was going for the single-season stolen-base record. He was one base shy of the tying the record of 118 set by St. Louis's Lou Brock back in 1974. It was August 26 and the last game for a while in Oakland. The A's would be leaving on a long road trip the next day. So the hometown fans wanted the record broken then and there. That puts a lot of pressure on the umpires.

Rickey had just one little problem that afternoon. He didn't get on base until he singled in the eighth inning. By the time Rickey got ready to run, we were down to three umpires. Larry Barnett, who was supposed to umpire second base, got sick. No wonder. He was chewing tobacco and drinking cold milk before the game, and that would make Godzilla sick. So in the fourth inning, Larry started having stomach and chest pains. At first, he thought it was a heart attack. "Larry," I said, "if you'd stop washing down that damn tobacco with cold milk, you'd feel a lot better."

Larry was barfing so bad that he wanted to go the hospital. But all he needed was some Pepto-Bismol.

With Larry hugging the toilet back in the umpires' room, I was left to work both second and third base. Which was no picnic considering that Billy Martin was over there in the A's dugout breathing his bad breath down my neck. The tension was thicker than a chaw of Red Man. We were all waiting for Rickey to run. But there was one more roadblock. Fred "Chicken" Stanley just happened to be standing on second base. Rickey had nowhere to go.

So Chicken Stanley just walked off second base and gave himself up. I couldn't believe my eyes at first. But Chicken Stanley was just standing there between second and third, begging shortstop Alan Trammel to tag him out. Trammel obliged, of course.

I'm country and I'm from Hooks, Texas. And I didn't think that was right. I thought about sending Chicken Stanley to the showers. But everybody's nerves were on edge anyway. So I held that thought.

So the stage was set. Third base coach Clete Boyer was over there yelling, "Durwood, we need this one! Durwood, we need this one!" And I tuned him out. So here I was, umpiring second and third base at the same time, waiting for Big Rickey. I could make history by calling him safe at second and, a pitch later, calling him safe at third. And, after all, I'm just a good ol' boy from East Texas. Good golly.

Off went Rickey like a rocket. To the credit of the Tigers, they were conceding nothing. Catcher Bill Fahey had called for the pitchout. Pitcher Milt Wilcox delivered. Henderson broke for second, and there was a big cloud of dust as the ball arrived. It was a perfect throw by Fahey and a bang-bang play. Trammell made the tag and I called Henderson out. (Oh, my God, I thought. I'd just declared war against the Kremlin and Billy Martin.)

But Rickey barely protested. He just got up, dusted himself off, and trotted back to the dugout. I didn't, however, need to turn around to know the devil himself was gaining ground on my backside. In all of my twenty-something years of umpiring, I've never met a more mean-spirited and intimidating manager than Billy Martin.

I whirled just as Martin arrived and met him face-to-face. Billy started tearing his shirt off. He was popping buttons and he was peeling down. Billy hollered, "If you're going to do this to me, I'm going to be naked when you do it." I think he was making another reference to unnatural sex acts. But I wasn't sure. So I ran him right out of the game. Nobody, not even a hot-tempered Billy Martin, accuses me of that kind of stuff.

Then I tossed A's coach Charlie Metro for arguing with me. A's center fielder Dwayne Murphy walked past and said, "What's wrong with you, Durwood? You got a hot date after the game?" I tossed him out, too. I was sending them out of the game at fifteen-second intervals—it looked like a conga line. The A's bench was riding me hard. So I walked over to the dugout, put my hands on my hips, and screamed, "Any of you sonsabitches who want out of this game, just keep yelling." I glared at Clete Boyer, who was now the acting manager, and said, "I'm going to throw everyone you've got out. I'm going to clean this bench out." Fellow umpire Rocky Roe got between me and the dugout and tried to push me away. Rocky had a lot of nerve. Shoot, Rocky yells back at the dugout more than I do.

I remember thinking about an incident back in 1896 when a National League umpire had the entire Cleveland Spiders ball club arrested and taken to jail. I was wondering if I could do the same with the A's. Just put Billy Martin in handcuffs and lead them all down to the lockup.

Boyer finally settled his team down, and we finished the

game. But I knew we had the gauntlet to walk. In Oakland, you have to walk about fifty feet past the crowd on the way to the umpires' room. I looked at Rocky and said, "Partner, get ready for the longest walk of your life."

Rocky glanced at me and said, "Durwood, I'll go anywhere with you, partner. But why don't you go first?"

Those A's fans threw everything they could find. They threw beer, cups, coins, hot dogs, buns, peanuts, and programs. They even threw an expensive sports jacket that I think Rocky still wears. Finally, we reached the safety of our dressing room. But we knew they would be waiting for us after the game. Our rental cars were in the players' parking lot, and getting through that crowd would be like fighting the Alamo again. A security guard came in and asked if he should move the cars into the stadium so we could leave through another exit.

By now, Barnett had barfed up all the chewing tobacco and milk. He hadn't seen the final five innings. He told the security guard, "That won't be necessary."

In unison, Rocky and I yelled, "It's necessary! It's necessary!" I looked at Barnett, and then I looked at the security guard and said, "This man doesn't know what he's talking about. He's been in here barfing while we've been out there fighting the wars. Get the darned cars in here!"

The Oakland fans hooted and hollered at us we left. But we sped away safely and headed for San Francisco International Airport. About halfway across the Bay Bridge, a cold reality hit me with the force of a Nolan Ryan fastball. We'd be flying to Milwaukee for the Brewers-A's series. We would be following Billy Martin and Rickey Henderson, and all of those people I just threw out of the game, right into Milwaukee.

My life in the major leagues was about to get even weirder.

The next day broke beautifully in Milwaukee. There's nothing like a clear, crisp September day in Wisconsin. I was still a little gun-shy about the A's and their fans and Billy Martin. But the team was staying across town. So Rocky and

I decided to take a walk through downtown to get some exercise and do a little shopping.

We were walking along, talking, and my mind kept wandering back to the events of the day before. Who could blame me for looking over my shoulder? A few blocks from the hotel, I noticed that a couple of guys wearing dark suits and sunglasses were following us. Every time we'd duck into a store, they would duck into that store right behind us. Every time we stopped, they'd stop. I finally said to Rocky, "We've got problems, partner. These dudes are following us."

We decided to stop around the next corner and confront these guys. As they turned the corner, I stepped out from the shadows and said loudly, "You guys are following us!" One of them removed his sunglasses and looked me squarely in the eye. He had these serious-looking eyebrows. "No, son, we're not," he said. "We're here to protect you."

They both pulled out badges—from the Federal Bureau of Investigation.

The man who'd pulled off his sunglasses moved closer and said in a low, gravelly voice, "Son, you've received a lot of death threats. You should probably return to your hotel." I thought about my wife and my two children back in Texas, and I felt sick inside. I was used to being away from home. But at that moment, I felt a million miles from Hooks. Until then, I never thought there were people in this game who would hurt you. But over the previous twelve hours, the American League office back in New York had been receiving death threat after death threat against me. I really didn't feel scared. But I did feel pretty darn betrayed.

The thing about our business is that you go to work every day in the friendly confines of a beautiful major league ballpark. You feel as if you're getting away from all the troubles of the world. In some respects, you're living in a fantasy world. But on that day, I felt like I was driving my rental car straight into the jaws of a monster. The four umpires barely spoke as we dressed in the bowels of the stadium. The unspoken tension weighed on all of us. Rocky finally said,

"Now, Durwood, when we get out on the field, I want you to go stand over by yourself. I don't want that killer getting us all with one bullet." Even that weak attempt at humor helped a little.

Thankfully, Rickey Henderson singled to open the game. He took off flying for second on the next pitch. My fellow umpires still kid me by saying that I'd signaled Rickey safe even before the ball got past the pitcher's mound. I don't know if that's true. But even according to my standards, I gave Rickey an exaggerated safe sign. I felt as if my arms were stretching to the sky. I looked like a bird ready to take flight. My hat flew off. When I yelled "Safe!" they probably heard me all the way to Green Bay. Rickey had tied the record.

Two pitches later, Henderson took off for third and arrived several steps ahead of the ball. As he stood there beaming, Rickey pulled the base out of the ground and held it over his head. The record was his. He was feeling a rush of glory—and I was feeling a fabulous rush of relief. I looked into the stands and wondered if those two FBI guys were still following us.

You know you're in a stressful profession when you see seemingly healthy men going early to their grave. We've lost three active umpires to heart attacks since I got into the major leagues in 1977. Another was killed in the street just outside my hotel room one night in Arlington, Texas.

I never would have suspected that a big and strapping Nick Bremigan would be a heart attack candidate when he went down in July of 1989. It was the fifteenth year of his major league career. He was as healthy as they came.

Lee Weyer was six-foot-five and full of life. He was loved by his fellow umps because he didn't mind admitting a mistake. Lee was at third base when Hank Aaron clouted historic home run number 715, and he was there when Pete Rose broke Ty Cobb's all-time hit record in 1986, and he worked twenty-three World Series games. And he left us in one heartbreaking moment during the 1988 season. He was fifty-three.

We all knew that Big John McSherry was overweight when he dropped dead of a heart attack on Opening Day at Cincinnati's Riverfront Stadium in 1996. But we still didn't expect to see him topple over and die right before they threw the first pitch. Big John was a giant of an umpire—physically, mentally, and emotionally. He deserved a better fate.

John was an umpire's umpire. When he missed almost a year because of heart problems, I dropped a card and said, "John, just in case I forgot to thank you for everything." He wrote me back and told me how proud he was of me.

I'd see John at a union meeting, or we'd cross paths at an airport, and he'd grumble and say, "Well, Durwood, I guess you made it to the majors in spite of me."

What really gave John a lot of happiness is that he saw his boys make it the major leagues. Then he saw them excel. He enjoyed watching Ed Montague, Al Clark, Steve Palermo, Mike Reilly, and me make our way in umpiring.

John McSherry was the most precise umpire I'd ever seen. He made every move exactly the way he'd taught it at umpiring school. When you saw John McSherry, you saw the portrait of an umpire. He was smooth and surprisingly quick on his feet for a big man.

It's easy to say that John was a fat guy and that he never got a handle on his weight problem. He had an irregular heartbeat. But John was in his twenty-fifth season in the major leagues. That is a lot of wear and tear on the body.

On April 1, 1996, the day he died, John knew he was sick. But he put on the shin guards, the chest protector, and the mask. And he took his spot behind the plate. John was the crew chief, and he felt a sense of responsibility to his guys. That's why he didn't take a deserved day off. He'd already told the National League office that he'd fly to New York the next day to have a full physical examination. If John had lived one more day, he might still be with us.

The hardest death for me to accept was that of Lou DiMuro on June 7, 1982, in Arlington, Texas. We had just finished up a game and were back at the hotel a few blocks from the park. Lou looked tired. He wanted to know if I wanted to go out and grab a late sandwich with him.

"I'm going to have to pass," I said. I wish now that I'd gone. Lou might still be with us today.

Lou walked a few blocks to a bar-and-grill. Back then, we didn't make a lot of money and our per diem wasn't that high. We didn't have the luxury of rental cars so Lou was on foot.

He'd been on medication for a hip injury, and I knew that Lou wasn't feeling well. Lou was sitting with Darrell Johnson of the Mariners, and Darrell said it was clear that he was feeling disoriented. Returning from the rest room, Darrell discovered that Lou had walked out without saying good-bye or paying his tab. And that's not the way that Lou DiMuro operated. That wasn't his style.

Lou was trying to cross the street next to the hotel, and witnesseses said that he stopped on the median. It was clear to the witnesses that Lou was in some kind of distress. Without warning, he stepped into the middle of the dark street. The driver of the car didn't see Lou.

I was packing my bags in the hotel room when the phone rang. The desk clerk said, "Mr. Merrill, we have some bad news. One of your partners has been hit by a car just in front of the hotel."

About half in shock, I said, "Oh no, he hasn't."

And the clerk said, "Yes sir, he has."

I bolted through the door and ran down the hallway to the lobby. I was sprinting through the lobby when the ambulance started up and headed off screaming down the street. So I grabbed one of the local cops and asked him to drive me to the hospital.

I could sense that the end was near when I walked into the emergency room and there was Lou lying on one of the tables. I removed the rings from his fingers and took out his wallet. I looked the doctor squarely in the eye and said, "Is there anything that can be done?"

The doctor shook his head and said, "No sir, he's gone."

I gathered Lou's stuff and went back to the hotel. There, I stood in the shower for more than thirty minutes, just crying my eyes out. Larry Barnett and Mike Reilly were also on the crew, and we faced an eerie task. One of his had to go into Lou's room and pack his stuff. Having gone to the hospital, I was still an emotional wreck. Larry and Mike couldn't make themselves do it. So we waited for Al Clark, who was part of the incoming crew. He went into Lou's room and packed his belongings.

Larry, Mike, and I flew on to Milwaukee for our next series. But we didn't work the next game. Today, if something like that happened, I would just go back home to Hooks. I don't know if I would have the strength to handle it. But back in 1982, we missed only one game.

Like many umpires that I've known through the years, Lou worked through a lot of pain. In fact, he pushed himself too far. The doctors had told him that he'd need a replacement hip, but Lou just kept taking his medication and trying to move on down the road. Meanwhile, the hip continued to degenerate.

It was Lou DiMuro who I replaced on a part-time basis during the 1976 season. Dick Butler would call me up from Triple-A to work in Lou's place for a few games. I was on the crew with Rich Garcia, Davey Phillips, and Bill Kunkel. After working a series or two, I'd sit in the stands while Lou limped around the field. I was the fifth member of that crew for a lot of games. The harsh reality is that Lou should have retired that year. But just like John McSherry and some of the others, Lou gave less consideration to his own health than he did the game of baseball.

This is what I hope: The young umpires who are coming into the game today should appreciate what we have gone through and what we have done to make their lives a lot better. Without us, they wouldn't be making the big salaries, and they wouldn't have the voice of a strong union. They wouldn't be working with a strong and dignified group of umpires. The John McSherrys, Nick Bremigans, Lee Weyers, and the Lou DiMuros helped make umpiring such a great profession. Let's not forget about them.

Earl, Billy, and the Boys

KNOWING THAT BALTIMORE manager Earl Weaver was in the dugout made a lot of umpires sick. Some would complain of upset stomachs. Umpire Ron Luciano blamed Weaver for a bleeding ulcer. Others just couldn't cope with the thought of dealing with that midget. Earl, when he got into one of his moods, could get downright ugly.

One night in Baltimore that rascal was showering me with expletives from the dugout. Utility infielder Pat Kelly, a religious man and part-time preacher, was sitting next to Earl. "Skip," Kelly said, "you need to learn to walk with the Lord." Weaver shot back, "F——you, Kelly. You need to learn to walk with the bases loaded."

That was just Earl.

My good buddy Steve Palermo summed it up pretty well when he said, "Earl Weaver is a militant midget. He just uses us umpires as props in his circus act. We're straight men for his comedy. But baseball is not a circus, and the game is not Earl's show. It's not 1892 anymore."

Bravo, Stevie.

Managers are like no other breed in the sports business. They wear uniforms, even though they don't play in the games. Managers don't get to call plays, they don't wear headsets, and they don't carry little grease boards around for the purpose of drawing up the last-second shot. They usually don't have Gatorade buckets poured over their heads, and they don't get carried off the field on the decklike shoulders of a 325-pound tackle. Still, most of the time, the pressure of winning is on them like stink on a fresh cow chip.

Job security in the major leagues for a manager can be as unpredictable as the stock market. They receive way too much credit when the team's winning, and far too much blame when it's on the skids. I've always felt that a manager is directly responsible for the outcome of about fifteen games a year. That's less than 10 percent of the games played in the regular season.

Managers get hired, fired, and then recycled more than your favorite soft-drink can. If a guy gets fired by one team, there's a pretty good chance he's going to pop up with another team the next season. So what's the point of this madness other than to prove that baseball really is a good-ol'-boy network?

Another silly aspect of baseball is all the arguing that goes on between managers and umpires. There is so much verbal sparring that some fans probably think these little brouhahas are staged for the purpose of keeping everybody awake. I know that I've been in a lot of doornail-dead ballparks when the fans are sitting on their hands and then all of the sudden the home team's manager comes running out of the dugout and you would have thought that the public address announcer had just promised free beer for the rest of the game. There's nothing like a good nose-to-nose argument to get fans on their feet.

You might assume that umpires and managers were born to argue, kind of like cats and dogs, Democrats and Republicans, New York cab-drivers and anybody they encounter. Ejections were way up early in the 1997 season, mainly because umpires felt we got an overall raw deal after Robbie Alomar used umpire John Hirschbeck as a spitball target. We got mad because Robbie's five-game suspension was put off until the next season and that his owner, Peter Angelos, picked up the tab on his fine. So managers bore some of the brunt of our frustration. April was "zero tolerance" month for umpires in both leagues.

One thing I've never understood about baseball is why

managers are allowed to run onto the field without warning and get right into an umpire's face, bad breath and all. When I first got into professional umpiring, I often asked why managers have such freedom in baiting umpires from the dugout and basically accosting us on the field. I was told that it's always been that way and that, for some reason, the fans like it.

I had more than my share of donnybrooks with managers early in my career. I'd stand a few feet from the dugout, hands on hips, and yell, "If you want to fight, then let's get it on!"

In the May 20, 1981, *Washington Post* sportswriter Thomas Bowell described me thusly: "Umpire Durwood Merrill is a vast side of beef of a man who looks like nobody in the NFL would faze him very much. Everything from his slow, composed drawling speech to his snakeskin cowboy boots proclaims him a confident fellow who was created to stay calm and strong at the center of a crisis."

Boswell provided this description in a story he was writing on Earl Weaver and his troubles with umpires. I'd just thrown Earl out of a game in Baltimore. The sportswriter asked me why I did it, and I thought I provided some valid reasons.

"All Earl did was dance circles around me like he was a clown," I said. "He flung his cap in a perfect spiral. He clapped his hands three times about an inch in front of my face. He kicked dirt on home plate twice. And then he mockingly gave me an umpire's heave-ho. I thought that was enough."

Earl was mad because I'd just run Eddie Murray out of a game when the great Orioles first baseman refused to step into the batter's box. He'd been dillydallying around for about thirty seconds. I warned him, and then I signaled for the pitcher to pitch, and I rang up a strike on big Eddie. All Eddie did was call me a mother forker. So I sent him packing into the rat-infested tunnel beneath that hellhole called Memorial Stadium.

Earl said, "You can't throw out a great player like Eddie

Murray. He'll be in the Hall of Fame someday." I yelled, "In that case, I'll just throw out the future Hall of Fame manager!"

It was my first time tossing the man, but the ninety-seventh ejection in fourteen seasons for Mr. Weaver. Among my fellow umpires, there was some real venom toward Earl before his retirement after the 1986 season. By the time that Earl officially retired for the final time, he had been tossed ninety-two times by American League umpires.

Larry Barnett provided this insight into Earl: "Once you run Weaver, he's like a recalcitrant child who can't accept authority and its enforcement. He goes through the whole logbook on everything you've ever done to him. I've never seen him do anything funny. No, I take that back. I once saw him slip and fall coming out of the dugout. That was funny."

The hate between Palermo and Weaver was mutual and intense. Earl once said about Steve, "If I didn't respect the umpire's uniform, he might be dead." Stevie didn't work many Orioles games one season because the league office feared a complete meltdown between him and Earl. He was assigned a late-season series in Baltimore. Normally, Earl sends one of his coaches to home plate for the exchange of lineup cards. Cal Ripken Sr. was walking toward home plate when Earl whistled and signaled for him to come back. He grabbed the lineup card and then came marching toward home plate like he already had a beef with Stevie.

Approaching home, Earl started flailing his arms and yelling, "Where the hell have you been? You've been costing me money!"

"What the hell are you talking about?" Stevie snapped.

"The commercial people," Earl said. "They want to make a commercial of you and me arguing. But you haven't been around this year. You're costing me forty thousand bucks."

Stevie flashed Earl a wry smile and said, "Stick around, big boy. I have a feeling we're going to make a commercial tonight."

The feud between Earl and umpire Ron Luciano actually began in the minor leagues back in the mid-1960s. They couldn't stand each other from the moment they set eyes on each other. Wouldn't you know that in 1969, when Earl was promoted to the Orioles, Luciano would also get his promotion to the major leagues. They were on a collision course from the moment they walked into The Bigs.

At times, it appeared their rhubarbs were some kind of a put-on, like a carnival sideshow to help sell tickets. It wasn't. They despised each other. Luciano once said, "I don't care who wins, as long as it's not Weaver's team."

Marty Springstead and Weaver were often like two prize-fighters squaring off in the ring. I was right in the middle of one of those main events, kind of like a referee. It was September 15, 1977, and the Orioles were trailing the Yankees by a game and a half in their division with two weeks left in the season. The umpires and the managers gathered at home plate before the game, and Earl started bellyaching about a tarpaulin in the Toronto bullpen. He wanted it moved. We all laughed. That tarp was blocking nothing and bothering nobody, and Earl was just playing more mind games.

Marty said, "It's not in the way. Let's go." Marty was dead right. Earl didn't have a legitimate gripe, but he still wouldn't put his team on the field.

Marty walked over to the Orioles dugout, put his hands on his hips, and shouted, "What do you want me to do, Earl? Choose up sides?"

When ten minutes passed, Marty did something no umpire ever wants to do. He forfeited the game in Toronto's favor. What a shame. Toronto was in its first year of existence, and the Blue Jays back then played kind of like a Double-A team. It looked like an easy win for the Orioles, who finished the season two and a half games behind the Yankees. As umpires, we all felt sick that we had to take that game away from the Orioles. But Earl painted us into a corner. He cost his team a critical game in the midst of a hot pennant race.

I know why my umpiring buddies considered Earl a sad

clown, but there were times when I thought his act was kind of funny. Earl, you see, never really got to me, and his little banty rooster act sometimes made me giggle. Guys who are five-six and weigh 160 pounds soaking wet aren't intimidating to me because, after all, I'm a vast side of beef.

At the height of the 1979 pennant race, Earl got tossed from a game in Oakland, so he hid in the bathroom and tried to manage through a knothole in the door. Richie Garcia raided the john and demanded, "What are you doing in here?" Weaver snapped, "I'm in here throwing up because you guys make me sick." Richie helped settle Earl's stomach, sending him straight to the showers.

I was behind the plate for Jim Palmer's two hundredth win of his career. Palmer was just rocking along, leading the Cleveland Indians 3–0, but Baltimore catcher Rick Dempsey wasn't having a good night. Four smoking line drives hit by Dempsey had somehow landed in the glove of outfielder Rick Manning. Dempsey was kind of a hard guy anyway. So he was really tough to deal with on a night when he really had a right to bitch.

Over in the dugout between innings, Dempsey was kicking over the water cooler and slamming bats into the rack when Earl said, "Take it out on Durwood! I'm tired of hearing about it."

Rick said, "What happens if I get kicked out?"

"Don't worry," Earl said. "I'll pay the fine."

In the top of the ninth inning, Rick came dragging up to home plate in his catcher's gear. He said, "I'm tired. I ain't going to play no more."

I looked at him sternly and said, "Rick, all I need is three more outs."

"Durwood, dammit, I'm tired," he said.

"In that case," I said, "why don't you just take a hike? Bring me another catcher."

Earl came out of the dugout to let me know who the backup catcher would be. He said, "Dammit, Durwood, you cost me money. I told Dempsey to take the whole thing out on you. But I never thought you'd toss him."

At first, I wasn't going to recommend a fine for Dempsey. He'd gone so meekly. But when I heard Earl was paying the fine, I said, "Ch-ching, ch-ching, ch-ching." It was time to take Mr. Weaver to the bank.

If Earl felt persecuted, imagine what was going through the mind of the man who followed him as Baltimore's manager, Cal Ripken Sr., when he tangled with Rocky Roe.

Rocky, who really hated Earl, was getting irritated one night with Cal Ripken Sr., who kept coming out of the dugout to complain about everything except the time of day. Some people said Cal Sr. got the managing job because he had two sons—Cal Jr. and Billy—on the Birds roster.

Cal Sr. was giving Rocky the business when Rocky struck back. "Look, Cal. Let me tell you one thing about your managing career. If you hadn't had a couple of good nights with the missus, you wouldn't even be a major league manager!"

Old man Ripken went ballistic, and Rocky had to run him. Maybe Rocky was right. Cal Sr. was gone as manager in two seasons. Cal Jr. remains one of baseball's darlings, and Billy is still a fine utility infielder.

Marty Springstead got out of umpiring in 1985 because the job of American League supervisor of umpires had come open. Some thought he left the field because he knew that Earl was about to finally retire. Earl took the 1983 and 1984 seasons off before returning in 1985 and then hanging it up for good after the 1986 season.

Truth is, Marty and Earl actually laughed and joked around behind the scenes. Yep, I was with Marty and Earl during their so-called wars. They didn't have a raw hatred for each other. They didn't threaten to bomb each other's car. Marty would say to Earl, "You know, if Timex really wanted to test their watches, they'd put one on your bottom lip. We'd see if that watch could take a lickin' and keep on tickin'."

Before he retired, Earl was asked about his combative relationships with umpires. He said, "The thing that surprises me about umpires is the amount of integrity they bring to the game. It took me a while to realize what a good game they would give you the night after a blowup."

Rocky recently ran into Earl at a golf tournament. Earl told him, "You guys have a lot more integrity that I ever gave you credit for. I'm not apologizing. I'm just saying that you guys were right ninety-eight percent of the time. And I don't know anyone with that kind of batting average."

I don't think any of my comrades attended his Hall of Fame induction. I know some guys who'd still like to take a poke at Earl's nose. He was that ugly to the umpires.

But when Earl stepped to the lectern on the steps of the Hall of Fame, you would have never thought we'd had a problem with the guy. This is what he had to say about umpires: "And now it's time to recognize a group of baseball people that very seldom receive credit for a job well done. This group being the umpires of the American and National League. I'm serious when I say their integrity and honesty is and must be beyond reproach. They accept the players' and managers' ire, and they never let it affect their call. Now, counting balls and strikes and close plays on the bases, they must have made over a million calls while I was managing. And except for those ninety-one or ninety-two times I disagreed, they got the other ones right. So to them, I want to say thanks for your patience and understanding and keep up the good work because the game can't be played without umpires."

My, what a few years away from the pressure of managing will do to a man.

Billy

Billy Martin: Just the sound of the name could give you the chills. I dreaded a confrontation with Martin more than with Weaver because Billy never forgot anything. Billy would come back on you for something that happened five years ago. That kind of offense is a straight ticket out of the game.

I never found Weaver to be that way. He could let things pass.

Earl couldn't hold a candle to wild Billy Martin. At least Earl didn't have that dark and intimidating side. Earl was more like a yapping Chihuahua nipping at your ankles all the time.

Billy was so adept at looking for loopholes that I thought about hiring him as my tax man. He was like a Nolan Ryan fastball. During Ryan's heyday, I used to say there was Nolan's fastball and then there was everybody else's fastball. With managers, you had your arguers and then you had Billy Martin. He was down and dirty and vicious. Dr. Freud would have loved Billy Martin, who had more personalities than Reggie Jackson had cars.

Actually, Billy could be a nice guy when you got him away from the ballpark. I always believed that if your wife or mother needed a life-or-death operation, and it was going to cost $100,000, and if Billy Martin had the money, he'd send you a check. That's just the way he was. But if you called a pitch he didn't like in the ninth inning, he'd be the first one up on the dugout steps yelling, "I hope she dies!"

Billy wasn't fair when he argued, and you just couldn't reason with the man. He was personally vindictive, and there were times that he really wanted to fight and he would use anything at his disposal to win an argument—including the real personal stuff. If he thought an umpire was a stiff drinker, he'd say, "Can't wait to get to the bar, heh?" If he'd heard that a guy was having trouble with the missus at home, he'd snicker, "Got a hot date tonight?"

Billy and Joe Brinkman got into an animated insult-swapper one night at home plate even before the game started. Billy was still mad about a call Joe had made the night before. One insult led to another. Billy called Joe a cough sufferer, and Joe had the pleasure of tossing him out of the game. Then the national anthem started playing. The two men paused, took off their hats, and stood at attention. The moment the anthem stopped, they started screaming at each other again.

Billy really wanted you to cheat for him. He also believed that if a call wasn't going his way, you were cheating him. I could always feel his presence over in the dugout, and I really didn't like it.

It's not surprising that Billy was at the center of one of the most controversial plays in the history of baseball, and that he would try to use his entire bag of tricks to swing the game his way. The Yankees were leading Kansas City 3–2 when George Brett slammed a Goose Gossage fastball into the right field seats to give the Royals a one-run lead.

Over on the Yankees bench, coach Don Zimmer noticed that Brett had been using perhaps too much pine tar on his bat. Pine tar is a black, sticky, and gunky substance that hitters put on their bats to help improve their grip. Eventually the stuff winds up on their pants, their jerseys, and their helmets. According to the rule book, you're not supposed to have more than eighteen inches of pine tar on your bat.

As George rounded the bases and his teammates came out to congratulate him on a great clutch homer, Billy started yelling at his catcher Rick Cerone, ''Check the bat! Check the bat!'' Then Billy came running out of the dugout and demanded that home plate umpire Tim McClelland examine the bat for a pine tar violation. McClelland deferred to crew chief Joe Brinkman, who really had no choice in the matter because pine tar was all over the bat and it extended far beyond the eighteen-inch limit.

Rule 6.06(A) states that a batter shall be out when he hits an illegally batted ball. Brinkman strung together some rules and decided that Brett should have been called out because he had clearly done something illegal. The umpiring crew walked toward the Royals dugout and McClelland signaled Brett out, thus ending the game, sending George into a mad fit at home plate. If Brett hadn't been restrained, I'm sure that he would have punched Joe in the nose, and that would have cost him a bunch of games and a bunch of money.

The Royals protested the decision, and wouldn't you know that American League president Lee MacPhail upheld the protest, thus deepening the mess and sending some of my fellow umpires into orbit. MacPhail ruled that pine tar would not improve the distance of the ball and, therefore, rule 6.06(A) didn't apply.

The Great Pine Tar Incident would take on the elements of a spy novel. Everyone wondered what Martin would have up his sleeve when the game was to be resumed about four weeks later with two outs in the ninth inning and the Royals leading the game (thanks to Brett's now legal home run) 4–3.

Fortunately, umpire supervisor Dick Butler heard from a source inside the Yankees that Martin did, indeed, have a card up his sleeve. Billy was going to appeal to the umpiring crew that Brett had missed a base during his home run trot. Since there would be a change in umpiring crews (Brinkman's crew would be working in Seattle) Billy could cause some confusion and possibly have grounds to protest the game.

Mr. Dick Butler figured out a way to stop that. He had Brinkman's crew sign an affadavit that Brett and U. L. Washington, the Royals player who was on base at the time, had touched all the bags. As soon as the game was resumed, Yankees pitcher George Frazier stepped off the rubber and tossed the ball to first baseman Ken Griffey, who stepped on the base. First base umpire Tim Welke signaled safe. Billy then walked confidently out of the dugout and approached umpire Davey Phillips, who had the affadavit in his back pocket.

When Billy made his appeal, Davey pulled out the piece of paper and stood there waiting for Billy to explode. "He looked like he'd just seen a ghost," Davey said. "Billy had this whole thing mapped out. And we took away his little plan with one little piece of paper." Billy lost the appeal, his potential protest, and the game 4–3 when the Yankees failed to score in the bottom of the ninth inning.

Umpires didn't like Billy's antics, and we grew weary of his trickery. But I'll still have to give him credit for his ability to turn teams around. Look at what he did with the Texas Rangers, transforming them from misfits to contenders in the mid-1970s, and with the Oakland A's, converting them to a play-off team in 1981. He always had a way of putting a spark back into the Yankees. But he wasn't effective for the long haul because the players always caught on to his act. Billy had a way of self-destructing and so did his teams, and I wasn't sad the day he got out of baseball.

Lou

Lou Piniella: Coming up as a player under Billy with the Yankees, Sweet Lou didn't learn all of his lessons well. Oh yeah, he learned to argue like a desperate lawyer. But at least he didn't learn to hold a grudge or to throw tirades at the drop of a hat. Don't get me wrong. Lou is feisty, but he doesn't go around getting into fights in strip joints like Billy did.

Lou and I've had a lot of fun through the years.

During a game between the Yankees and Angels in Anaheim in 1985, well-liked Angel Don Baylor got hit by a pitch. There was some bad blood brewing between the teams, so the benches emptied and the field suddenly looked like a saloon brawl from an old Western movie. It's the job of umpires to restore the peace, and I've always thought they should issue handcuffs and nightsticks for such duty.

It's also the responsibility of the manager and his coaches to break up fights. So when I saw Sweet Lou, then the hitting coach, starting fights, ol' Durwood felt his blood pressure rising. Lou had just finished a ten-year stint as a Yankees player, and maybe he was a little confused. But I had no time to explain the rules to Leaping Lou.

I collared Piniella at home plate and started pushing him backward. I walked him more than ninety feet, past the Angels dugout, and then I pancaked his butt. I pushed his backside to the ground and I pinned him. I held him to the ground while he proceeded to tear my shirt off. I heard him grunt, "Dammit, Durwood, you're a strong sumbitch."

It was my luck that a television cameraman filmed our

little tango. It led the one of the late sportscast that night and was the talk of baseball for several days.

Lou and I have a lot in common in that we both like to cut up and we're both type A personalities. Sometimes I think there's a big kid hidden inside both of us.

It's always been fun to argue with Lou because he can burst into a tirade with the best of them. He'll rant and rave and throw his cap. Maybe he did learn that from Billy Martin. But the next day, Sweet Lou will be patting you on the back, laughing with you, just forgetting the entire episode. That's the way it ought to be. Baseball is no place to hold grudges because baseball is a game, doggone it.

Sometimes Lou will throw one of his fits, and I'll just laugh in his face and say, "Lou this is good. Please keep it up." Then the next day, he'll say, "Did I really do that? Tell me I really didn't say that."

On September 10 of the 1996 season, I reversed a call in Seattle that could have changed the face of the postseason. The Yankees were leading the American League East and the Mariners were still chasing Texas in the West. They met in Seattle in mid-September.

Seattle's Paul Sorrento hit what appeared to be a home run to center field. Rocky Roe, umpiring second base, hustled into center field to make the call. Rocky thought he saw the ball clear the fence before landing in a fan's glove. From his angle, though, Rocky didn't realize that the fan had reached three feet over the center field wall to make the catch. So Rocky flashed the home run sign.

From third base, I had a better angle. I saw the fan, a man in his mid-twenties, run down the aisle and lean far over the wall. Clearly, it was a case of fan interference. I instantly reversed Rocky's call, giving the Mariners a double instead of a home run.

Lou came roaring out of the dugout. "Who is the crazy sumbitch who reversed that call?" he screamed at first base umpire Davey Phillips.

By now, I'm half jogging across the infield toward Lou.

**Earl and I went toe-to-toe on
more than one occasion.**

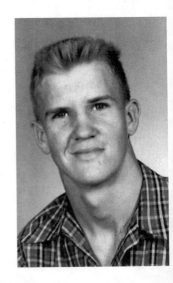

Heck, was I ever this young?

Coaching football and working with kids was a great part of my life.

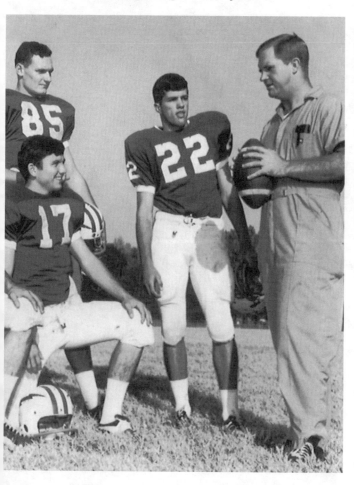

**Here I am with my good friend
Steve Palermo (left) down in Puerto Rico.**

My patented "Big Out" call

Here I am meeting President Bush before he threw out the first pitch in Texas in April of 1991.

Here I am with two great men— Colin Powell and Steve Palermo.

My wife, Carolyn, is a wonderful
and important part of my life.

Sparky Anderson,
one of the greatest
managers in the history
of baseball, was also one
of the greatest arguers.
(Sparky Anderson)

"Here I am, big boy!" I hollered. "I made the call, blame me, Lou?"

Lou, with venom spewing from both ears, shouted, "Why'd you have to stick your damn nose in that play? That's Rocky's call. Besides, Durwood, you can't see that far!"

I had the comeback for Lou that I'd been waiting to deliver for quite some time, and I knew that he was going to explode just like the Seattle scoreboard.

Chuckling, I said, "Lou, son, I can see all the way to the sun. And the sun is ninety-one million miles away."

Lou went off like a Roman candle. Pretending to be one of those soccer-style sidewinders, he tried to kick a little dirt on me, but he kept missing. I kept thinking about an NFL kicker who couldn't put the ball through the goalposts.

"Lou," I said, chuckling again. "I'm over here."

Lou finally kicked a little dirt on my shoes. I lifted both arms into the air, like an NFL referee, and yelled, "It's good!" Then I ran Lou's butt right out of the Seattle Kingdome.

Yes, I was right. The *Seattle Post-Intelligencer* reported the next day that the fan admitted catching the ball over the wall. Because he had pulled this little stunt once before, the Mariners decided to bar him from the Kingdome for the rest of the season.

The next day, Lou walked up to me, put his arm around my shoulder, and said, "I was wrong again, podnah. But, Durwood, I sure put on a show, didn't I?"

Lou handles his players just like he treats the umpires. He'll scald their butts, especially the pitchers, if they make mental mistakes, but the next day he might meet them at the clubhouse door with a hug. He's the kind of guy I could play for.

Tommy

Tommy Lasorda: People still ask why I had such knock-down drag-outs with this guy. We just didn't click. I never asked him, and he never asked me. I think, though, that if Tommy and I were off somewhere eating Italian food, we would get along great. I think if we ever did a banquet together, we'd have a fine time. But every time I did one of his games, he always said something to rub me the wrong way.

During spring training in Florida, Rocky always checked the Dodgers schedule to see when I'd be behind the plate against Tommy. Rocky would be there if he could because he knew there was going to be a fight.

When I walked on the field, the Dodgers players would start yelling, "Durwood, herrrrrrrrrrre's Tommy." Dodgers catcher Mike Scioscia once told me, "We're taking bets in the dugout on which inning you'll run Tommy out of the game."

Here's the weird part. Managers rarely get thrown out of Grapefruit League games down in Florida because it's a time when everybody is pretty mellow and the players are out there working on fundamentals. Nobody cares. But I had to throw Tommy out of three spring training games.

The first time I tossed him was in Lakeland. The Dodgers were playing the Detroit Tigers, and Tommy started chirping in the first inning. He'd yell, "Sparky Anderson runs that damn [American] league over there." He was trying to imply that he also controlled the umpires. So I shot back, "Watch this run, Tommy!" I jacked him right out of the game.

Another time, the Dodgers were playing Kansas City in Baseball City very early in spring training, and Tommy was sitting in a chair about twelve feet from me at home plate. He yelled, "The pitch was low."

I hollered back, "So what? What do you think I've been doing? Calling balls and strikes all winter?"

He yelled, "What do you mean, so what?"

I threw my right hand into the air and yelled, "So what this! You're outta here."

The next inning, Joey Amalfitano, their third base coach, walked by and said, "Hey, Durwood, you know what's funny? Tommy wanted to get thrown out of the game. He knew they'd just delivered his fried chicken to the clubhouse, and he was ready to eat.''

That was before he got on his dern diet powder and lost all those pounds. Do you know what we do with Tommy Lasorda's diet powder around Hooks, Texas? We use it to fill up potholes at the farm.

Tommy had the filthiest mouth of any manager I've ever encountered, including George Bamberger, who once used the F-word five times in a seven-word sentence. Just like Earl Weaver, I couldn't stay mad at Tommy. Maybe someday we can break a loaf of Italian bread together.

In spite of all of our problems, I was happy for Tommy on the day that he was inducted into the Hall of Fame in Cooperstown. The Dodgers didn't get around to naming him their manager until he was forty-nine years old, and then he had to follow a legend in Walter Alston. You have to admire a man who has the will to follow his dreams, along with the patience and the perseverance to make sure those dreams come true.

Tony

Tony LaRussa: Arguing with this guy on the field, you make doggone sure that you think before you talk because he's a great manipulator of words. After spending seventeen years in the American League with Tony, I always got the feeling that we were arguing in the courtroom, not on the baseball diamond. The man knows baseball and the rule book and all of its interpretations as well as anyone in our business. He really could have been a great lawyer.

Truth of the matter is that the less you say to Tony, the better off you will be in the long run. When our arguments start running long, I say, "Tony, gotta go. We've got a baseball game that we need to play. Gotta go now."

Tony wasn't the first major league manager to use the computer, but I think he probably perfected it before anyone else. He and his staff work endless hours, entering information and working on matchups that might provide the slightest edge. One afternoon, Tony had one of his coaches, Rene Lachemann, working on a series of color-coded sheets in the dugout when I walked by and yelled, "Hey, Rene, where did you get that pretty coloring book? Tony's gonna have you do crossword puzzles next."

I had to run Tony out of a couple of games. Neither time was it a case of his becoming rude or obnoxious or saying any of the magic words. Both were cases when his team was getting pounded and he wanted out of the game because he just couldn't stand it anymore.

One night against the Rangers, his Oakland A's were having one of those nights when nothing was going right. Tony just kept arguing, even though he knew the argument was over. I said something like, "Tony, do you want me throw you out of the game? Just say so, because we can make this pretty easy." He nodded and I just yanked him out of the game.

I was preparing to work the plate during an exhibition game between the Cardinals and the Rangers in the spring of 1997. Tony walked up to me and said, "Durwood, you've been the best umpire in the American League the last five years. It took me a long time to appreciate your work. It took me a long time to appreciate you because I thought you were a hot dog. But I really think you're the best."

To some people, being a hot dog means that you really don't care about your work. However, people discover sooner or later that I'm as conscientious about umpiring as anyone who's ever been in this business. As I accepted Tony's compliment and walked away, I wondered if Tony was really being sincere, or if he was just blowing oxygen up my skirt. I really wondered if he was just setting me up for interleague play, which would start in about ten weeks.

I would find out later that he'd said the same thing to *Dallas Morning News* columnist Randy Galloway, who started writing about baseball back in 1972 and really knows a lot about the game. Because I respect Tony so much, and

I know how dead serious he is about managing baseball, I felt pretty good about the job I'd been doing.

Sparky

Sparky Anderson: I guess you could say he was my hero, although I didn't want him to know that.

When Sparky Anderson came over to the American League during the 1979 season, he was like a god to a lot of people. Managing the Reds for nine seasons, he'd gone to four World Series, winning two. So I decided that first season to assert myself and try to get his attention. I was umpiring at third base when Sparky came out of the dugout to challenge a close call on a triple. I let him chew on me for a while, and then I sent him straight to the showers.

"What do you mean?" he said with a puzzled look.

I cracked, "This is what I mean: I can't walk on water. And neither can you!" I was just trying to take him down a few notches. I don't think that Sparky ever forgot that.

Just about every time I saw him after that, he'd pull his britches legs up and say, "You know, Durwood, I'm still trying."

Sparky came roaring onto the field one afternoon, mad as hell at one of my calls. He was determined to scald me for this one. It was a steal at second base, and I called the opposing runner safe. Sparky came out yelling at his shortstop, Alan Trammell, "Tram, did you get him?" Trammell said he did, though he was dead wrong.

So Sparky started chewing on me. I looked at him and said calmly, "Let me tell you one thing, Sparky. I'm not going to get no better."

That just disarmed him. He shrugged and laughed and said, "I guess there's no reason for me to argue because I'm not going to get no better, either." Then he turned and jogged back to the dugout.

For years, Sparky went around the league telling people,

"Durwood and I have a pact. Neither one of us is going to get no better."

The last time Sparky came out of the dugout on me I'd called one of his players, Juan Samuel, out for leaving second base too soon. Juan didn't even come close to tagging up. Sparky said, "Let me tell you what I'm going to do, Durwood. I'm going to look at the instant replay. If you missed the call, I'll be back." In my younger days, I would have bellowed, "Let me save you a trip! You're gone." But I had a lot of respect for for Sparky, and I didn't want to toss him out of the game.

Managers like to have one guy around to check the television replay monitor after a controversial call. That guy will run up the tunnel, and then he'll hustle back down and tell the manager if the umpire got it right. I always knew when I got a call right. After listening to them bitch and moan for about five minutes, there would be nothing but dead air coming out of the dugout.

Sparky would use clubhouse man Jimmy Schmakel as his TV guy. He'd yell, "Hey, Schmake, what'd you think about the call?" And Schmakel would respond, "You know, Sparky, I think he got it right." That would send Sparky into orbit. "I don't want to hear that," Sparky would yell. "Then why the hell did you ask me?" Schmakel would fire back.

One last thing about Sparky. He was a great manager, and if he doesn't make the Hall of Fame, those voters need to take a Breathalyzer.

Ralph

Ralph Houk: If there was one manager who could shake ol' Durwood up, it was this man. Ralph is mostly remembered for replacing Casey Stengel as the Yankees manager in 1961 and leading New York to World Series titles his first two years. The Yankees went to their third straight World Series under Ralph in 1963, but lost in four games to the Dodgers. He'd be replaced the next year by Yogi Berra and return to manage the Yankees again from 1967 through 1973.

His managing career was winding down with the Detroit Tigers in 1978, and my major league career was just getting legs. My second year in the big leagues I thought I was doing a fine job one afternoon behind the plate at Tiger Stadium. Wilbur Wood, the great knuckleballer, was on the mound for the White Sox, and his ball was just dancing all over the park. The toughest pitcher for a plate umpire is a knuckleballer because the doggone thing might drop two feet in the blink of an eye.

With two outs in the ninth, Detroit shortstop Alan Trammell faced an oh-two count when Wood delivered. About four feet from the plate, the pitch looked like a perfect strike. I raised my right hand and "stri . . ." was already out of my mouth. Then that ball fell like it'd been dropped from a table. The pitch bounced about a foot in front of the plate. But it was too late. I'd already called strike three. The game was over.

This day, I had no escape hatch. To reach the umpires' room, I would have to walk through the Tigers dugout and down the tunnel with the players, the coaches, and, yes, Tormentor Houk. He glared at me as if I'd stolen his World Series ring. His eyes cut through me like cold bayonets.

"Got a hot date tonight, Durwood?" he said. "Couldn't you have waited for one more pitch?" I wanted to tell him that I didn't drink or smoke and I certainly didn't even think about running around on my wife. But those words were stuck in my throat.

Houk's biting words rocked me. Here I was, a young umpire who was still a little sensitive to criticism. Furthermore, I knew that I'd clearly blown that third strike call to Trammel. Heck, everybody in Tiger Stadium knew I embarrassed myself.

I don't know if it was what Ralph said or how he said it. But I didn't sleep very well that night, and the next morning, I asked Marty Springstead what I should do. He said, "Durwood, you just need to walk up to the man and explain yourself."

With my heart in my throat, I approached him the next afternoon. "Ralph," I said. "I really have no excuse for what happened yesterday. I just missed it. But I didn't do it intentionally. I really tried."

Houk put his arm around me and said, "Tex, you worked a great game yesterday." We walked out to the plate together. All the while, I was thinking, Is this the same man who took my head off yesterday?

About a decade later, Ralph was doing some consulting work for the Minnesota Twins. In the ninth inning of an exhibition game down in Florida, the Twins and Yankees were tied. Twins infielder Al Newman, a little bowling ball, was rolling down the third baseline. He slid across home plate so hard that he cut my legs out from under me. I flipped end over end like a kickoff. Lying on the ground, all I could see was Houk over in the Twins dugout laughing and yelling, "Safe! Safe! Safe!" After a rough start, Ralph and I had a lot of laughs through the years, and that was one of them.

Bobby

Bobby Valentine: American League umpires weren't always entertained by his baiting and taunting from the top step of the dugout. He was run out of seventeen ball games by seventeen different umpires in one season. That tells the fans and the league and the sportswriters that Bobby, not the umpires, was having a problem. It all came to a head in Minnesota during a confrontation between Bobby and Larry Barnett. Bobby charged out of the dugout and yelled at Barnett, "Hey, Larry, how much money you got on this game?" I think that's when the proverbial you-know-what hit the fan. There was a big meeting between Bobby, the Rangers, and the league office. Bobby got hit with a big fine. I think he learned a valuable lesson from that. He needed to take stock of where he was and what he was doing. Bobby started getting more control of himself. He started growing up.

Bobby has always known the game of baseball. His wife

says Bobby has a type A-plus personality. I would agree. Players loved to play for him. I think he proved that with the New York Mets in 1997. What a fine job he did in his first year in New York.

I always liked Bobby Valentine, and at first, I thought he was fair to umpires. He would come and speak his mind, and then he would get off the field. But the pressure started getting to Bobby. That's nothing new in our business. I've seen many other Bobby Valentines in our business. Baseball will take your sanity if you let it. I've seen a lot of other managers who lost control and couldn't get it back. Pretty soon, the manager is taking it out on everybody in sight and umpires are big and easy targets.

Valentine got rolling one night in Boston, and I thought I was going to need riot gear to break up the fight between him and my good friend Steve Palermo. Those two were ready to tear up Fenway Park. It was one of those games when the Texas Rangers couldn't find a pitcher who could keep the ball in the park. The Red Sox were launching pitch after pitch over the Green Monster in left field. Valentine and the pitching coach were wearing out the grass from the dugout to the mound.

Now, if there's one thing that an umpire can't stand, it's a game that drags along needlessly. We have three-and-a-half-hour games in the American League where the final score is 3–2. There's just too much scratching and chewing and worthless dialogue in the American League. It's enough to make a religious man like me want to cuss.

This game in Boston was crawling along when Rangers third baseman Steve Buechele walked to the mound. He just wanted to give a pep talk to his pitcher, but Palermo, who was umping at first base, told Buechele, "Get your butt back to third."

Buechele told Palermo to mind his own business—well, something like that. And he got his butt thrown right out of the game. So here came Valentine from the dugout with both barrels loaded. It was showdown time for a couple of Italian gunslingers.

This argument degenerated pretty quickly.

"I'll kick your ass," Valentine said to Palermo.

"No, I'll kick yours," Palermo shot back.

I kept wondering when one madman was going to invite the other madman to a fight in the parking lot. No sooner had the thought crossed my mind when Valentine screamed, "Meet me in the parking lot after the game!"

Whoa, Nellie. We're talking about a couple of full-grown adults here.

I would later call it the meeting of the Italian minds. In one sense, it was kind of funny. Then you think about the anger involved, and it wasn't funny at all. The real problem is that the two men were too much alike.

Joe Brinkman was our crew chief that year, and he got a call the next day from American League president Bobby Brown. Brown asked Joe to intervene in the Palermo-Valentine feud. Joe did the smart thing by convincing the two combatants to have breakfast together one morning. Being the curious type, I took a table in the same restaurant not too far from the scene. You know, I've always enjoyed a good fight.

About thirty minutes later, I looked over to see the two men standing up. Instead of slugging it out, they were hugging. I laughed until my ribs ached.

My reason for digging up Valentine's temperamental past is to make a point about Bobby's current state of mind. He's a changed man. I've seen him deal with the pressures of baseball, and I've seen him smile in the face of adversity. And in 1997, I saw him do a doggone good job of managing the New York Mets.

This you must realize about Bobby. He can motivate his players and he has a dynamic personality. If he'll just put aside the needless bouts of temper, this man could become one of the best skippers in baseball. I think he's typical of a man getting a second chance, a reprieve if you will. He got fired by the Rangers, and then he did a self-imposed exile in Japan. I think he went through a lot of self-examination over there. When Bobby finally made it back to the major leagues, I think he appreciated it more. You can see that in his eyes.

His players used to call him "Top-Step" behind his back because Bobby always stood on the top step of the dugout, barking at the umps. Now he relaxes on the bench, and he doesn't pick a fight unless he believes he's completely right.

Over the years, I've tried not to hold grudges against managers, with the exception of Billy Martin. With that in mind, I give you the top twelve managers of my time in the major leagues—the last couple of decades in baseball. These are the guys I saw up close and personal. Some too personal. Some too close.

My main criterion for rating managers is what they did with their great teams. The great ones, like great jockeys, know how to boot their teams home in October. Here is my list:

Durwood's Dozen

1. Tom Kelly: Twice in his life, he had a chance to win the World Series. He did it both times. If he had the Yankees' talent year after year, he would be in the postseason every year.

2. Sparky Anderson: He won the World Series with two different teams. He turned the kids into champions in Detroit.

3. Earl Weaver: He may have been the most consistent manager that I saw in the major leagues.

4. Tony LaRussa: He had the ability to build and add and keep putting the pieces together. When it came time for him to win, his team was ready.

5. Billy Martin: He could develop a team as fast as anyone in the game. But he lost a few as quickly as he built them.

6. Jim Leyland: Winning the World Series added new credibility.

7. Bobby Cox: If he can maintain this winning level, he'll be due even more credit.

8. Tommy Lasorda: I never could get along with him. But his enthusiasm for managing made the Dodgers one of the best teams of the last twenty years.

9. Lou Piniella: Lou has taken Seattle places they've never been before.

10. Felipe Alou: Most managers would pull their hair out in Montreal. Every time he gets a superstar, the Expos give him up to another team.

11. Joe Torre: He got the Yankees to a certain point and then took them over the top. Here was a man ready to stay away from baseball. Then he walked into the toughest job in managing, and his blood pressure never went up.

12. Mike Hargrove: He's been to the World Series twice and, with improved pitching, will soon win one.

My honorable mentions for top managers would be Johnny Oates of the Rangers, Phil Garner of Milwaukee, Terry Collins of Anaheim and Bobby Valentine of the Mets.

Collins sure showed the folks in Houston that he wasn't worthy of managing there. All he did was coax California from last place to the top of the A. L. West standings for a good part of the 1997 season.

Johnny Oates was let go in Baltimore and brought Texas its first division championship. He also happens to be one of the nicest guys in all of baseball.

What kind of manager would I be? I'd know what buttons to push and I could motivate because I did that for years as a high school coach.

But I don't think that I could manage baseball. I'd be too

emotional. To be a good manager you have to be able to throw off losses, and I'm not going to do it by getting into the booze. Bob Lemon once said that he left every lost game at the nearest bar. I couldn't even find the nearest bar.

Down on the field every day, I can see the strain in the managers' faces. I can look right into a man's eyes and see if he has been winning or losing. Managing is no cakewalk. It might appear to be a fantasy game of pushing buttons and moving men around on a chessboard, but it's much more than that.

Another problem with managing in this era is trying to handle the players' million-dollar bank accounts. Managing is often a matter of peeling back the scalp and looking into the mind. That little game becomes even more complicated when you add the pressure of megabucks.

Some players are motivated by money. The more they're paid, the faster that engine runs. Others become laconic with millions and millions in the bank. They become fat and sassy, and they stop working at the game. Yet another group of players becomes paralyzed by payola. They think, Oh, my God, they're paying me so much that I've got to get the winning hit today. They end up choking at the plate with two outs in the bottom of the ninth.

Walk in a manager's shoes sometime and you'll see how the almighty dollar can affect performance. Then you'll come to understand just how tough the job is today in baseball. As I become older, and I see the rich getting richer in baseball, I truly believe in the adage that money causes pain, not gain.

Managers today prepare a lot more than the old guys. You'll see them arriving ten hours before a game with the strap of their laptop computer case slung over their shoulder. They use the football approach with all of their computer data to analyze every situation. Everything from the color of their eyes to color of their socks is used to set up certain situations.

Sparky Anderson said the old-line managers managed by the seat of their pants. They played a lot of hunches. But today, managers play percentages, trying to get that left-handed hitter matched against that right-handed pitcher. It's a constant strategy game going on out there. I think that's why you see fewer and fewer warlike confrontations between managers and umpires. Managers today are more from the thinking-man's school.

I don't think managers today like to fight as much as their predecessors. They want to help their ballplayers win more. They just don't care as much about attacking umpires. Managers used to believe that if you beat on an umpire long enough, he'd cave in. Today's managers have wised up and they know abuse can backfire on you.

When I first got into the major leagues in 1977, managers would chart each pitch thrown by a pitcher. For instance, if Roger Clemens was throwing nothing but fastballs to Reggie Jackson, and he was hitting them out of the park, they would change to the curveball to Reggie. It wasn't very scientific stuff. Basically, it was a lot of common sense. But nowadays, they chart not only the pitch but the location and the velocity. They chart where the batter hit the ball. Today, they leave no stone unturned.

Most managers know the right buttons to push. So what separates a great manager from a mediocre one is motivating the players over the long haul of a season. Sparky Anderson was a great manager because he could handle all the egos on a team. You've got twenty-five helium-inflated egos. Job One is keeping the prima donnas happy.

As far as handling the role players on your ball club, I think that Kelly and Anderson were two of the best. They knew how to keep everybody awake in the dugout happy because they made sure the backup guys got plenty of plate appearances. I noticed that Valentine did that with the Mets in 1997 and it paid some huge dividends.

A guy that deserves another shot at managing is Kevin Kennedy, who had a conflict with Boston general manager Dan Duquette and got fired after the 1996 season. Kevin knows the game of baseball and he's a great motivator. I would hate to see him get passed over and then forgotten. I thought he was one of the most personable guys I'd been around in a long time.

Mostly, umpires just want managers to be fair when they're conducting their business. Of course, a fair manager will stand up for his players, but he won't get carried away when he knows the umpire is probably right and the player is just throwing off steam. A fair manager will come out of the dugout and get the frustration off his chest, and then he'll go back and sit down and let the game go on without badgering everybody within earshot.

I'll say that managers can be the funniest and yet the most ornery people that I've ever known in baseball. They'll make you laugh and some have even made a few umpires cry. One minute, you'll be joking with the manager, and then next minute he'll be blowing bad breath in your face. What I've tried to do over the years, dating back to Billy and Earl, is to understand the manager and the countless crises he's got to face every season. All you had to do at the end of the 1997 World Series was to look into the eyes of Cleveland's Mike Hargrove to know the pain this game can inflict. There probably is nothing more complex in all sports than the umpire-manager relationship. Somehow, based on what I've experienced through the years, I doubt that the dirt-kicking and the screaming and the cussing will ever stop.

Thank You, Reggie and Junior

I KNOW THAT BASEBALL is a game of Big Greed and uncaring robots, a hard business that's fouled the air and broken hearts the last few years. What a doggone shame, because there was a time when baseball could compete with Mama's fresh-baked hot apple pie.

Call me a shameless dreamer, but a vision lives in my mind's eye, and like a cat hair, I can't get it out. Truth is, I don't want it to go away. This is baseball the way I want to see it, a game played for simple enjoyment. It is the pleasure of being at the ballpark, eating a mustard-and-relish-covered hot dog, chasing down a foul ball, and smelling the fresh-cut grass. It is a cool evening with real folks sitting down the baselines in their folding lawn chairs. It is about dogs chasing kids who are chasing fireflies. It is Ken Griffey Jr. relaxing in the Seattle Mariners dugout in the seventh inning, eating a Snickers bar.

That's right. Not too long ago, I peered into the Mariners dugout between innings, and there was Junior, laughing and joking with his buddies while his feet dangled underneath the bench. The Snickers bar was about half-eaten.

As I paused to watch, I knew my mind was going back in time. I was seeing a twelve-year-old Little Leaguer in a baggy dirt-stained uniform. And as I stood there, Junior never stopped smiling or laughing or punching one of his teammates in the arm.

When I want to revisit this feeling, I turn to The Kid.

Junior Griffey is the closest thing we'll ever see to baseball done right. Watch him while you can because baseball's money machine surely will, before long, eat him up and spit him out like so much Red Man chewing tobacco.

The Kid's such a wonder because he's having fun every day of the season, and I really think he'd play a pickup game for nothing. He doesn't need to do a bunch of soul-searching back at the hotel after going oh-for-four at the plate. He's not afraid of chasing a few bad ones at the plate, or lapsing into a mild slump, or overthrowing the cutoff man. Deep inside, he knows that baseball is a game that sets you up for failure and, by gosh, there are going to be some tough times. That's why his personalized license plate reads, FEAR NO ONE.

In April 1997, I was working an afternoon game at Tiger Stadium between the Mariners and the Detroit Tigers. Standing just behind third base, a line shot was hit right at my head. I ducked and landed on my backside as the ball rocketed into left field. Little did I know at the time that a TV camera had focused on my fall, and as I lay there on my back, the TV broadcasters were having a little fun at my expense. "Look at his shoes," one of them blurted. "Durwood's got on Junior's shoes!"

A few weeks earlier, I'd gone out and bought of a pair Nike cross-trainers for the same reason that a lot of people buy shoes—I liked the way they looked. But I didn't know that they were Griffey models because instead of his name, they had his likeness on the back: a batter taking a big looping swing. I was walking around Tiger Stadium one afternoon when the players started giving me the business for wearing the Griffey shoes. I kept saying, "Show me his name on these dadgum things." That's when they pointed out the logo on the back.

It just so happens that Griffey's marketing man was watching the game on the afternoon I got all the free airtime. The next day, I was standing in the Tigers dugout when Junior came running by. He stuck a piece of paper in my top shirt pocket and said, "That's my marketing rep's phone number. Give him a call and he'll send you some more shoes.''

I did and he offered to send me a pair of Junior's latest model. But I added, ''I can't really accept them unless you send shoes for the entire crew. We'll need four pair.'' The next day, the shoes arrived, and for several weeks, we were as coordinated in our footwear as the Beatles back in the early 1960s. We had the best-looking shoes in all of umpiring.

What I really like about Junior Griffey, other than he wears great shoes, is that he never whines when you call a strike on the corner. He's got that in common with George Brett and Rod Carew and Reggie Jackson and, yes, even Mickey Mantle. These guys rarely whined about the strike zone and never sent me a dozen roses after a three–home run day. The Kid doesn't need favorable calls from the umpires to hit over .300 every year while driving in 150 runs and smacking 50-something dingers. Great hitters could care less about the umpires.

When I say that Junior Griffey is one of my favorite players of all time, I'm sure that somebody is going to call for a congressional investigation. All I've got to say about that is this: ''Hah!'' The world is too full of conspiracy theories. Besides, how can you pick on a kid who eats a Snickers bar in the seventh inning?

I've often wondered if Junior would have been eating nails instead of candy bars if he'd somehow landed in that alien place called Yankee Stadium instead of sleepy Seattle. A long time ago, when he really was a kid, he said he'd never play in the Bronx, and I don't blame him. He was taking batting practice one afternoon in the House That Ruth Built when one of the anal retentive Yankee snoop dogs threw him off the field. Seems they don't let the sons of superstars take batting practice on their hallowed ground, even if his name is Ken Griffey Jr. This all happened when Ken Griffey Sr. was playing for the Yankees in 1983. Junior Griffey has told me more than once that he'd rather give up his Nike commercials than play in that crazy town.

Which brings me to a man who was a beaten dog before his five-year sentence in New York ended after the 1981 season. I'm talking about the straw that stirs the drink, Reggie Jackson.

There were times when Reggie seemed tormented by the game and all of the chaos flying around him in New York. Baseball became a fat chip on his broad shoulder. There were times, at his own admission, that he darn near had a nervous breakdown. Oh, I know that Reggie was able to block out George Steinbrenner and some of the other demons that haunted him, like Billy Martin, because he had some great games, and he delivered dramatic and unforgettable blows in the postseason. But he had to deal with a mental jackhammer that never stopped pounding him down in New York. Billy once said of Reggie and Steinbrenner, "One is a born liar and the other is a convicted felon." The "liar" was Reggie and the "convicted felon" was Steinbrenner, who received a felony conviction in 1974 for making illegal contributions to Richard Nixon. That little outburst caused Steinbrenner to fire Billy the very next day.

Billy and Reggie were always at it, beginning with his first season in pinstripes in 1977. In June of that year, Billy thought Reggie was loafing on a fly ball to right field. So, in the midst of the inning, he sent a reluctant Paul Blair in to replace him. Reggie, after returning to the dugout, asked Billy for an explanation, and the two almost went to fist city.

Here's a question I'm going to ask Reggie Jackson someday. I'm going to walk up and say, "Just how much better could you have been if you'd been happier at times?"

In some ways, Reggie and New York were a match made for Broadway. He had the flamboyance and the love of the nightlife and the guts to swim with the big sharks in the world's biggest fishbowl. But I still contend that the crush of it all nearly broke him down. You've got to give the man credit for believing in himself. But, boy, what a price he paid for that fame.

I really think that Reggie's happiest days were his first few seasons in Oakland, even though he didn't get along with owner Charlie O. Finley. Everybody knows that Charlie O. was a tough old coot who threw nickels around like manhole covers. But even though he fought for his freedom from Oakland, Reggie felt he got a better all-round honest deal from old Charlie than he did from Steinbrenner, who liked to give him mental spankings.

Some people of his era thought that Reggie Jackson was a pompous ass. Actually, I thought Reggie was a lot of things. Smart. Abrasive. Proud. Childlike. Generous. Unsure. Colorful. Insecure.

I think he was pompous as a player in that he had tremendous confidence. You could even see the confidence in Reggie when he struck out because he did it with such vigor. You never could break the man's spirit, at least not on the ball field. I always knew that Reggie was in the batter's box because I could feel his presence, just like I knew it was Nolan Ryan or Catfish Hunter on the mound. I could close my eyes and feel Reggie Jackson just a few feet away. Confidence just oozed out of his body.

There are two types of ballplayers, and good managers can easily separate them. Hitters like Reggie, with the game on the line, will say, "Get out of my way and give me the damn bat." Others will slide down the end of the bench, hoping to be out of sight and thus out of mind.

With the game on the line, Reggie was a madman starved for center stage. He was just like George Brett and and Wade Boggs during their prime. He's just like Junior Griffey is today. Every great player must have a monster ego, and I know that Reggie put his on display a little more frequently than others. But when he had a pool cue in hand, he wanted to run the table. When he had the dice in his hand, he wanted to break the casino.

I've seen Reggie take the monster swing and miss and almost fall down. Then, he'd turn to the catcher and say, "Don't let him throw it again. If he throws it again, you'll never find it." Nine times out of ten, the next pitch would be so far outside that you couldn't reach it with a tree limb.

I've also seen Reggie play a pitcher like a poker hand.

That pitcher would nibble, nibble, nibble until Reggie knew which card was coming next. Then, *ka-Boom* and good-bye baseball.

It was September 17, 1985, and Reggie was going for one of baseball's great milestones, his five hundredth home run. When you think of Reggie Jackson and the great drama of his career, you think of the New York Yankees and the Oakland A's. But on this night, he was in the uniform of the California Angels, and at age thirty-eight, his career was fading gently into the burnt orange horizon beyond the Pacific.

But I learned that evening that nothing was wrong with his eyesight. With Kansas City's Bud Black on the mound, the first pitch dipped and caught the dirt inches in front of the plate. Black threw another pitch and Reggie hollered, "Durwood, check that ball. There's a little spot on it."

I wondered to myself how he could possibly see a dirty spot on a ball that was traveling ninety miles per hour. But I called time-out anyway and examined the ball. And, indeed, there was a tiny red speck on the ball. Anaheim's infield back then had a red clay mixture.

So I stuffed that baseball into my bag and threw Black a clean new baseball, and we were back in business. Reggie slammed Black's next pitch about twenty rows deep into the right field seats—about 420 feet—and the Man had his meeting with history. Reggie managed to get the home run ball back from a fan, but I kept the spotted one. It has Reggie Jackson's autograph on it and remains part of my memorabilia collection.

Nobody ran around the bases after a home run like Reggie Jackson. The signature of that home run trot was Reggie dipping his shoulder as he approached the base and then cutting a half-circle around it. It was like he was saying "I'm going to get every ounce out of this." Reggie was one of the first big sluggers to pause at home plate and admire his home run. It made a lot of pitchers mad, and I'm sure some of them felt like they were being showed up. But to me it was art.

When people talked about Reggie's arrogance, I could see

it, but then I couldn't see it. In the decade I spent with him in the major leagues, I think that I got to see another side of Reggie. Maybe it was the real side. Like some other players, he liked to take sanctuary down in the umpires' room, where he knew he couldn't be found by the media or Billy Martin. We'd sit and talk about his collection of cars. Reggie had an entire warehouse full of expensive wheels back in the Bay Area. During those times when it was just him and me, Reggie could be Reggie. He loved our little cubbyhole under the grandstands where he could get out of the rat race and let down his guard.

You know what Reggie really liked? The southern fried chicken that I made and brought to the ballpark from time to time. One afternoon at my daughter's house just west of Fort Worth, I cooked up about fifty chicken breasts, along with gravy and potatoes and rolls. I think it took Maria three days to clean up the kitchen after I got through.

I brought the whole batch to the umpires' room at old Arlington Stadium when the Yankees were in town. Guess who was the first one through the door? Reginald Martinez Jackson.

"Hey, Durwood, man," he yelled when he walked through the door. "I hear you think you can outcook me at chicken. That's impossible, man. You didn't grow up in the ghetto."

Well, I showed Mr. October a thing or two about frying up a mess of chicken. My ace in the hole is my late mother's old country recipe to which I've added a couple of my own touches. According to the recipe, I'll flash-fry the chicken and then bake it in the oven. So it's really a baked fried chicken. It's a lot more juicy that way. Because the skin is the bad part of the chicken, I'll strip it off first. When I dip the chicken in milk, I'll add a couple of shots of Tabasco. With most fried chicken, the seasoning is right on the top. I'll take a sharp knife and cut my chicken all the way down the bone so my seasoning goes all the way through. When you take a bite into my chicken, you're going to taste the seasoning all the way down.

It seems that baseball and fried chicken have always gone hand in hand. Mickey Mantle used to have a fried chicken restaurant in Dallas, and even though they cooked up a pretty mean clucker, the place went belly-up. Mickey told me that he thought their motto killed them. It was "The only piece of chicken better than this, the rooster got." No wonder the Mick went bust in the chicken business.

I learned one thing pretty quickly about advertising my fried chicken. All I had to do was serve a large helping to Reggie Jackson and pretty soon the word was all over the ballpark. The Yankees and the Rangers were knocking down the umpires' door trying to get my chicken. Dick Butler, our supervisor, was there early and he got his share, too. There was enough finger-licking in the umpires' room to the make the Colonel want to fry hamburgers.

At first, I wondered why Reggie took a liking to me, because we seemed so different. Reggie lives for the bright lights and the big city. I crave the country and the fresh air. But one day, we were sitting around the umpires' room when he looked me in the eye and said, "Durwood, you're the Reggie Jackson of umpiring."

Now, I've never thought of myself as the straw who stirs the drink. Shoot, I don't even drink. Maybe you could call me Mr. October because I've worked a lot of play-offs, including three of the last four postseasons. But I never belted four World Series home runs on four straight swings.

Flamboyant? Possibly. I am the most impersonated umpire in all of baseball, and my hat does fly off a lot when I punch out runners on base paths. I do call my strikes with two fists. And, in my younger days, I did throw out a lot of people for wearing the wrong aftershave.

Talkative? Yes, indeed. I'll talk your ear off about cars, cows, cotton-pulling, knee surgery, exotic birds, and politics. I've always thought I could do my own radio talk show of any kind because I just love to talk and I study a wide range of subjects. Reggie and I are a lot alike in that regard.

Let me tell you why I think that Reggie and I got along. Because we both grew up poor—him on the second floor of a dry-cleaning and tailor shop near Philadelphia, and me in the cotton fields of western Oklahoma. We both had to overcome a lot of hard knocks, and there were plenty of mountains to climb. Nobody gave us a thing when we were kids, but that didn't keep us from dreaming. We both viewed sports as a vehicle to transport those dreams. So we rode the big train for as long as we could.

More than anything in my life I wanted to get away from the farm because I didn't want to chop cotton and bale hay anymore. I'm sure that Reggie got tired of pressing other people's suits. We both loved football before baseball became our sport. Not many people know that Reggie played a couple of seasons for Frank Kush—one of the roughest, toughest, meanest coaches ever—at Arizona State.

The first time that I saw Reggie I thought he would be taller. I guess he's not much over five-ten. But his forearms looked like a side of beef, and they were a raw source of power. Football helped him develop the muscles in his arms, and that's why he pounded 563 home runs.

Reggie loved taking the stage in baseball because he hungered for the white-hot spotlight. Equally frustrating, though, was the fact that people regarded him only as a jock. Even today, he wants to be regarded as a man of commerce. He told me about the long conversations he'd had with power brokers, people like movie mogul Marvin Davis and Edward Bennett Williams, the great lawyer who once owned the Washington Redskins and the Baltimore Orioles. Reggie thought he could handle himself with any boardroom bully in the country.

He was in the Bay Area one day when he got a phone call from a rich married couple in New York. They wanted to buy one of his Rolls-Royces. Reggie said they'd agreed on a price of $100,000. Reggie picked the couple up at the airport and drove them to the warehouse. And, just as he promised, the Rolls-Royce was there in mint condition. The man pulled out his checkbook and said to Reggie, "Let's see, you said eighty-five thousand." And Reggie said, "You know, my mother wanted this car. I guess she'll end up with it now. Ya'll just get a taxi and head on back to the airport."

Reggie said to me later, "Durwood, they just thought I was a dumb black boy. They thought they could take advantage of me. They found out pretty quick that they couldn't."

Because Reggie was so outspoken and flamboyant, and since he flaunted his ego, I think he was misunderstood. Reggie, in some respects, is an insecure guy, and he has trouble showing people his true side. As a player, he kept the real Reggie locked in a back room where even the media couldn't get to him. That's too bad, because during our conversations in the umps' room, I think I got to know the real Reggie.

After winning two straight World Series, Reggie and the Yankees were trying to get back into the A.L. East race in early September of 1979 when my umpiring crew hit town. New York was squaring off in an all-important four-game series against the Orioles, who were rolling like an East Texas freight train. Since Baltimore had a six-game lead, the Yankees really needed to sweep the series.

It had been a tough emotional year for the Yanks. Thurman Munson had died in a plane crash on August 2, Sparky Lyle had come out with a controversial tell-all book called *The Bronx Zoo,* and Goose Gossage had missed two months of the season after injuring a finger during a locker-room fight with Cliff Johnson. Rumor had it that manager Bob Lemon, the zookeeper, was about to be showed the front gate.

The umpiring crew took the subway to the Bronx because back then we didn't worry too much about our safety, even though the Yankees fans were the rowdiest in all of baseball at the time. It took cops wearing riot gear and riding horses to get them off the field after the 1978 World Series. We were wearing our sports jackets and ties, and a lot of people recognized us. But nobody gave us any trouble.

The game turned out to be a classic. With the score knotted at one, the Orioles were batting in the top of the ninth. With the go-ahead runner at third, Al Bumbry stepped to the plate for the Orioles. Goose Gossage had opened the inning, and he was throwing smoke. There were two outs. You could almost feel Yankee Stadium rocking and swaying around you.

Somehow my life was about to become entangled with perhaps the most popular Yankee of the time—Bobby Murcer. He had broken in as an eighteen-year-old phenom in 1965. He shared a Yankees record of four consecutive home runs with three of the biggest names in their history—Babe Ruth, Lou Gehrig, and Johnny Blanchard. For God's sake, he had come out of Oklahoma to take over the center field position from his idol, Mickey Mantle, in the late sixties. And in 1979, he was the Yankees captain.

On this night, Murcer was playing left field when the left-handed hitter Al Bumbry slapped one of those nasty slicing and sinking line drives his way. Murcer broke perfectly on the ball. He dived and scooped with his glove and came up with the ball. But I knew deep in my heart something was wrong. Maybe it was just instinct. But I knew the ball had short-hopped into Murcer's glove. With more than fifty thousand fans cheering Murcer's feat, I raced into the outfield from second base and threw both arms into the air. I signaled that Bumbry was safe. The go-ahead run scored from third as I was waving and yelling, "No catch! No catch! No catch!" From the way they acted that night in Yankee Stadium, you would've thought that I'd shot Murcer in the heart with a .44 magnum.

Suddenly I was surrounded by third baseman Graig Nettles, shortstop Bucky Dent, second baseman Willie Randolph, center fielder Mickey Rivers, Gossage, and Murcer. They were yelling things at me that we could never get into print. A fan in the stands threw an old baseball that hit me on the shoulder. Thankfully, Billy Martin was taking one of his many respites from managing the Yankees, or we would still be there arguing. But the mild-mannered Bob Lemon did have a few choice words for me.

After the Orioles had won 2–1, we were back in the umpires' room when two New York cops walked in. As I undressed on my stool, one of them glared down at me and said, "How did you get here, and how do you plan to get out of here?'' He was shocked when I said we'd taken the subway to Yankee Stadium. ''Sir, you won't be going back on the subway tonight,'' he said. ''They'll maul you. We've already had several death threats.''

I'll say this about Yankee Stadium security. They are the best in the American League. Given the baloney they have to put up with every night, I guess they have to be the best. So I was driven back to my hotel in a New York squad car while the other umpires took a private taxi.

The next morning, I grabbed all the New York newspapers from the corner newsstand and my eyes feasted upon one of the most beautiful pictures I'd ever seen. A *New York Daily News* photographer had captured a diving Murcer with his glove about two inches from the ball as it was bouncing on the outfield grass. I could've sat down and cried. I read every story about the play that I could get my hands on. Basically, the sportswriters raked my butt over the call. George Steinbrenner was quoted as saying, ''That call by Durwood Merrill just might cost us the pennant.'' But the *Daily News* picture told the whole story.

I got some public support from a strange source. Orioles manager Earl Weaver said, ''When Durwood has to make a call like that, he'll make it. He's not intimidated. Besides, my bullpen saw it and they said Murcer trapped the ball.''

Thank you, Earl Weaver. For all the trouble you gave me all of those years, that's the nicest thing anyone's ever said about me.

The New York cops drove me back to Yankee Stadium for the Saturday afternoon ball game. The first person I encountered in the umpires' room was John Stephens from the American League office. With the expression of an undertaker, John said, ''Durwood, there have been more death threats. You don't have to work today. We can go with three umps. Maybe you should sit this one out.''

Heck no, I wasn't sitting. In all of my years of umpiring, I've never been intimidated by anyone or anything. Besides, I had the newspaper with the picture right there in my hand.

If somebody was going to harm me, at least they'd say afterward that I was right about the call.

As we walked onto the field, fellow umpire Marty Springstead said, ''Now, Durwood, you stood there like a big ol' oak tree last night and got the call right.'' Then he chuckled and said, ''But please don't stand next to me at home plate. When they start shooting, I don't want to get hit.'' After the lineup cards had been presented, and before they played the national anthem, I sprinted down to my position at first base. To thunderous boos, I might add.

Reggie Jackson, on his way to right field, stopped and stood right next to me while they played the anthem. ''Durwood,'' he said, ''I understand. I've been in these situations before, too. You didn't see me over there arguing last night. I had a perfect view of the play. The ball bounced. I saw it bounce, but I didn't want to say anything because I'm up to my butt in alligators as it is. You made the right call, buddy. Hang in there.''

When the anthem ended, Reggie sprinted out to right field before I could kiss him and tell him how much I appreciated the moral support. The warm spot in my heart that I'd always had for Reggie Jackson got warmer that day.

As I stood behind first base and got ready to call the Saturday afternoon *Game of the Week*, I fully understood the hell that Reggie went through every day in that madhouse called Yankee Stadium. No one took a shot at me that afternoon, and I never rode the New York subway again. And I was glad the next day that Yankee Stadium was in my rearview mirror for a long time.

Almost a decade later, after Reggie'd retired from baseball, I was in the bowels of Dodger Stadium, getting ready work the plate in the 1988 World Series between Los Angeles and the Oakland A's. I hadn't heard from Reggie for a while and had missed our heart-to-heart talks around the umpires' room.

I was getting dressed at my locker when I felt a tap on my shoulder. I turned and there stood Reggie with the patented smile. ''Just wanted to come by and wish you luck, big guy," he said. "You're the man and I know you can do it." Seconds later, George Brett walked up to my locker. "You know I wouldn't let you walk out onto the field without saying good luck," he said.

Needless to say, I had chills all over my body. Two of the best sluggers in the history of the game had dropped by for old time's sake. I was working on a six-man crew with Darrell Cousins and Larry McCoy from the American League, along with Bruce Froemming, Doug Harvey, and Jerry Crawford from the National League. I looked around and all five of those umps were standing there with their mouths wide open. They couldn't believe that two superstars like Reggie and George would take time out just to say hello. I was close to those guys and there was a lot of mutual respect.

As I sat there and buckled up my shin guards, I realized how lucky I was that my life had collided with so many wonderful people. Baseball, in spite of all the baloney, can still be a beautiful thing. Thanks, guys.

Great hitters carry an aura to the plate, and you can feel their confidence when they dig in. That confidence won't wane when they get two strikes against them. In fact, you can feel their determination start to grow. Great hitters like Wade Boggs and Don Mattingly and Carl Yastrzemski always tried to use the whole field once they got two strikes on them. Striking out never entered their minds.

I've always thought that a great hitter looked good even striking out. A great hitter would even sting the ball on a fly out. I've talked to a lot super swingers about hitting, and I hear the same thing from Rod Carew, Boggs, Jackson, Yaz, Mattingly, and all the rest. They say the ball is no more than a foot from the pitcher's hand when they've already identified the pitch. They've already recognized the rotation of the ball to determine if it's a fastball, curve, slider, or sinker. Now all that's left is getting that pitch into their hitting zone and deciding where to hit it. Here are some notes on some truly great players I've seen.

Yaz

Carl Yastrzemski: When I first got into the major leagues in 1977, I spent a lot of time in spring training at Winter Haven, Florida, the home of the Boston Red Sox. Yaz was thirty-two at the time, and he was ripping up the American League. When the day's exhibition game was over, I'd normally wait around for an hour or so at the Chain of the Lake Parks because the traffic was so thick.

The Red Sox kept their batting cage covered with a big tarpaulin around the sides and on the top. After the games, you could always hear a *whap-whap-whap* coming from the cage, but thanks to the covering, you couldn't see who was in there. I knew, though. It was Yaz.

They once said that Ben Hogan was such a force in golf because he hit practice balls until his hands bled. If baseball had a Ben Hogan, it was Yaz, who was inducted into Cooperstown in 1989 with 3,419 career hits. Even as I was leaving Winter Haven on those cool late spring afternoons, Yaz would still be smacking baseballs all over the diamond.

No wonder this guy was one of the greatest hitters of all time and the last to deliver a Triple Crown in 1967. I have no doubts as to why he played twenty-three great seasons in the major leagues. The man worked his butt off every day of his career, and that's why he was still knocking the cover off the baseball when he was thirty-eight, thirty-nine, and forty years old. Most guys at that age are just hitting pitchers' mistakes. Yaz was a living testament as to how far hard work will take you.

Bo

Bo Jackson: I'll never forget the first time I saw this guy run up the side of a wall at old Memorial Stadium in Baltimore to make a catch. He was running parallel to the ground for about six seconds and looked as though he was defying gravity. I was umpiring at second base that night, and I ran into the outfield to make the call. All the while I was saying to myself, "No, I just didn't see that." God knows he was strong enough to do superhuman things.

He could run and he had that awesome arm from the outfield that cut down a lot of runners. I saw him field a hit off the wall one night and fire the ball all the way home on the fly. He cut down the runner and almost made him cry. That throw looked like a rifle shot coming in from left field.

Bo was just learning to hit when he suffered the horrible hip injury while playing for the Raiders in the 1990 play-offs against Cincinnati. He was destined to have a long and great career in the major leagues when the injury occured. I was working the plate when Bo had his first at-bat following hip replacement surgery. As legend would have it, he hit a shot into the right field seats. But he did it with nothing but arms. Because Bo was never able to roll his hips over, he didn't regain the powerful stroke that we'll all remember him by.

Cal

Cal Ripken Jr.: If the stress is getting to him, I've never been able to detect it. He's the same guy every time that I've seen him. The day after manager Davey Johnson moved him from shortstop to third base, he looked like he'd been there all his life. They say that sometimes he gets tired, and I'm sure that he does, but he never lets down.

Cal grew up in a baseball family. His dad was a player, a coach, a manager, and a man who knocked around some in the minor leagues. Cal is just like his dad, a pretty serious man. Brother Billy, on the other hand, is kind of a happy-go-lucky player. This is not to say that he's not a dedicated player. But he doesn't have the work ethic and the focus of his brother. Cal doesn't laugh and joke much on the field. He's one of those guys who stays in his concentration zone, so I don't bother him much. I don't want to break his focus.

Of all the games I've umpired involving Cal Jr., I don't

think I've ever seen him make a mental blunder. Baseball is more of a mental game than a physical one. The man is human, and I'm sure he's made some boo-boos in those games. I just never saw it.

In sports, the body will only give you so much every day, especially when you're playing the 162-game regular season schedule and your team is a semiregular in the postseason. I've heard coaches and managers say for years that they want a 100 percent effort out of their players. That's just not possible. Some days, the body will give you 70 percent and other days it might be 73 percent. What makes Cal Ripken Jr. so special is that he'll give you every ounce of effort his body can provide him on that particular day.

Is Cal a great player? Yes, because he has great knowledge of the game and he knows where to set himself up for every situation.

George

George Brett: He had a demanding father who believed that baseball is an endeavor, not a game. George's father once told him, "If you're going to play, you're going to play it right and you're going to play it hard." So the first term that comes to mind when I think of George Brett is hard-nosed.

I first saw George in the Cal League in 1972, my first year in umpiring. He was promoted to Double-A in about a month, and there was a good reason for it. George Brett had as good an eye for hitting the baseball as anyone I'd ever seen. The blue-collar work ethic was with George all the time. But he also had that boyish foolishness about him. One moment he could be dead serious about winning a game, and the next minute he's falling apart laughing. The whole ball-park could be dead silent, and George would be over in the Royals dugout laughing at something. What I really loved about George is that he could also laugh at himself. That's a good trait to have in the game that is constantly setting you up to fail.

When they get into a hitting slump, most players can be as grumpy as an old bear. You can see it in the way they walk around the field. I'll bet these same guys are loads of fun around the house. George, though, was never moody and acted the same almost every day.

Tony

Tony Gwynn: As the years pass, I'm beginning to think there's a better chance that Roger Maris's sixty-one–home-run mark will fall before we'll see another .400 season. As Tony Gwynn continues to age, the odds are rising against a hitter eclipsing Ted Williams's last .400 season all the way back in 1941.

What Tony tried to do during the 1997 season was meet the inside pitch in front of the plate. That came at the advice of Ted Williams himself, who told Tony that he wasn't being aggressive at the plate. The result was more base hits, more RBIs, and a decent run at the .400 mark.

I love to see Tony Gwynn swing the bat, and thanks to interleague play, I've been able to see more and more of him. He's also one of the nicest people you'll ever want to meet in your life.

Junior

Ken Griffey Jr.: If you ever held Junior's bat in your hands, you wouldn't believe that he can hit the ball that far with it. The thing weighs thirty-two ounces and looks like a little black Little League bat. It's the same bat that twelve-year-olds swing every summer night in ballparks all over America. Only Junior swings it for rocket home runs, screaming line drives, and singles that bring home the winning run.

As a young hitter, Junior was pretty carefree, and the critics said he didn't pay enough attention to the gentle nuances of the games. He didn't study pitchers as he should. That might just have been a lot of stupid noise. I do know this. He seems to be getting lacquer tough as a hitter. Oh, he's always had the great swing. Not only does he have the same exquisite swing, he's starting to study pitchers more intently, and I think it's starting to show.

As the years go by, Junior is setting up pitchers. He might look bad on a pitch in the first inning, and then he'll come back two innings later and pop the same pitch out of the park. These days, most hitters study their own hitting videotapes more than they do the stock market. But Junior rarely sticks his head into the video room. He'll occasionally go in there to check the positioning of his hands.

Junior's not a big fan of weight lifting, but if you had that kind of bat speed, you wouldn't lift iron either. The Kid's just a natural.

One night at The BallPark in Arlington, I was working second base when Junior sent a rocket into the stratosphere. Way up in center field, the Rangers have a target marked off that reads 501 FEET—WIN A SUIT OF CLOTHES. Even before I turned around, I said to myself, "There goes the suit of clothes." I really think the mark in center field is farther than 501 feet. Junior didn't hit the target that night, but the ball climbed and climbed until it almost took my breath away. It rattled around in one of the upper decks for a doggone long time.

Wade

Wade Boggs: There was always something magical about watching him hit. Wade could put wood on the baseball almost at will, and during his salad days, he had the best eye I'd ever seen in baseball. Regardless of what happens the rest of the way, I truly believe he belongs in Cooperstown.

The sad part is watching a great hitter in decline. The best years are clearly behind Wade. You know an older hitter is struggling when he fouls off a pitch that he used to send on a rope into the gap. You see it when he can no longer handle the inside pitch. Just like Jose Canseco, he's developed a blind spot on the inside part of the plate. The eyes are going. He was such an intricate hitter that he really depends on good eyesight. I really think he's going to have a hard time getting to three thousand hits as he finishes his career in Tampa Bay.

When hitters start going bad, they want the umpire to be sensitive to their problems. They don't want you to call that inside pitch that they can't hit anymore. They almost want the plate to be round. They want to you stop calling pitches on the corners. Not only do they want the plate to be round, they want it to be about six inches in circumference.

Raffy

Rafael Palmeiro: I was working first base one night in Baltimore, and he was irritated about striking out. Raffy said, "Durwood, Rocky [Roe] just called me out on a third strike that was three inches outside." Then he shook his head and said, "But, dammit Durwood, it's my own fault. I should have never put myself in that position. I should have hit the ball long before I got two strikes."

Now, how many ballplayers are going to say something like that? Not many, brother. In an age of selfish and greedy players, Rafael Palmeiro is just a very special man. He's a different breed because he just doesn't make excuses.

I don't think I've seen a better attitude in a ballplayer when it comes to being honest about the game and being honest about himself. Even more important, the guy can still turn on the ball. The Texas Rangers made a bad mistake by letting Raffy go the free agent route to Baltimore. He'd still be popping forty a year into the right field porch at The BallPark in Arlington.

Juan

Juan Gonzalez: A man with great talent, but also one with a brittle side. He's had a variety of injuries through the years that have kept him down for several weeks at a time. If I were the Texas Rangers, I would make damn sure that my $40 million investment doesn't play any more winter ball down in Puerto Rico. That's where he injured his thumb, which kept him out the first month of the '97 season. I know it's important for those people in the Caribbean to see their national heroes during the off-season. But Juan also needs to think about his career. Even the late Roberto Clemente, the greatest player and national hero ever from Puerto Rico, limited his playing time down there in his final years.

Juan has said that he plans to play 162 games during the 1998 season. Well, that will take more promises. The biggest requirement will be committing himself to a mind-set. In late August, when his body starts talking to him, he must be willing to go on. Just like a football player who is bruised and beat up, Juan is going to have to learn to play with pain. I don't think there's anyone in baseball who believes that Juan Gonzalez is that durable.

Tino

Tino Martinez: I've been fooled by this guy because I never thought he'd make the smooth transition to New York as he has. I really thought he'd be a twenty–home run man. But that right field porch at Yankee Stadium is just right for his bat. There was a time back in July and part of August that it looked like he might chase Roger Maris's record in September. Maybe the day will come when he'll truly challenge the mark.

Whether his numbers have been a fluke, I don't know. You're just never sure if a guy like Tino can keep it rolling. What's his mental makeup? When he first got to the Bronx, I wondered if he even had the discipline to play in New York. He didn't seem to like the city or anything about it. But he learned to adjust, and that's the biggest job in all of baseball.

*   *   *

Putting together a list of the best hitters I've seen over the last couple of decades is a tough task. But here goes:

Durwood's Dozen

1. Rod Carew: Never saw a pitch he couldn't hit. I worked a game against Minnesota when Nolan Ryan threw a four-hitter. Carew got all four hits. To every other hitter on that day, the ball looked like an aspirin. Carew told me it looked like a volleyball.

2. Wade Boggs: Best two-strike hitter I've ever seen. Most hitters melt down with two strikes.

3. George Brett: At some point during his at-bat he knew exactly what the next pitch would be. I've never known a hitter that positive. The master at setting up the pitcher.

4. Carl Yastrzemski: One of the toughest outs in the history of the game. He simply went with the pitch and used the field like a master.

5. Tony Gwynn: Now that he's following the advice of the great Ted Williams, the .400 mark is possible. I'm looking forward to seeing more of this hitting machine in interleague play.

6. Junior Griffey: Makes the game look easy. He's an extremely rare talent. The happy-go-lucky style makes his play seem effortless. But don't be fooled. He works hard.

7. Don Mattingly: Just a darn great pull hitter who could drive any pitch before he hurt his back. He had the lightning-quick bat.

8. Barry Bonds: The only thing that can stop Barry Bonds is Barry himself. He has a world of talent and an extremely quick bat. But he's got to stop fighting

with the people around him. He needs to take a course in Junior Griffey diplomacy.

9. Reggie Jackson: A fearless man and the best clutch hitter of my time. He craved the bat in tight situations. If I were facing a firing squad and there was a batter who could save my life with one hit, I'd pick Reggie.

10. Kirby Puckett: Best bad-ball hitter I ever saw. I really believe that Kirby could have hit a bouncing pitch. I really loved that he made us stout guys look good.

11. Mark McGwire: No one hits a louder home run. If Junior Griffey doesn't break Roger Maris's sixty-one home run mark, this guy will.

12. Larry Walker: Takes a football mentality in the game of baseball. He hits with the power of a linebacker and absolutely loves the game.

Given the configuration of today's new ballparks, and all of the short porches, I predict certain doom for Roger Maris's single-season home run record of sixty-one. Take, for instance, the dimensions of Oriole Park at Camden Yards in Baltimore. You can drink three beers and pee out of that place.

I believe Junior Griffey will be the one to break Roger's mark because of his great disposition. I've never seen anything rattle him. Believe me, September is going to be tougher than boot leather on the man with a legitmate shot to catch Maris. The media is going to come out of the woodwork, and they're going to have cameras in his face every step of the way. He's not going to be able to eat a Big Mac without somebody shoving a microphone in his face. If Junior were sitting on sixty home runs with a week to play, the drama would inspire the biggest road show this side of Ringling Brothers. But Junior has the personality and the character to handle it.

When Roger Maris was chasing Babe Ruth's mark in 1961, the pressure was so bad that his hair started falling out.

Here was a man who'd hit only twenty-nine homes runs the year before and really was a nobody. When the New York media started tracking his every move, he almost fell apart. When Roger hit number sixty in the 159th game of the year, he was so mentally exhausted that he asked Ralph Houk for a day off. Number sixty-one came mercifully during his second at-bat on the final day of the season.

Staying healthy, having a lot of luck, getting a lot of at-bats, and holding on to your hair will be four key ingredients in chasing the record. The tough month will be September when you're going to need between eight and thirteen dingers. You'll also need to be a cool and fresh cucumber in the month of September when fatigue normally sets in.

For Mark McGwire to break the record, he'll need to stay healthy for once. I have little doubt that 162 games in a St. Louis uniform would get him pretty darn close to the record. But McGwire is always pulling something.

For sluggers like Frank Thomas and Fred McGriff, they're going to have to play every day of the regular season to catch Roger. They've both proven to be injury-prone.

Joey Belle has pretty good work habits and can really power the ball when he's in form. But I think he still hasn't made the adjustment to Comiskey Park in Chicago. You can just read the frustration on Joey's face when he hits one to the warning track at Comiskey because he knows it probably would have been out at Jacobs Field in Cleveland. Joey keeps so much anger inside, and he broods so much, that I don't think his disposition is right to handle the tension down the stretch. In 1997, when he got the big contract, he couldn't handle the pressure and deliver the goods.

I think today's travel creates a disadvantage. Players are crossing many more time zones than Roger did back in 1961. Roger didn't have to traverse the width of this country like Junior does. The same could be said about Babe Ruth, whose travel in one season was about one-fifth the miles that Junior will cover. I really believe that crossing all those time zones can produce wear and tear on the body. Travel is the hardest thing that you do in the baseball business. Moving three times a week is enough to send your body into a spasm. Just playing the games can be a relief because you're trained to do that. But sitting on an airplane and arriving in a new town at five in the morning will break you down in a hurry.

The man who finally breaks Maris's record will have reached one of baseball's near impossible dreams. When Roger hit number sixty-one in 1961, we didn't know how special it really was. Do you realize, though, that it's been thirty-seven years since the record went down? From Ruth in 1927 to Maris in 1961 was only thirty-four years. That tells us that the next home run champion really will be of a different breed. That's why I think Junior will someday be the man who'll hit the magic number sixty-two.

Fastballs, Curveballs, and Knuckleheads

IT WAS A SMOKING HOT late afternoon in Texas. The sun hovered just above the horizon, cooking the earth. The hottest time of the day in Arlington is about five-thirty in the heart of the summer when you can roast a brisket on the sidewalk. In a couple of hours, I'd be behind the plate for the Rangers and Baltimore Orioles. So I should have been sitting under the air conditioner in the umpires' room, contemplating the meaning of the strike zone. Instead, I was standing down the third baseline with sweat forming tiny rivers behind my ears.

Why the punishment? It was my grandson Dustin Durwood's twelfth birthday and he wanted to get some players' autographs. He had a couple of friends in tow, and they were working the field just before the start of batting practice, having a great time.

Far into right field, through the glare and steam, I could see Nolan Ryan running his off-day wind sprints. Nolan's shirt was so damp with sweat that he looked like he'd just walked through a car wash. Nolan is a guy with a pretty level head, somebody you could always trust and a guy you just liked to be around. There was nothing fancy or pretentious about him. He always went about his baseball business with workmanlike precision, and he worked his butt off to stay in shape.

With a lot of pitchers, you never could figure out what they were thinking. They might say the darndest things. I've heard some people say that Roger Clemens has a bad head and I assume he got that reputation from getting tossed out of the first game of the 1990 American League Championship Series by plate umpire Terry Cooney. Terry claimed that Roger yelled a few magic words at him from the mound, so he sent him to the showers in one of the more controversial umpiring calls of that decade.

Maybe Roger marches to a drummer that the rest of us can't hear. But I really don't think you can be an effective pitcher in the big leagues unless you've got a few screws loose up top. Why are pitchers Looney Tunes? Because they sit around for four days waiting for something to do. Because on that fifth day, every hitter on the other team is trying to take their head off. They live a lonely life on that island called the pitching mound.

The really successful pitchers in the major leagues are generally ornery, irritable, and even mean when they get to the mound. Some have flown straight out of the cuckoo's nest. Even though he's one of the nicest guys I've ever met in my life, Nolan was a mean motor scooter when he took the mound. Other guys with that mean streak are Baltimore's Mike Mussina and, of course, Clemens. Among the old-timers who pitched with the red ass were Hall of Famers Bob Gibson and the late Don Drysdale. When they toed the rubber, they didn't care about your wife or your kids or that you once bought them a beer and a steak down at the neighborhood saloon. They just wanted to send you back to the dugout with pain in your heart and the bat on your shoulder.

On that red-hot afternoon in Texas, as the sweat-covered Nolan Ryan sauntered toward the Rangers dugout on the other side of the field, he somehow spotted our little group. He walked all the way across the infield and hollered, "Hey, what's wrong with you, old-timer? Don't you have the plate tonight?" I explained that it was Dustin's birthday, and Nolan said, "Why don't you let me host this birthday for a little while? You go on back and rest."

Not many ballplayers would volunteer for that kind of work. He escorted those boys to the Rangers and the Orioles clubhouses. They played Ping-Pong and got enough autographs to start a baseball-card store. All because Nolan Ryan is one of the real people in baseball. Dustin still talks about the best birthday party of his young life, and I don't think those boys will ever forget that afternoon with the Strikeout King.

Which brings me to this tale of two Nolans. On the one hand, he's one of the nicest and most genuine people I've ever met in baseball. Nolan grew up in Alvin, Texas, and he never really strayed from his peaceful small-town manner. He celebrated his sixth no-hitter by eating pizza in his hotel room with his wife, Ruth, and some friends. No champagne or loud music. A simple life for a simple man.

But on his day to pitch, look out. Nolan always viewed the batter as the enemy, a man who was there to challenge his turf. He was out to blister the hitter's backside. He had that hard, menacing glare and he wasn't putting up with any funny business. I've seen a lot of hitters like Reggie Jackson and Barry Bonds stand at home plate and admire their work as the home run sails into the stands. But doing that to Nolan would have been foolish. Your life would have been on the line next time up because Nolan was a hard man with a long memory if you showed him up.

Take the night at old Arlington Stadium in 1993 when he drilled White Sox third baseman Robin Ventura squarely in the ribs. Robin is a couple of inches shorter, considerably lighter, and fourteen years younger than Nolan. But he charged the mound anyway without much planning. Nolan got Robin in a headlock and hit him seven times right on top of the noggin. It was like a good hard set of noogies and the fight was over in the first round.

I walked up to Robin a couple of weeks later and said, "What in the world were you thinking?" Robin said, "I made one big mistake. I didn't know what I was going to do when I got to the mound. But Nolan did."

Lesson learned.

Here's a trivia question: Who got seven hits one night off Nolan Ryan and didn't score? Robin Ventura, of course.

The way Nolan lived his life in baseball kind of reminded me of a line from an old Kris Kristofferson song: "He's a walking contradiction, part truth and part fiction." One moment, he could be the kind and caring Uncle Nolan, the most considerate man in baseball. But on his day to pitch, you got the feeling that Godzilla had just entered the building. Before the game, he might give you that good ol' Texas how-ya-do. But he could turn stone-cold fierce when he walked onto the field.

Completing this horror show was the Ryan grunt. If you ever sat behind home plate when Nolan was pitching, you know what I'm talking about. He sounded like a four-hundred-pound German shotputter with bad gas when he turned the ball loose. It was *Uhhhhhhhaaaaaaaaahhh*. Some people called him the doctor of grunt.

Nolan needed the guile of a gunslinger to accomplish what he did in baseball—7 no-hitters, 5,714 strikeouts, 324 wins, and 61 shutouts. Five times he finished a season with more than 300 strikeouts. Nobody's going to get within fifty miles of his lifetime strikeout record.

Some nights the hitters just had no hope of catching up with the Ryan Express, a pet name for his fastball. The pitch made them irritable. If you called a strike on the corner, all you heard was bitch, bitch, bitch, bitch. Some outings the fastball was so fast and heavy that you could hear the catcher groan when he caught it.

When Nolan had proper rest and was totally healthy, there was no one who could deliver that kind of heat. Johnson's ball has never been as unhittable. How quick was Nolan's fastball? He could throw it through a West Texas sandstorm without getting it dirty.

Contrary to what some people said, Nolan wasn't a one-dimensional pitcher. There were nights when the fastball was clocking in the upper nineties and the curveball was hitting eighty-nine on the radar gun. At that speed, the curve would break so hard that it'd take your stomach away.

For the first three innings, he'd occasionally mix in the curve just to let you know it was there. Mostly, he would just blow you away with the gas early on. Then he'd go to work on the curveball, which just corkscrewed the hitter into the ground. Batters had to lace their shoes up tight when they came to the plate against Nolan.

Mickey Rivers would dig in at the plate and I'd holler, "Strike one!" Mickey would mumble, "I know, Durwood. I didn't see it. But it dern sure sounded like a strike when it went by."

Hitters normally don't have much to say about the pitcher after they settle into the box. But Gary Gaetti, a pretty fine hitter, was facing a sizzling Nolan one night when he blurted, "There's no damn way. I didn't even want to be here tonight."

Kent Hrbek had some great years with the Twins. But he was hacking and missing one night against Nolan when he laughed and said, "Just forget it. If he doesn't come off that fastball, there's no way I'm hitting that, man. I might as well go sit down."

I was working first base on a cool July night at the Oakland Coliseum in 1990 and I could sense something powerful in the air. Ryan was on the mound for Texas, and his pitches sounded like cannon fire. About the third inning, I strolled up to home and said to plate umpire Don Denkinger, "Nobody's touching this guy tonight." About three innings later, Don walked down the first baseline and recited my prediction back to me.

The A's were hearing a lot of Nolan's pitches, but not seeing much. In a display of pure brute force, he got his sixth no-hitter that night. Pretty soon, he'll be celebrating his Hall of Fame induction with pizza and Kool-Aid.

I hear that Early Wynn, whose twenty-one–year career ended in 1963, may have been the meanest pitcher of them all. A hitter would dig into the batter's box and he'd start walking toward home plate. "That's right," Early would growl at the hitter. "Just keep digging, big boy. Because pretty soon, they're going to be digging a big hole for you anyway."

Then Early would fire a fastball about an inch off the guy's chin and you knew he wasn't bluffing.

A pitcher needs a middle linebacker's mentality and the toughness of a jackhammer bit. The Yankees' David Cone, who could have played linebacker, is what I call a junkyard dog because he'll knock you out of the box without blinking. He's got a better-than-average fastball and a real hard slider. Those two pitches help set up one of the best change-ups in either league. Guys with three strong pitches are going to give you consistently good outings.

Mussina looks like a nice guy before he walks to the mound. Then, as he glares down at the batter, you know he's singing off-key. If I were hitting, I wouldn't get too close to the plate with him on the hill because Mussina might just give you an earful.

I was behind the plate in 1984 at Comiskey Park for Jack Morris's no-hitter against the Chicago White Sox. I wouldn't have wanted to step in the batter's box that afternoon, either. By the fourth inning, he had the look of a man ready to kill. His eyes were coal black and he kind of looked like Dracula without his cape.

Another nice guy who turns surly on the mound is the Rangers' Bobby Witt. I think the biggest reason he solved those terrible control problems is because he got deadly serious about his work on the mound. Early on, Bobby couldn't have hit a bear in the butt with a baseball from five feet.

All of these guys I just mentioned take on their Satan's glare when their day to pitch rolls around. Other days, they laugh and joke and they might even baby-sit your kids.

A lot of people like to compare Nolan's fastball to the bullet that Randy Johnson throws up in Seattle. The radar gun clocked his fastball at ninety-nine miles per hour seven times while whiffing nineteen A's batters in a game in 1997. He maintained a level of ninety-seven miles per hour into the ninth inning and, brother, that's bringing the heat.

John Kruk said he once shook for fifteen minutes after facing Randy Johnson in an All-Star game. Maybe so. But I've never seen anyone as intimidating as Nolan on the mound. Just for pure paralyzing fear, Randy couldn't compare to Nolan. I saw a lot of hitters shake in the box against Ryan.

Even though he let the Mariners down in the 1997 division playoffs against Baltimore, Johnson is one of the top three pitchers in the game, along with Greg Maddux and Roger Clemens. In spite of having surgery on a herniated disk in his lower back before the '97 season, he has put together four seasons that are unmatched in major league history. He had a record of 44–6 during one stretch. No full-time starter has done better in this century, not Sandy Koufax or Lefty Grove or Sal "the Barber" Maglie.

At six-foot-ten, the Big Unit has a mighty big advantage with those long legs and that big stride. He looks like a big hairy half-tarantula as he goes into the windup. Instead of throwing from sixty feet, six inches, he sometimes looks like he's delivering from about fifty feet, five inches.

Johnson's arm is thirty-eight inches long, which means that he's actually delivering the ball three feet behind a left-handed hitter's back. The amazing part is that the ball winds up on the outside part of the plate, causing the left-handed hitter to lean so far forward that he's almost falling on his nose. The scary thing about Randy is that he's still a little wild and you've got to worry, as John Kruk once did, if that next fastball is going to slip out of his hand and send you into the land of ringing phones and flashing lights.

After Johnson started the 1989 season with an 0–4 record, the Montreal Expos dumped him. He was picked by Seattle, and I was behind home plate late that season when the Mariners met the Twins at the Metrodome. He was wilder than a spring weed growing on my ranch in East Texas. Some of his pitches were hitting ten feet up the backstop.

In four innings that day he hit seven Twins, and those guys were walking around with big red welts on their bodies and anger radiating from their eyes. Now, Randy was doing his best, but he couldn't have hit downtown Minneapolis with his fastball. The safest place in the ballpark was home plate. He couldn't have found the five-sided dish with a volleyball. I ducked every time he released a pitch and, after a while, I kind of felt sorry for ol' Randy because his career was on the line and we all wondered if he was ever going to develop decent control.

In the fourth inning, Don Denkinger walked several feet down the third baseline and hollered, "Dur, do you think you ought to warn him, Bud?" When a pitcher goes that wild and starts hitting batters, the home plate umpire will normally pull off his màsk, walk toward the pitcher's mound, and deliver a stern warning. If the pitcher hits one more batter after that warning, the umpire sends him to the showers.

I pulled off my mask and walked out from behind home plate. Then I walked down the third baseline and hollered loud enough for every fan in the Metrodome to hear, "Don, he can't do no better!" Everybody in the Minnesota Twins dugout fell down laughing. It broke the tension. Minutes earlier, the Twins were ready to charge the mound and drag Randy into the streets.

Thankfully, it also motivated Seattle manager Jim Lefebvre to pull Randy's backside out of the game. When the game finally ended, my fellow umpires were laughing so hard at my little remark that they had tears rolling down their cheeks. Larry McCoy walked into the umpires' room and dropped straight to his knees. Fortunately for everyone in the American League—the hitters, the home plate umpires, and the fans sitting nervously behind home plate—Randy found his control.

Still, you worry about a fastballer who depends so much on his spine to generate velocity on the ball. The guy isn't muscled-up like a lot of pitchers that we've been seeing in the 1990s. Nolan Ryan depended so much on the power of his legs that he didn't start to develop arm problems until his next-to-last season and he pitched until he was forty-six.

After a game, they pack Randy in so much ice that he looks like a snowman. He takes anti-inflammatory medication, and I've seen him walking around bent over like an old man. You just wonder how much longer he can throw that big fastball with that kind of lower back pain.

Another pitcher who got a second chance was Tommy John, who had laser surgery performed by Dr. Frank Jobe on his pitching elbow. There were a couple of years when Tommy really wondered if he would ever pitch again. Here was a man who really appreciated the talent that God had given him. When he was able to pitch again, he went to work every day with a smile on his face.

I really think that Tommy was the Greg Maddux of his time. He could pinpoint the ball as well as anyone I'd ever seen. Later in his career, he proved that if you can pitch around the plate, you can stick around the major league.

Some people said that Tommy catered to the umpires and that he had us wrapped around his little finger. Not true. Yeah, he came to the umpires' room, but he wasn't asking for any favors. He hung around us because he liked to talk about things other than baseball. You can't always get that kind of conversation around the clubhouse.

He had one of the best minds in baseball, and he could talk about anything from baling hay to raising cows to raising kids to Washington politics. Tommy understood that there was life beyond baseball and that there was more to the game than wins and losses.

What touched me is how he handled the downright frightening accident involving his young son, who fell out of a window and landed on his head two stories below. I remember being around Tommy during that tough period of his life, and he never let down, never gave up hope. Instead of asking "Why me?" he talked about the great job that the doctors were doing. He talked about the benefit of prayer. And his child pulled through.

We saw a similar return to greatness during the 1997 season in the wonderful form of Roger Clemens, one of the best pitchers I've seen in my twenty-one years of umpiring. When the Boston Red Sox didn't give Roger a raise after the 1996 season and he decided to sign with Toronto for $8.5 million a year, I knew he was bound to become a man on a mission. He'd gone 39–40 in his last four years in Boston and that just didn't sit too well with the Rocket. Plus, getting the cold shoulder from Dan Duquette, the Red Sox general manager, must have been unsettling for a man with that kind of competitive fire.

Boy, was I right about Clemens. Even though he turned thirty-five in August of that season, the man was Godzilla on the hill in '97, putting together one of his best seasons and winning the Cy Young award for the fourth time. The glare was back. Baseball relearned a great lesson about Clemens; pitching, regardless of your physical state, is still a matter of energizing your attitude.

As I've preached so many times, pitching is about trying to win, not about avoiding losses. Roger spent the better part of the off-season willing himself to the top of his game once more. He came into spring training in the best shape of his life. His weight was down, and you could sense that he was carrying around a lot more fire in his belly. Since we are both Texans, I spent a lot of time observing and analyzing this man during those thirteen seasons in Boston. The Red Sox clearly mistook Roger's spate of injuries as a red flag that his body was breaking down. They didn't realize he still had the attitude to overcome aches and pains and to reignite that competitive fire.

Roger Clemens is a self-made throwback to the men with real competitive juices—guys like Gibson and Drysdale. You might even go back as far as Dizzy Dean in making comparisons to Roger. A line drive broke Dizzy's toe in the 1937 All-Star game, but because he was stubborn and strong-willed, he refused to let the injury heal. Instead of taking several weeks off, as the doctors had prescribed, his competitive streak kept him pitching. Compensating for the broken toe, he changed his pitching delivery and ruined his arm.

I umpired three of Roger's games during the 1997 season and was amazed that he'd become such a consistent spot pitcher. I don't think I've ever seen a pure fastballer adjust to his limitations and become a control pitcher that quickly. He's not blowing hitters off the plate anymore. Nowadays, he's throwing the fastball in the high eighties and low nineties and instead of blasting the ball by you, he's telling himself, "I've got to make a pitch." His slider is improving with every outing, and he's using the split-finger pitch as a kind of change-up. Now that he's in the mid-thirties, the guy realizes that he's got to rely more on his head than his arm.

Making his Cy Young season even more memorable is the fact that he won it on a mediocre ball club, one that finished dead last in the American League in hitting. If he'd been playing with a contending team that provided a lot of run support, there's no telling what his final numbers might have been.

Can Roger Clemens keep up this pace for two or three more years? I don't know, and I'm not so sure he knows. Given their pathetic attendance in 1997, I don't think the Toronto Blue Jays can continue to pay him that kind of big moolah. Their record was greatly improved from 1996 to 1997, but they finished so far behind the Orioles and Yankees in the A.L. East that they couldn't have seen first place with a telescope.

So no one is sure where Roger is going to be pitching the next few seasons. If he winds up with a genuine contender, one that can provide run support every night, he might just need more shelf space for all of those Cy Youngs.

Something that Clemens said to *Sports Illustrated* writer Gerry Callahan made me want to give the guy a standing ovation. Roger said, "I see some guys walking around the clubhouse before a start, and they're afraid to lose. I tell them, 'If you don't want them to beat you, they're not going to beat you. It's all up to you.'"

It seems that guys with chicken hearts have infested our game the last decade or so. They are haunted by the fear that the batter is actually going to hit the ball. They don't understand that hitting is just part of the game, just like spitting and scratching and yelling at umpires. Even a shortstop with a .216 average is going to slap a duck fart (another name for a Texas Leaguer) into left field from time to time.

Umpires like to say that a pitcher "spit the bit" when he couldn't handle the pressure. That's an old racing term for a horse that quits in the home stretch. Just like an old nag, some pitchers shut down long before they hit the wire because they can't handle the pressure of a base hit.

Another thing I've never understood about major league pitchers is why they don't all keep track of the umpires' tendencies. We all have different strike zones. Wouldn't it be wise to keep a chart (even if it's just a mental chart) of all the umpires in both leagues? Hitters do. There's not a .300 hitter in either league who can't tell you the exact strike zone of every umpire in their league.

Don't you think that guys like Wade Boggs and Tony Gwynn and Junior Griffey and Barry Bonds study umpires and their strike zones? Pitchers should pay more attention. I've known pitchers who'll toss a great game—maybe a three-hitter—and three hours later they've forgotten who was behind the plate.

A lot of pitchers today have six-inning mentality. They believe that success is pitching until the sixth inning. Somebody should tell these guys that baseball's last thirty-game winner, Denny McLain, completed twenty-eight of his thirty-one wins. Heck, you couldn't blow Bob Gibson off the mound with dynamite because he always wanted to go nine innings. Do you think the great Sandy Koufax went out there saying to himself, "Man, if I can just pitch into the sixth inning I'll be all right"?

This is Durwood's simple formula for success in pitching: You've got to be able to bounce back after a rough inning, or even a tough game. If a pitcher gets blown away in the first inning, and then throws six scoreless innings, he's a big leaguer. If he loses a game 8–2 and then comes back to throw a three-hit complete game, his name is likely Orel Hershiser.

I got my first up-close view of Hershiser in the second game of the 1988 World Series when I was behind the plate. He looks like a bookworm and pitches like a bulldog. He threw a three-hitter that night against Oakland and never missed the catcher's mitt. This isn't to say he threw one pitch down the heart of the plate. He just worked the corners all night and drove the A's crazy.

I saw the resiliency in Hershiser nine years later at Jacobs Field in Cleveland. Mark McGwire had just hammered one of the hardest shots I'd ever seen. It hit the Budweiser sign on the left field scoreboard with howitzer force. I swear the ball was still rising when it creamed the beer sign. It was one of those moments when you just stand there with your mouth wide open and say, "God almighty, Mama, did you see that?" The whole ballpark just fell dead silent.

Orel walked off the mound and strolled within about five feet of home plate. He shrugged, smiled that boyish smile, and said to me, "Can you believe that I threw that pitch?" Then he went back to work like nothing had ever happened.

Of all the ingredients I've seen in pitchers over the last twenty-one years, resiliency is the most important. Pitchers, after all, are always digging holes, so they'd better keep a shovel handy at all times to dig themselves out.

The *Sporting News* hit upon a pretty revealing statistic. Did you know that 40 percent of the pitchers in our game have been released at least once? We've been recycling a lot of bad arms. Or have we been recycling a lot of broken psyches?

Here is my take on the revolving door with major league pitchers: I believe the ones who continually fail actually have strong arms and good stuff. You can't battle your way through the minor leagues and make The Bigs without some talent. At some point, you've thrown a 90 mph fastball, or you've had a good mix of pitches. You've posted some good numbers against men who can swing the bat.

But the dividing line between success and failure in pitching is the neck. You might have the strong arm and body to get the job done. But you don't have Hershiser's resiliency or Ryan's toughness or Cone's grit or Mussina's mean streak. Guys who are foundering need to loosen or tighten some screws and stop worrying so much.

Which brings us to pitching coaches. It is the job of the pitching coach to help the manager handle the staff. Mostly, though, it's his job to massage broken egos. He's got to build confidence at times when all seems lost. He must do the impossible—sell some self-esteem to a man too mentally broke to pay attention.

Ray Miller, now the manager of the Baltimore Orioles is a pitching guru for all time. He pumps up his starters. He tells them, "You go out there and get us nine innings tonight. Our bullpen needs the rest, and we're depending on you." That's why Scott Erickson, Jimmy Key, and Mussina are pitching into the eighth and ninth innings.

If your starters are flopping in the fifth inning, and you've got to use three relievers to clean up the mess, think about the toll taken on the bullpen. By September, those guys will be walking around with their tongues dragging on the ground. Just look at what happened to the California Angels in 1997 when they were contending for the American League West title and their pitchers started going down.

When I got to the big leagues in 1977, every team had five starters and, shoot, you could throw a blanket over the first four. The fifth one might be so-so, but he'd win some games for you. Every team had a closer who could get three doggone outs in the ninth inning.

Pitching did improve somewhat in the American League in 1997. Eleven of the fourteen teams improved their ERA. But nothing could have been worse than what we saw in 1996 when the leagues combined to set records for home runs, runs, walks, and earned runs. The game's overall ERA of 4.60 was the highest since 1930.

As Rangers manager Johnny Oates told the *Sporting News,* "The bottom line is you just can't pitch as bad as this league did in 1996." Even though pitching isn't what it used to be, I've seen some great ones in my umpiring days. Here's my list:

Durwood's Dozen

1. Nolan Ryan: Just think what his record might have been if he hadn't played for such sorry ball teams.

With that kind of velocity, some hitters never got a good look at his pitches.

2. Tom Seaver: Mr. Terrific had it all. He made every pitch work for a long period of time and was the most consistent hurler that I saw.

3. Jim Palmer: A little like Nolan in that he could get away consistently with the high fastball. Wanted to pitch in his underwear. (Heh-heh.)

4. Roger Clemens: Continues to be a great pitcher even without the big fastball. Great competitive fire keeps him going and he might just have two or three more twenty-win seasons in him.

5. Greg Maddux: Can throw strikes with his eyes closed. Deadly on a two-two count. I would love to have this guy on the mound every time that I worked home plate.

6. Jack Morris: He hated every batter he faced. I would agree that he was the pitcher of the 1980s. A real nice guy. (Heh-heh.)

7. Randy Johnson: Not quite as dominating as Nolan. But he can still scare the dickens out of hitters. Needs a haircut. (Heh-heh.)

8. Jim "Catfish" Hunter: He was a control freak. Catfish didn't need the overpowering fastball because he was deadly sharp with the slider and curve. You couldn't rattle him.

9. Tommy John: A surgeon. He would throw the ball two inches outside to see if it fit my strike zone. If it did, he threw the next one three inches outside. He proved you could pitch in the big leagues with an 83 mph fastball.

10. Rollie Fingers: He was paid to get three men out and he did it longer than anyone. Great split-finger pitch and the best mustache in baseball.

11. Don Sutton: I was glad to see Sutton inducted into the Hall of Fame. Nobody was sharper at the tail end of his career.

12. Orel Hershiser: Tommy Lasorda said it all when he nicknamed him "the Bulldog." He could get pounded one day and throw a three-hitter next time out. Still going, like that battery-powered bunny.

Honorable Mentions: Rich Gossage, Dennis Eckersley, Sparky Lyle, and Ron Guidry.

Hitters had eyes like saucers when Goose Gossage marched to the mound. He didn't fool around and he didn't throw junk. His fastball would make some hitters wet their pants. Goose was typical of closers from that era in that he had one intimidating pitch and liked to stick with it.

Dennis Eckersley's success is more linked to control. His slider might be the best I've ever seen. The Eck gets creamed, though, when the slider isn't right on the button. But, like all of the great relievers, he hungers for the ball in the tight spots and he doesn't live in mortal fear of giving up the clutch home run because he knows that sooner or later it's going to happen. When it does, he just shrugs his shoulders and goes on to the next batter, or he gets himself ready for the next game.

A guy I loved watching pitch they called "Looziana Lightning." There were times when I could hear Thurman Munson groan when Ron Guidry threw the hard sinker. It must have weighed two hundred pounds when it hit the mitt. Ron had one of the best seasons ever by a pitcher in 1978, going 25–3 with an ERA of 1.74. Only Guidry and Roger Clemens have compiled a season ERA under 2.00 since the American League went to the designated hitter in 1973.

What you really appreciated about Sparky Lyle was the fun-loving attitude. The Bronx Zoo was his life and he lived it to the fullest. He became the first American League reliever to win the Cy Young award in 1977 because he never let the pressure knock him off stride. He'd have the bases loaded, and he'd look down at the batter and snicker.

From the first few games of interleague play, I could see a big difference between the American and National League pitchers. An American League pitcher will go to nibbling when he gets two strikes on the hitter. Conversely, the National League pitcher will come right at you, even if your name is Ken Griffey Jr.

With an oh-two count, the American League pitcher will throw it in the dirt, or two feet outside. That's why you see so many three-two counts in the American League and so many games that run over three hours.

Every pitcher in the American League should take a long, hard look at Greg Maddux. He's won four Cy Young awards because he throws about eighty strikes and twenty-five balls every time he goes to the mound. His strikeout-to-walk ratio during the '97 season was a phenomenal seven to one. He gets ahead of the hitter and takes advantage of the count and he doesn't believe in messing around.

What both leagues need is an influx of good young arms now that expansion is taking place again. I've seen potential talent in some young pitchers, but not as much as I'd like. Of the young guys who've caught my eye, Minnesota's Brad Radke would be at the top of that list. I worked the plate in one of his '97 appearances against Oakland, and he broke off those A's bats with the hard sinker. In his first couple of seasons, he liked to work around the plate, and like most young pitchers, he didn't have a lot of confidence. But the guy became an overnight Cy Young contender when he started challenging hitters, and now he carries a pretty big swagger to the mound.

A pitcher I liked from the start is Andy Pettite of the Yankees. Almost every left-hander is going to have some wildness at first, but not this guy. He throws strikes and gets ahead in the count. The fact that he can throw it just about anywhere he wants makes him double-barrel tough. He makes the batters hit the ball on the ground, and that's what keeps you in the ball game.

Yankees owner George Steinbrenner is a guy who doesn't mind spending money and rolling the dice. But throwing $11 million at Hideki Irabu, the fat Japanese pitcher, was almost like tossing it out the window. It was quickly apparent that his fastball was an impostor. When it started coming in flat, the Yankees were full of excuses. Oh, they said, the poor guy was out-of-shape. They said he wasn't accustomed to living in America and he wasn't accustomed to the food. Apparently he knows enough about food to order breakfast, lunch, dinner, take-out pizza, and twenty-four-hour room service.

One day in Yankee Stadium, I got a good look at Irabu from second base. He wasn't able to consistently throw his curveball over for strikes, and hitters were just sitting on his fastball, which is very hittable.

When things started falling apart, Irabu even started blaming the mound. He almost tore the rubber off the hill one afternoon until umpire John Hirschbeck threatened to throw his butt out of the game. Then he showed a lot of maturity when he broke off a shower head out of frustration in the Yankees clubhouse after a loss.

The scouts seriously overestimated his fastball, which hit the radar gun in the low nineties, not the high nineties as they first thought. Even Steinbrenner has seen through the guy and knows that he'll need time in the minor leagues to learn how to throw like a major leaguer. When Joe tried to protect Irabu, sending him out against the weak teams, he couldn't even handle Philadelphia, the worst team in baseball in '97.

Maybe the Yankees, and everybody else, are waking up to the fact that Japanese baseball isn't as good as advertised. In Japan, Irabu didn't see the talented hitters that he's seeing over here. He gave up a lot of home runs and was hit hard a lot. That's really a bad sign, especially for a guy who's seeing hitters for the first time and should be able to fool them a little. He just didn't see that kind of pop in the bat over in Japan.

Pitchers do the craziest things, and one of the hardest guys ever to figure out was Gaylord Perry, who never admitted that he threw the spitter, but we all knew he did. Gaylord verbally sparred with umpires who accused him of throwing the spitball and he even threatened to sue a couple. Another one of Gaylord's cheat pitches was the resin ball, which I also called the puff ball. He would reach down and get a handful of resin off the little bag and just cover up the baseball. That pitch would just explode out of a bank of white smoke and there was no way the hitter could hit it, or the umpire could call it. The only way to deal with the resin ball was to walk to the mound, pick up the resin bag, and throw it toward the baseline.

In spite all of his bitching and moaning, I did find a way to get Gaylord and his spitter out of the game one Saturday afternoon in 1980. He was pitching for the Rangers against Boston at Fenway Park. Everybody pretty well knew that Gaylord threw his spitball with K-Y Jelly. But he was a slick operator and the stuff was hard to find on his body. Many umpires came back empty-handed after a trip to the mound.

But at Fenway Park that afternoon, before the national TV cameras, I knew that Gaylord was throwing the spitter on just about every pitch by the seventh inning. The Red Sox players were hollering from the bench and I didn't blame them. If Gaylord had been throwing the doctored pitch every other inning, it would have been a different story.

It's pretty easy for an umpire to know that somebody's throwing the spitter. The ball will travel fifty-eight feet on a straight line, and in the final two feet, it'll drop like a twelve-pound shotput. There's no way you can throw that kind of pitch without cheating just a little.

When he left the mound between the seventh and eighth innings, I collared Gaylord before he got to the dugout. I said, "Mr. Perry, now you're going to make me have to take a stand. I'm going to have to come out and start hunting for your K-Y Jelly. Or, if you're so tired that you have to throw the greaseball at every batter, then you need to get out of the game.'' By gosh, he took himself right out of the game.

Later in his career, Gaylord was pitching a night game at old Arlington stadium. A foul ball arced over the stands and landed *ker-splat* against the pressbox window. It left a huge greasy splotch. After the game, *Dallas Morning News* sportswriter Randy Galloway approached Gaylord and asked him about the greaseball that had smudged the pressbox window. ''Oh that,'' Gaylord said. ''Well, it must have caught a big old fat mosquito on its way back.''

If you really want to catch the circus, check out the closers. These are the guys who pitch only one inning at the end of the game. They say that California's Troy Percival gulps down a gallon of coffee a night just thinking about pitching that one inning.

He kneels down behind the mound for about thirty seconds. Then he toes the rubber, and instead of looking for the signal, he bows his head like he just fell asleep. The first night I caught his act, I said, ''What in the name of Rollie Fingers does he think he's doing?'' Anaheim's catcher, Todd Greene, turned around and said to me, ''He's not through yet. This is going to take awhile.'' I couldn't figure out if he was praying or sleeping.

Percival throws the ball about a hundred miles per hour. Sometimes he doesn't know where it's going. Sometimes the batter turns it around. Sometimes Percival gets them on strikes. You're never sure what's going to happen.

The same can be said for the highest-paid closer of all, John Wetteland, who saved all four of the Yankees wins in the 1996 World Series. He was the Series MVP, but when the Fall Classic was over and the ticker-tape parade had ended, the Yankees were ready to say adios to Mr. Wetteland.

Yankees manager Joe Torre told me after the '96 season that he personally liked Wetteland, a good man who has done a lot of charitable work over the last few years. But he couldn't stand to watch him throw another pitch in a Yankees uniform. Wetteland scared the hell out of Joe and made the Yankees manager a happy man when he signed that $23 million contract with the Texas Rangers.

"He put us on the ropes every time he came in," Joe said. "I give him credit for what he did for the Yankees. But the guy was there to put out the fire, not to stoke it." If Joe sang in the shower, he might have been belting out "Thank God and Greyhound He's Gone" when Wetteland left town.

I thought that writer Tom Verducci pointed out some interesting stats in *Sports Illustrated* concerning Wetteland's World Series saves. He noted that John only had to pitch to 19 of the 232 Atlanta batters faced by New York pitchers. He got three of his four saves by entering the game with nobody on base and a lead of at least two runs, needing just two or three outs.

Wetteland is an ulcer waiting to happen. He's like dipping barbecued ribs into jalapeño juice. He'll come into the game with a 5–3 lead and walk the first two men just to make it interesting. By July 1, Wetteland had five blown saves, two more than he'd had the entire previous season. He blew a six-run lead to Colorado, and there were plenty of other times when he barely escaped with that ugly sweat-stained cap still on his head.

This is my suggestion to the Rangers. Decorate your dugout just like the cabin of a commercial airliner. Install oxygen masks in the roof of the dugout. When Wetteland walks to the mound in the ninth inning, drop the masks so everyone can strap one on their face and start breathing again.

Check out the guys in the Rangers dugout the next time Wetteland takes the mound. You'll think they're watching *Poltergeist*. They're all hiding their eyes. Someday, Oates will be asked to do a Maalox commercial if Alka-Seltzer doesn't get to him first.

You can't blame Oates, a fine manager, for going to Wetteland, because the Rangers paid top dollar for this man. Johnny knows that he's really got no choice but to use him.

If I had my druthers, though, I'd want a stopper like Milwaukee's Doug Jones, a no-nonsense guy. He'll take the ball from the manager and put out the fire before you can dial 911. You don't hear a lot about Doug. But I did a series between Milwaukee and Baltimore in early July of 1997, and he got the call three times in save situations. He converted all three without breaking a sweat. All he had was a slider and a change and a fastball that limped to the plate. But he had them popping up all over the infield.

Doug doesn't get $23 million like Wetteland. But while Wetteland is going to a full count on a lot of hitters, and walking plenty of them, Jones is just chopping them down.

Dennis Eckersley's been pitching so long that he faced Hank Aaron. Why does this guy keep rolling on like a mighty river at age forty-two? It's called confidence. He doesn't have closer's stuff. He throws the ball eighty-seven miles per hour, but he knows where every pitch is going.

During game one of the 1988 World Series, with me umpiring at first base, Eckersley gave up one of the biggest home runs in postseason history to the Dodgers' Kirk Gibson, who came limping off the bench in the ninth inning with a bad hamstring and banged it into the right field seats. Still, you've got to give Eckersley credit. He threw that pitch with a lot of confidence and it sure didn't put a damper on his career.

Eckersley possesses the right stuff that once belonged to guys like Dan Quisenberry and Fingers. Neither one of those guys had fireballing stuff. But they could throw strikes and neither possessed an ounce of self-doubt.

Closers don't throw nearly as many innings as they used to. During the Yankees' championship season of 1996, Wetteland pitched 63 ⅔ innings in sixty-two appearances. Eighteen years earlier, in the same number of games as Wetteland, Goose Gossage worked twice as many innings for that Yankee championship team.

Here's the biggest question about closers. If they're working fewer innings these days, then why do they break down more often than Mir? Why do guys like Mitch Williams and Rob Dibble flame in and flame out? Well, it goes back to the same principle I mentioned about starters. Just as starters need confidence, guts, and a short memory, so do closers. They need to take a few lessons from Orel Hershiser.

Reliever Norm Charlton has recently been lighting up scoreboards. But Charlton, a smart guy who graduated from Rice, once said, "In this job, you have to learn from failure." Right on, Norm. It doesn't matter how poorly you did last time out, pitchers must be resilient. Just about every great pitcher I've known had to deal with some kind of adversity in his life. If you can rally from adversity, you might just last a long time in this business and make a lot of money. That's what pitching is all about on the major league level.

Nuts, Fruitcakes, and Joey Belle

LOU PINIELLA AND I have carried on a love-hate relationship for more than two decades, and we've always been able to get over our spats and make up, kind of like an old married couple. But there was a time during his playing days in New York that I thought we were going to the mat. Seems that every time I umpired one of Lou's games in 1978, my second full season in the majors, I had to send his butt to the showers.

By the All-Star break that season, I'd thrown Lou out of four games. Must have been some kind of record. Dick Butler, the umpires' supervisor, called me one afternoon and said it was time for me to patch things up. "Durwood," he said, "the whole damn league is talking about this." So I went to fellow umpire Bill Haller and asked for some sage advice.

"Durwood, you've got to use some tact," Bill said. "You're from Texas and that means you're just a lot smarter than Lou. Just calm down and try to talk to the guy."

One hot Sunday afternoon in New York, Lou came to the plate at Yankee Stadium. The first pitch came in, I quickly rung up strike one, and he whirled and hollered, "Where was that pitch at?" Since I was determined to stay cool, I calmly called time-out and pulled off my mask. I pulled the plate brush from my back pocket, and as I started whisking off a spotless plate, I looked up and smiled at the big smart aleck. "Lou, you've been in this league almost a dozen years," I began. "You've hit three hundred six times in your career and you've been an All-Star. You were the rookie of the year back in sixty-nine. You guys were world champions just last year. But something went wrong along the way, Lou. One of your teachers didn't teach you that you don't end a sentence with the preposition 'at'!''

Boy, I could tell that I'd gotten to him because Lou looked dumbfounded. I slowly slid my plate brush back into my pocket, and I put on my mask and calmly went back to work behind home plate.

Seconds later, Lou called time-out and let his bat drop off his shoulder. He cocked his head sideways and, with that silly smirk, said, ''Well, then, Durwood, where was the pitch at—asshole!''

So much for tact. The expletives and the slobber started flying, and I had to send Lou back to the clubhouse to ponder not only his plight but his poor use of grammar. I can honestly say that after twenty-one years together, Lou and I still fight like Clinton and Gingrich. But after tempers cool, we normally have a big belly laugh about it.

Let me tell you a couple of stories that I use on the banquet tour during the off-season that are partly truth and partly fiction. In baseball, it's often difficult to separate fact from fairy tales. On the banquet tour, when it comes to telling funny baseball stories, you don't always let the facts get in the way.

After the Dodgers won the World Series in 1988, Bill Russell, one of the coaches, decided to invite Tommy Lasorda, the coaching staff, and the wives to his house for dinner. I'm sure you've heard Tommy harping about bleeding Dodger blue. Well, Bill and his wife decided to paint all of the toilet seats in their house Dodger blue. They used that quick-drying Krylon paint, which at the time was being endorsed by retired Reds catcher Johnny Bench. I can just imagine Bill and his wife having a big laugh as they went about their painting.

By noon, the commodes were painted. The Russells figured they'd be dry in plenty of time for the dinner party. About halfway through dinner that night, Mother Nature called Tommy and he answered. After several flushes, Tommy was still unable to get up because that quick-drying paint hadn't dried. He was stuck like a horsefly in wet asphalt.

Bill heard Tommy yelling and cursing, and he came running into the bathroom to find his boss now Dodger blue in the face. Bill went to tugging on Tommy, and pretty soon he realized that the old skipper was actually Dodger-glued to the seat. So Bill got a screwdriver and took the commode lid completely off. He wrapped Tommy up in a sheet, and together they headed off to the local hospital.

They looked pretty funny walking into that emergency room, and I'm sure the patients were wondering why Tommy was dressed in a sheet. On top of that, you could tell he had something stuck to his rear end. The nurses told Tommy to climb onto the examining table and to set himself on all fours. Wouldn't you know that a female doctor was on duty that night, and Tommy, not being at a loss for words, said, "Doc, have you ever in the world seen anything like this?" And the doctor smiled, winked, and said, "Well, now, Mr. Lasorda, I've seen ten thousand of those. But it's the first time I've ever seen one in a picture frame." I imagine that Tommy's face was probably Cardinal red at that point.

Everybody knows that Yogi Berra has said a lot of funny and goofy things in his life, and that he winds up in some pretty comical situations. During Yogi Berra Night at Sportsman's Park in St. Louis he said, "I want to thank all of those who made this night necessary."

On his approach to the game of baseball, he once said, "Half the game is ninety percent mental." About a popular restaurant in New York, he pontificated, "Nobody goes there anymore, it's so crowded." When his playing career came to an end in the mid-1960s, he eloquently stated for the record, "I really didn't say everything I said."

With his playing days over, Yogi was honored at the Waldorf-Astoria in New York, and as a token of appreciation for those great years, they gave him a twelve-foot grandfather clock. He couldn't find a bellman to help carry it, so he had to kind of muscle it through the lobby, walking the clock along on its legs.

So Yogi was grunting and sweating and walking that big grandfather clock along the marble floor when he reached the revolving front door. He got sucked through the door and, with the clock leaning precariously on his shoulder, stumbled onto the busy New York sidewalk. He bumped into a drunk and Yogi blurted, "Why don't you watch where you're going!" And the drunk shot back, "Why don't you wear a wristwatch like everybody else!"

Clete Boyer, who spent seven great seasons as the Yankees third baseman and played in five World Series, became one of my favorite guys in baseball. Not many baseball people can match his wit. He was on Billy Martin's Yankee staff in the early 1980s, and one afternoon those guys were riding me like a sweat-soaked mule. All I could hear from the dugout was that my strikes were high and that my balls were dragging the ground—or something like that.

I had Rickey Henderson at the plate, and he likes to get in that tight crouch. His strike zone is about as big as Billy Martin's smile. Calling balls and strikes on Rickey is like finding drinking water in the Hudson River. I called a strike, and somebody from the Yankee dugout yelled, "Pitch was low!" I called strike two, and the same refrain: "Pitch was low!"

Rickey grounded out for the final out of the inning, and I was glad to be done with him.

Since Clete was coaching over at third, he had to trot past home plate on the way to his post. I noticed that he kind of paused in front of home plate, but thought nothing of it. Then I noticed that he was standing in the third base coaching box, smiling like he'd swallowed the fattest canary in the Bronx.

I looked in front of home plate and there it was. Clete had stuck a golf tee in the ground. I guess he thought my strike zone was so low that his guys needed a tee to drive those pitches off the ground. So I got into my crouch to start the inning, and Clete yelled from third base, "Tee 'em up down there, big guy!'' I was laughing so hard that I was afraid to take off my mask. Tears were streaming down my face.

It was raining pretty hard one afternoon at Yankee Stadium, and Milwaukee was leading New York by five runs in the fourth inning. As you might expect, the Yankees wanted home plate umpire and crew chief John Shulock to call off the game. After five innings, a game becomes official, even if it rains enough to float the Ark. If John had called off the game right then in the fourth inning, the Yankees would have avoided a loss. But he just ignored their desperate whining, even though the rainstorm had developed into a downpour. Small rivers were starting to form on the infield.

In the middle of the fourth inning, Clete trotted over to the third base coaching box. Just before the first pitch, he popped open a big golf umbrella that had about fourteen different shades of red, blue, orange, and pink. He was smiling from earlobe to earlobe. Now, I probably would've laughed my butt off and told him to get rid of the doggone umbrella and stop showing me up. But Big John ran his butt right out of the game, umbrella and all.

Clete would be sitting in the Yankee dugout, listening to the bench jockeys hurling barbs at the umpires. He liked to join in the fun at times. But one afternoon he got tired of listening to a light-hitting shortstop giving the umpires the business. I think the guy was hitting about .205. Clete grabbed the little goober by the shirt and yelled, ''You ain't never going to be nothing but a two-oh-five hitter. So why don't you shut the f—— up before somebody realizes you're still around and they kick you out of baseball!''

I was in a fine mood umpiring second base on a sunny and clear spring afternoon in Toronto. But I had one little problem. I had rocks in my right shoe. Common sense told me that I should go to the dugout between innings to shake out those sharp little buggers. They were just killing me.

Instead, I knelt down between innings, untied my right shoe, and started shaking. I really thought nothing of it until

I heard footsteps and heavy breathing behind me. Then a body fell on me like a sack of wet concrete. I should have known it was that jokester Jesse Barfield, who was playing right field for Toronto that day. Giggling like a kid on the playground, Jesse said in that high-pitched voice, "Durwood, I've always wanted to do this to you."

"Yeah, Jesse," I gasped. "I always knew that you had some weirdness about you. Now get the hell off me, you big bear!"

Jesse Lee Barfield from Houston had one of the strongest arms from the outfield that I've seen in baseball. He won a couple of Golden Gloves and hit with power. That day, he hit me with a lot of power.

As my luck would have it, a photographer for the *Toronto Sun* fired off a few frames during Jesse's sneak attack. Next day, my butt was in hock once again with the American League office. Before my feet hit the floor that morning, the phone was ringing in my hotel room.

"Durwood," Dick Butler moaned into the phone. "Nice pictures of you today along with Jesse Barfield. You really made the American League office proud today."

"Oh, Mr. Butler, do you take the Toronto papers there in New York?" I asked weakly.

"No," he snapped. "The Associated Press picked it up, and now it's all over the New York papers. Why me, Lord?" Once again, I had to go by the American League office the next time I was in New York so Mr. Butler and America League President Dr. Bobby Brown could chew on my ears. All because Jesse Barfield decided to pull a crazy stunt.

I always had fun with Bo Jackson before his blossoming baseball career so sadly ended due to a football-related hip injury. Bo had a little stutter, and one afternoon, when I was working the plate, he looked back and said, "Durwood, wh-what's the count?" I told him it was two-two. Bo looked back again and snickered, "Th-thanks for sh-sharing that with me."

I can't say that I had a better relationship with anyone in baseball. Tears came to my eyes when he tore up his hip playing football for the Raiders because I knew this splendid all-round athlete would never be the same. I also knew that I would miss his great sense of humor.

I was umpiring second base one afternoon in 1989 when he was still playing for the Kansas City Royals. He was on his way to left field when he stopped and said, "Now, Durwood, has anyone ever dedicated a home run to you?"

"Bo, it's never been done," I said. "I'm not so sure that it's going to happen today."

Bert Blyleven was going that day for the California Angels, and he had the great curveball working. In the first inning, he struck out Bo and made it look easy. Same thing in the fourth. In the sixth inning, Bo went down swinging on three great-looking breaking balls.

As Bo trotted out to left field for the bottom of the sixth, I yelled, "Hey, big fella, thanks a lot for the home run. Next time you're up, why don't you take a boat paddle up there with you? You're going to need it!"

In the bottom of the ninth inning, Blyleven threw one of those long sweeping curveballs. Bo reached out and one-handed it into the right field seats. Not only did I get my home run, I was impressed with his raw power once again.

Then I realized that the man rounding the bases was still carrying his dadgum bat. When he stopped at second base, I knew what he was going to do. "You can't do that," I said, scooting away, acting like a man trying to avoid a hot stove. But he kept shoving the bat toward me. "You're going to get fined. Heck, Bo, they'll probably try to kick both of us out of baseball! Get the heck away from me!"

Bo reluctantly gave up and finished his home run trot. But after the game, he strolled into the umpires' room with the autographed bat: "Home run dedicated to Durwood Merrill." I still have it at my home in East Texas, and I'm still very proud of it.

There's one more thing about this story that I'm also proud of. That July, during the All-Star dinner, commissioner Bart Giamatti asked Bo to come to the lectern to tell about dedicating his home run to me. I'd been nervous about the whole ordeal because my bosses can be pretty sensitive to things like that. I figured I was going to get called again on the carpet in New York for something I had nothing to do with.

But after Bo's speech, Giamatti rose and had a few touching remarks. "What happened between Bo and umpire Durwood Merrill is what baseball is supposed to be all about," he said. "That is the essence of baseball to me. I just wish we had more cases of people having this much fun in our game." I never got to personally thank Bart Giamatti for his remarks. He died in office less than two months later, on September 1, 1989. Although it's a little late, I guess this is my chance to finally say thank you, Mr. Commissioner. You also helped make baseball a fun game.

If you really wanted to have fun around the game of baseball, you needed a ticket to see Pete Vukovich pitch before his retirement in 1986. He was an extremely likable nutcase in those ten seasons he played for four different clubs. Pete irritated a lot of umpires because of his antics, but to me he was always worth a great laugh. He liked to wear shoes of two different colors—usually one black and one white—and that was enough to confuse the heck out of a lot of batters.

Pete had one little habit that kept the umps on their toes. Between pitches, he liked to scratch around the rubber with his spikes. He was always digging, kind of like an old dog in the soft spots of your garden. Pretty soon, he'd have the entire rubber buried. That's when you really had to watch the guy.

The rubber, as most baseball fans know, is sixty feet, six inches from home plate. If Pete could make the rubber disappear, he'd start pitching about a foot closer to the plate. A lot of times between innings, one of the umpires had to trek to the mound and dig up the rubber. The rule book states that if you catch a pitcher throwing off the rubber, the umpire should call a ball. If there's a runner on base, it's a balk and the runner advances one base. We also had the option of throwing the pitcher out of the game. But with a guy as funny as Pete Vukovich, you wanted to keep him around.

They also tell me the guy's IQ was somewhere around 140.

Pete is now the Pirates' pitching coach, and I ran into to him during interleague play during the 1997 season. Later that day, I was telling one of the other Pirates coaches about Pete's old habit of burying the pitching rubber, and we had a pretty good laugh.

A couple of innings into the game, one of the Pirates players dropped a note off to me while I was standing at second base. It read: "Dear Durwood. I hear that you're still defaming me. Love, Vuke."

Another pitcher who was slightly off-kilter was Bill "Spaceman" Lee, who was with the Boston Red Sox in the '70s. A lot of the Spaceman's antics were really a put-on. He was a smart guy from USC and had a wide range of knowledge. But I really couldn't make heads or tails out of what he was saying. I remember that the Spaceman would sit on the corner of the dugout steps, and he always looked like he was in a different ozone layer than the rest of us. He wasn't a bad pitcher, winning 119 and losing 90 with an ERA of 3.81. Spaceman was a big part of the Red Sox staff during some great years.

But he said something pretty peculiar to a sportswriter there in Boston, and the quote made it into the morning newspaper. He said he liked to sprinkle marijuana on his morning waffles. I've never been around marijuana and sure as heck wouldn't smoke it. But putting it on our waffles isn't something that Mama and I would do on the ranch back in East Texas. I sure as heck don't think it would taste too good.

Some of the funniest people in baseball are the umpires. Over the years, I've really gotten a kick out of just being around my umpiring buddies. I like to crack jokes, and the umpire rooms are normally pretty lighthearted when I'm around. One night I was trying to psych myself up to work the plate with Nolan Ryan on the mound. That is one of the toughest jobs in our profession. Umpires always kept a close eye on the pitching schedule to see when you'd draw the dreaded plate against Nolan. We called him the train because the fastball thundered to the plate.

A few minutes before the first pitch, I was bouncing around the umpires' room, kind of like a heavyweight prizefighter preparing to enter the ring. I always thought that if I breathed real hard, I might draw some extra oxygen into the brain. So I was doing the Durwood Shuffle, and Richard "Hoggy" Price, the umpires' room attendant at old Arlington Stadium, was having a big laugh. As I ran through the door on my way to the field, I yelled, "Hoggy, I feel light tonight." And Hoggy yelled back, "Durwood, there's a reason for that. You forgot to put on your chest protector."

I had to run back into the umpires' room, pull off my shirt, and strap on the protector before I could go onto the field. Otherwise, I might've been killed by a Nolan Ryan fastball.

Working the plate one day at the Metrodome, the game was in the third inning when I had to hustle down the baseline to make a call at third. I said to myself, "Boy, I feel fast today." Then it hit me. I'd forgotten to put on my shin guards. So I called over fellow umpire Marty Springstead and said, "Spring, got a big problem here. I need to run back to the dressing room and put on my shin guards." We had to hold up the game for about ten minutes, but neither Texas manager Pat Corrales nor Twins manager Ray Miller complained. They both probably said, "Oh, that's just Durwood for you."

Going to the bathroom can be a real problem when you're umpiring a major league game. You've got about two minutes between innings, so you've got to hustle up the tunnel to the clubhouse. During a nationally televised game between the Rangers and White Sox in 1997, I took a bathroom break and realized I wasn't going to make it back in time. Since I was umpiring at second base, it wasn't the end of the world. The other two guys took up the slack. As a matter of fact, I stood over in the White Sox dugout until that half-inning was over. I didn't want to make a big scene by running back onto the field between outs.

As far as being nervous on the field, I guess my toughest game was a home plate assignment in the 1983 postseason between the Baltimore Orioles and the Chicago White Sox. I'd just finished my seventh full season in The Bigs and I knew that I was prepared for the job. I just didn't know if my heart could handle it.

I'm standing on the top step of Chicago's dugout when I see Bob Fishel from the American League office just a few feet away. I said, "You know, Bob, I'm so nervous that I can't even make spit." Bob looked at me with eyes as big as saucers and said, "You know, I'm feeling exactly the same way." Then I started thinking: What in the world is he so nervous about? I'm standing here with the mask in my hand, and I'm about to go out there and call balls and strikes in one of the biggest games of the American League season. So I kept watching Bob and wondering what the heck he was doing. Then, the big voice over the loudspeaker boomed, "Leading off and playing first base for the Chicago White Sox, second baseman Vance Law." All that doggone Bob was doing was standing there patting players on the butt and telling them when to run onto the field for pregame introductions. Some reason to be nervous. I just stood there and laughed until my butterflies just sort of flew away.

Regardless of what's at stake, the game's always been fun to me. A Saturday afternoon at Tiger Stadium in September of 1977 was a day that will stick with me the rest of my life. About three hundred miles to the south that day my beloved Oklahoma Sooners, ranked third in the country, were playing the fourth-ranked Ohio State Buckeyes in Columbus. When you grow up in the Oklahoma cotton fields, Sooner football flows into your veins like crude oil and you can't get it out. As a towheaded kid with no shoes, I started listening to Oklahoma football on radio back in the 1940s when Darrell Royal was the Sooners quarterback. Darrell, almost a decade later, would become the hated head coach of the Texas Longhorns. Also making his way in Sooners crimson-and-cream in those days was the great halfback Billy Vessels.

Almost three decades later, I would become a good friend of coach Barry Switzer when he was recruiting future Heisman Trophy winner Billy Sims out of Hooks. Barry gave me a lot of credit for persuading Billy to play for the Sooners, and a lot of people say I actually "delivered" the great halfback to Norman. But that would be exaggerating just a little.

My problem as I walked into Tiger Stadium that afternoon was I had no way to track the Oklahoma–Ohio State game that would feature Billy Sims at halfback in the wishbone. That was before I hit upon a remarkable idea. I knew that head groundskeeper Frank Feneck kept a small television handy, so I asked him to do me a favor. I convinced Frank to sit down at the third baseline, watch the Sooners and the Buckeyes on TV, and provide hand signals as a kind of running commentary on the game. Thumbs-up meant the Sooners had done something great, like scoring a touchdown. Thumbs-down meant that Ohio State had made a big play.

Thumbs were up and down all afternoon until the final seconds of the game. Ohio State led 28–26, but the Sooners had driven pretty deep into Buckeye territory. I heard Frank yelling, "Oklahoma is trying a field goal! Oklahoma is trying a field goal!" We had a break between innings, and I darted over to the third baseline and yelled, "What the heck is going on?" Frank hollered back, "You won't believe it. Ohio State called a time-out to freeze your kicker. And now he's standing in the middle of the field, leading the Ohio State band in their fight song."

In my mind's eye, I could see Uwe von Schamann standing at the Ohio State thirty-yard line, waving his arms like a band conductor. The guy had ice water in his veins, and he wasn't afraid of anything. Sure enough, he banged home a forty-one-yard field goal to beat Ohio State 29–28 in the final seconds. As Frank pointed his thumb to the sky, I did a big leg kick at second base. I bet those fans at Tiger Stadium are still wondering what the heck that umpire was doing out there.

To this day, Switzer still likes to speak on the banquet tour about the major league umpire who did a little jig at second base on the day von Schamann beat the Buckeyes.

I really think the game was more fun for the umpires back in the '60s and '70s, before big money became such a powerful influence and the steely cold pressure came along. Bill Valentine, who had a five-year umpiring career back in the '60s, had a serious run-in with Jimmy Piersall, one of the really nutso players. Jimmy was a fine baseball talent and probably the best outfielder in baseball for about ten of his seventeen seasons in The Bigs. But he did loony things. Jimmy ran the bases backward on his home run trot—from home to third to second to first—after hitting his career hundredth dinger.

One day, Piersall got mad at Valentine and started kicking dirt on home plate. Instead of kicking Piersall out of the game, Bill patiently handed Jimmy his plate brush. After finishing his tirade, Jimmy brushed all the dirt off the plate, calmly returned it to Bill, and continued to play. The crowd loved it. If you did something like that today, they'd accuse you of making a farce of the game.

We don't have a Jimmy Piersall in today's game. But there's a rascal who plays for the Chicago White Sox who acts a little goofy, and I like to ride him from time to time. He calls himself Albert Belle, but to me he's still Joey Belle, the name he used to go by. If he ever switches it back to Joey, I'll probably call him Albert.

Joey has done some bizarre things in his baseball career. One afternoon at the old Cleveland Municipal Stadium, a fan stood up from the left field bleacher seats and asked Joey if he'd like to come to his house after the game for a keg party. The timing of the invitation is pertinent to the story, since Joey had just declared himself a problem drinker and announced his intentions to quit cold turkey. So angry was Joey that he fired the ball into the stands and scored a direct hit to the fan's rib cage. He got sent to the minor leagues for that called strike.

Seems that Joey has this thing about hitting people with the baseball. A *Sports Illustrated* photographer somehow irritated Joey one day by snapping a few pictures. So Joey hit the guy in the back with the baseball.

I've always felt that I could relate to Joey, since he grew up in Shreveport, Louisiana, which is about an hour's drive from Hooks. That entire region of South Arkansas, North Louisiana, and East Texas looks the same and produces the same kind of people. They call it the ArkLaTex. So I cornered Joey one night in Cleveland and decided that I was going to lecture him about becoming baseball's bad boy. "Now, Joey," I began, "you know that we came from the same part of the country—me from Hooks and you from over in Shreveport. You know that we've both been lucky. Joey, by the way, how much money do you make every year? About six million. How is it possible that you can go around mad at everybody in the world? Me, I'm glad to be a major league umpire, getting to love the life I live, and live the life I love."

I paused and looked Joey right in the eye and said, "You know what we'd both be doing if we weren't in major league baseball. We'd both be back in the ArkLaTex pulling cotton. Think about that, Joey. You need to straighten up your act."

Joey, I'm sure, pondered my speech for about three seconds. It wasn't long before he was back in the news with yet another black eye to deal with. This time, he got mad at some kids for decorating his house with toilet tissue and eggs at Halloween. Seems that Joey didn't have enough candy for all of the trick-or-treaters, and when they abused his house, he decided to chase them in his car. That little stunt attracted national headlines and landed Joey a courtroom appearance.

The next season, when I was working a game in Cleveland, Indians manager Mike Hargrove sent Joey to home plate for the exchange of the lineup cards. I had poor Joey trapped like a rat. I cocked my right eyebrow at him and said, "Joey, next time you don't have enough candy at your house at Halloween, will you please call me? As a matter of fact, Joey, I'll wire you the candy if you're in that kind of a bind." All of the other umpires started howling with laughter. Joey actually smiled before he walked back to the dugout.

I think I should add this about one of baseball's finest hitters. I once gave Joey some advice about dealing with umpires, and he took it to heart. I told him that umpires aren't the enemy, but if you treat us that way, we'll become your biggest nightmare. You rarely see Joey explode against the umpires. Actually, on the field, he's polite and workmanlike. He kind of reminds me of a great hitter named Richie Allen, later to be called Dick Allen, who never got along with the media. But on the field, Allen was a gentleman and one of the easiest guys the umpires ever worked with.

Oh, I know that Joey isn't always an angel on the field. He got thrown out of a game in 1997 by one of the National League umpires, who'd called him out on strikes. He hardly deserved it. All he did was drop his bat and helmet as he walked back to the dugout. It's not like he spit on the guy or anything.

Another thing I'm proud of Joey for is the way he shouldered the blame for the White Sox's woes his first season there. He admitted that if he'd hit better, especially in the first half of the season, they wouldn't have needed the fire sale that owner Jerry Reinsdorf conducted right after the All-Star break. Joey gathered the beat writers around him one day and was candid about his play. Way to go, big fella. Looks like neither one of us will need to pull any cotton after all.

Actually, I've known some guys in baseball who did more moaning and complaining than Joey. These are the guys who like to drink their whine with dinner. These are the guys who just love to bitch.

Durwood's All-Bitch Team

Paul O'Neil: In the five years we've been together in the American League, I've never been able to make the guy happy. That's why Paul is the lead-off man on my all-bitch team. He bitches and moans so much that even his Yankee teammates are tired of hearing about it.

This is Paul's simple formula for calling balls and strikes when he's in the batter's box: If he doesn't swing at a pitch, then it's automatically a ball. If he swings, there's no question that it was in the strike zone and he made the right decision.

When some hitters swing and miss, they'll ask the plate umpire if the pitch was indeed a strike. They'll turn around and say, "Ump, where was it?" If the guy's been a friendly sort and hasn't been thrown out of a game lately, most umpires will tell him the truth. "A strike on the inside part," the ump will say.

But if the batter is Paul O'Neil, forget it. Paul whirled on me one night after swinging at a really bad pitch and demanded, "Durwood, where was it?" Trying to remain calm, I said, "Paul, if you're so damn smart, why don't you figure it out. Why do you need me back here anyway?"

It's pretty common knowledge that Paul and I have a banter going, and noses do get tweaked in our little discussions. But for the most part, we try to keep it civil. We were standing down the third base line at Yankee Stadium one afternoon, and we were laughing and joking about something. I said to Paul, "You know, I've always wanted to body-slam your ass." He growled, "You know, Durwood, this is as good a place as any. Let's get it on."

A couple of Yankee players started moving toward us, thinking we were serious. That caused both of us to laugh real loud.

I have a confession to make about Paul. In some ways I like the guy, especially his nickname, Jethro.

George Bell: When I was putting together my all-bitch team, I almost placed this guy ahead of Paul. The problem with George is that he really didn't bitch. Instead, he wanted to fight most of the time. George was a Latin player who had a temperament to show for it.

It was the second day of the 1982 season, and I had the plate in Toronto. The first strike I called on George almost tore his little heart out. I thought he was going to cry. Then, when I called strike two, it really ruined his day. He cussed at me in Spanish, and I guess he didn't realize that I'd spent a couple of winters umpiring off-season ball down in Puerto Rico. "George," I said, "you know better than to call a grown man that." Now George was gritting his teeth.

The next pitch, he grounded sharply to the third baseman, and I guess he thought he couldn't beat it out. So, after taking a couple of steps toward first, George spun around and started running straight toward me. Given the crazy expression on his face, I figured that George was going to keep running and bump me into the backstop. He was in that red-alert I'm-going-to-kick-somebody's-ass mood. But he pulled up short and ran off a string of magic words—cough sufferer and mother forker—that got him run right up the tunnel and out of the game.

B. J. Surhoff: His own teammates nicknamed him B. J. Surlyhoff, so don't blame the umpires for hanging that moniker on him.

I'm convinced that B. J. wouldn't believe it was a strike if his wife called it on him. There never was a strike called on the man that he didn't moan about.

But I'll give him some credit. He is a self-made player who didn't have a lot of talent. His uniform is dirty most of the time. Baseball has never really come easy for him, so I guess it's okay if he complains some of the time.

Carl Yastrzemski: This selection to my all-bitch team is going to surprise a lot of people. The Yaz man has always been known as a highbrow Bostonian who held himself above the unwashed masses of baseball. He was articulate and walked like an aristocrat.

Truth is, I loved the man as a hitter and absolute workaholic. He worked longer in the batting cage and the fitness room than anyone I've ever known in baseball. That's the biggest reason he was able to last twenty-three years in the major leagues and why he went into Cooperstown on the first ballot.

But when you called a strike on this guy, he could be curt. He wouldn't even look up or give you the dignity of a facial expression. It was, "The pitch was outside." Like he knew it was outside and you were dead wrong about the stupid call.

Eddie Murray: Another guy who is headed for Cooperstown's Hall of Fame, and my all-bitch Wall of Shame. He could sting you with expletives faster than a Muhammad Ali jab. Eddie was one of those guys who kept to himself and didn't converse with many people outside of his circle. He doesn't sign many autographs, and he avoids fans like the plague. You wouldn't exactly call him bubbly.

I got on Eddie's bad side one night in Baltimore back in 1981. I called a strike that he didn't like. So he wandered out of the box and started staring at the sky. I said, "Come on, Eddie, let's play ball. Get back in the batter's box and let's go." When Eddie kept staring at the sky, I signaled for the pitcher to pitch and I called a strike. I've never known a man who could cuss that fast. I had to send him back to the clubhouse to wash his mouth out with soap.

George Brett says the funniest stunt he's ever seen in baseball actually involved me. Wouldn't you know it?

We were in Kansas City for a Sunday afternoon game between the Royals and the White Sox. With the speedy Willie Wilson at first base, Royals second baseman Frank White drilled a pitch into the left field corner. Before they tore up the plastic rug at Kauffman Stadium, a well-hit baseball would ricochet like a pinball down in those tight corners. I instantly knew that both runners would be trying to make hay as the left fielder tried to corral the crazy ball.

It also meant the umpires were going to have to pull off one of the toughest maneuvers in our profession: the Rotation.

That day, Jim Evans was at third base, Darrell Cousins at second, Ted Hendry at first, and I was behind the plate. With the ball bouncing around in the left field corner, Evans was forced to leave his post at third and sprint into the outfield.

In unison, Cousins was supposed to shift from second to

third, and Hendry from first to second. You can understand how tough this can be. It became doubly difficult when I noticed that Cousins got a slow break at second. So I was forced to take off sprinting for third base because I thought the throw would be coming there.

I really didn't anticipate that Willie Wilson wouldn't stop at third. But the big ex-halfback just kept steaming around the bag, and he was churning for pay dirt. The dust was flying as the White Sox third baseman took the relay throw and whirled to throw to the plate. A very close and exciting play was developing, but we had a problem. Nobody was home.

You can imagine my dismay as Robin rifled the ball to the plate and Willie went into his slide. Standing about five feet from third base, I steadied myself and tried for the best angle you can get from eighty-five feet away. Since I'd gone to church that morning, I guess the good Lord decided to smile on me. I saw the play as clearly as if it had been right in front of me.

Now came the tough part. As thirty thousand fans held their breath, and the ballplayers from both dugouts became eerily still, I started clomping toward home. Think about all of the stupid gear I was wearing. I had knee pads stuck under my pants. I had a chest protector stuck under my shirt. I was wearing steel-plated shoes that weighed about forty pounds apiece. And I had an oval protector stuck in my crotch that is commonly called a cup. I had on enough plastic and steel to stop the Terminator. I must have weighed close to four hundred pounds.

Surely I sounded like a herd of buffalo as I trundled toward home plate. In fact, the only other sound in the ballpark was Brett laughing like a spotted hyena over in the Royals dugout. In these tight spots, there's only one way to react. It was time for some Durwood Dramatics. About five feet from home, I leaped as high as I could. I landed so hard just inches from the plate that I'm sure they heard the rumble all the way into Kansas. I brought down my right hand with a powerful stroke, and at the top of my lungs, I screamed, "OUUUUUUUUUuuuuuuuuuuut!"

Before my theatrics were over, twenty-four Royals players, six coaches, and a manager were cursing me in unison. The lone dissenter was none other than George Brett. The only reason he wasn't standing on the top step of the dugout, yelling his silly head off, is because he was lying on the floor of the dugout laughing his guts out.

Needless to say, Royals manager Dick Howser was in my face before I could say Abner Doubleday. He was hollering and cussing and calling me everything but Tex Watson. Then, without warning, he started to laugh.

"Now, Durwood," he suddenly blurted through the laughter. "I know that I don't know everything. But are you sure he was out?"

My head was overamping and I said the only logical thing that registered in my mind. "Sure as I can be, Dick," I said. "Only problem is that I overhustled the play."

I guess that stood as the understatement of decade.

I've known a lot of the good guys in baseball, and Milwaukee's Robin Yount, even though he called me Dagwood, ranks pretty close to George Brett just for having fun. Robin was a nineteen-year-old phenom when he broke into the majors as the Brewers' shortstop in 1974. He put together twenty great seasons and a lifetime batting average of .285 that might someday get him to Cooperstown. But Robin also had a sneaky side, as I found out one night in 1992.

It was the bottom of the ninth inning and the Twins were trailing the Brewers 4–2 in Minneapolis. Even with two outs, there was still plenty of hope with runners at second and third and Kirby Puckett, one of the best hitters ever, at the plate.

Puckett lifted a towering fly ball into the Metrodome lights. Because of the white ceiling in that oversized garage, a fly ball often disappears. But Yount got a great break on the ball and raced to the fence. He leaned over that silly piece of plastic, also known as the Glad Bag, to steal Kirby's home run shot. I would have sworn on my life that Robin Yount caught that ball.

Robin was one of the best all-round fielders I'd ever seen. The ball indeed stuck in the webbing of his glove. He pulled back from the fence and started running toward left field, where he gave Greg Vaughn a high-five. I raised my big fist and punched the air with the out sign. Game over. Crank up the organ and turn out the lights.

Everybody in the dome was packing their stuff, getting ready to go home. They posted a 4–2 final on the scoreboard. Then, as Robin came running past me, I yelled, "Hey, Robin, let me have the ball! Let me have the ball!" He stopped, shook his head, and laughed. He opened his glove to reveal nothing but leather. The ball was somewhere beyond the center field fence. I could feel my heart sinking right into my shoes.

I started waving and waving and waving. Kirby had turned to run back to the dugout. But I got his attention. I was twirling my right hand, leaping as high as I could, and shouting, "Home run! Home run!" I should have yelled, "Robin Yount is a cheating rascal!" But I didn't. As Kirby and the two other Twins runners rounded the bases, I said a little prayer. "Thank God I asked Robin for that baseball."

The scoreboard operator added three runs for the Twins in the bottom of the ninth. Minnesota 5, Milwaukee 4.

I should've been mad at Robin Yount. But I wasn't. My eyes, however, hadn't deceived me. "I did catch the ball, Dagwood," he told me the next night. "But when I hit the fence, it popped out of my glove."

I know that Robin Yount is still out there somewhere, kicking back and telling stories about the day he almost fooled Dagwood. I know that he's having a big laugh on me. But, Robin, let me remind you of something that you should have learned that night in Minnesota. The umpire is always right.

The Art of Making
the Call

FOLKS AROUND THE AMERICAN LEAGUE
say I've sent a few pitchers to the Hall of Fame before their
time because my strike zone tends to swell like George M.
Steinbrenner's ego. They say that if my strike zone got any
bigger, it'd spill over into the next county. They're exaggerating, of course.

Wade Boggs, a great hitter with the best eye I've ever
seen in baseball, gets a little frustrated with my strike zone.
He likes to stand in the box, cock his head sideways, and
holler, "Durwood, keep it up and you're going to put that
damn guy in the Hall of Fame."

The next pitch will come in and I'll say, "Wade, there's
another bitch pitch." He'll just grin and say, "Well, excuse
me, Durwood, while I bitch a little."

Umpires in the American League are constantly badgered
for what is called "squeezing the strike zone." Me, I only
squeeze ripe fruit and Mama's hand. I guess I've squeezed
a few batting averages the last twenty-one years in the major
leagues because they say my strike zone is bigger than the
Green Monster at Fenway Park.

Now, don't jump to any conclusions. I don't particularly
favor the pitchers of the American League, and I think a
good percentage of them should be gift-wrapped and air-
mailed each December as Christmas fruitcakes. We've got
more impostors pitching baseballs in our league than we've

got two-faced congressmen in Washington pitching lower taxes.

Let me tell you about one of the biggest controversies in all of baseball that doesn't involve corked bats, spitballs, or Joey Belle's temper. I call it the War of the Strike Zone. Over in the National League, my more esteemed compadres generally have what is considered a larger bull's-eye for the pitchers. It's been said through the annals of time that a National League umpire is more apt to call the low strike than the American Leaguer. Maybe that's why a sinkerballer like Kevin Brown sets the league on fire when he leaves the Texas Rangers of the A.L. for the Florida Marlins of the N.L. and why Greg Maddux has more Cy Young trophies than Bayer has aspirin.

Thanks to the advent of interleague play, I've umpired quite a few National League teams lately. One afternoon in Anaheim, the Angels were playing Colorado when Rockies slugger Larry Walker stepped to the plate. Because he was hitting lights out, and his batting average was hovering around .400 at the time, the Angels wisely walked him. As the final pitch came through, and I called it ball four, Walker flipped his bat toward the dugout and yelled, "Those pitches would've been strikes in the National League."

As Larry trotted toward first, I laughed, and I thought he would be doing the same. Instead, he wasn't even grinning and looked pretty doggone serious. I had to assume that Mr. Walker was agitated with what he considered the ever-inflating strike zone over in the National League. It certainly didn't sound like an endorsement for my brethren from the so-called senior circuit, and I guess they're not perfect after all.

Defining the strike zone may be the toughest task in baseball. It's kind of like analyzing Jerry Reinsdorf's brain waves on the day he dismantled the Chicago White Sox while they were still in the thick of the 1997 A.L. Central race.

To understand the strike zone, you must first become acquainted with the bizarre dimensions of home plate, which kind of looks like a five-sided monster. According to the official rules of baseball, ''Home base shall be a five-sided slab . . . a 12-inch square with corner filled in so that one edge is 17 inches long, two 8 ½ inches, and two are 12 inches.'' Nothing in the whole wide world is shaped like home plate, and maybe that's the reason that bugger has caused so many nightmares for umpires, hitters, and pitchers through the years. If there's one thing it doesn't look like, it's a plate.

The problem is establishing the dimensions of the strike zone—the imaginary box, if you will. To make a strike zone, you must paint four lines on nothing but thin air. Then, for nine innings, or about 310 pitches, you've got to make sure that your strike zone doesn't blow away on the next gust of wind. With the strike zone, you can't hold it in your hand, hug it, kick it, or break a Louisville Slugger over it. You can't take it to dinner or spill mustard on it. Truth is, it's nothing but dead air.

Again, according to the rules of baseball, the width of the strike zone encompasses the seventeen inches of the plate. As far as depth, it's supposed to extend from the knees to the uniform's lettering just below the shoulders. I hear that the last umpire to use a strike zone that extended to the letters also traveled by wagon train from ballpark to ballpark. No umpire has rung up a letter-high strike since the batter was called a striker and an umpire was called a scout. Today the strike zone in both leagues is from the knees, or just below the kneecap in the National League, to the top of the belt. That means we've stolen about four inches from the strike zone since somebody invented it.

A few years ago, then–league president Dr. Bobby Brown decided he was going to put his foot down and set us all straight on the strike zone. He decided it was high time that the rules of the game be enforced. He was going to take no prisoners. Dr. Brown marched out the rule book, and he started rattling sabres. Then he hopped a plane from New York to Florida, where he gathered the umpiring troops during spring training and laid down the by-God law. Dr. Brown was acting like the Harry Truman of baseball.

"I want the strike zone to be called just like this, from the letters to the knees, just like it says in the rule book," Dr. Brown said. Then he pulled out a life-size chart of the batter and the strike zone. Everybody was quite impressed, and quite clear on Dr. Brown's strike zone. Since Dr. Brown was a doctor in real life, we knew he understood the human anatomy. I think we all saluted, wiped the relish and mustard off our shirts, and went back to work.

For more than a month in spring training, the American League umpires proudly followed the mandate of our dear boss in New York. We called strikes from the letters to the knees and upheld our pledge to do so. We carried our rule books close to our hearts. Each morning, we looked into the full-length mirror and muttered to ourselves, "From the letters to the knees. From the letters to the knees."

All was going well with the new and improved strike zone until the faxes, the memos, and the phone calls from Dr. Brown stopped coming. Suddenly, the machinery in New York went dead silent. Then the season started, and we went back to the same old strike zone. We learned through the American League grapevine that Dr. Brown's chart had been chucked in the trash can back in New York. Seems the owners had gotten wind of our president's plan and demanded he stop tinkering with our sacred little imaginary box. The owners didn't give a good dadgum about following the rule book. They just wanted runs, runs, runs, and more runs. An expanded strike zone, they figured, would favor the pitchers and thus cut down on run production. And that's not what the American League stands for. Putting butts in the seats is all that matters.

Some great men and some fine scholars have tried to define, redefine, and refine the strike zone over the years. Most of them, like Dr. Brown, have failed in midtheory. Take, for example, Fay Vincent, baseball's commissioner for three years before he was run out of office by the National League owners.

I was in my hotel room at the Kansas City Hyatt one morning in 1991 when the phone rang and it was Fay. He said, "Durwood, I want you to have breakfast with me this morning, and I want you to tell me about the strike zone."

I thought, Finally, here's a commissioner who wants to hear it from the horse's mouth. He'd heard enough from guys like Tim McCarver, the catcher-turned-broadcaster, who wouldn't know a strike zone if it was painted on his face. Like most baseball people, Fay wanted to know the difference between the A.L. and the N.L. strike zones. I shot straight with him when I said, "Fay, if you've got thirty umpires in the National League, and thirty in the American League, you're going to have sixty different strike zones. That's just human nature. We know that no two humans are alike, and therefore no strike zones will be the same. I know that probably isn't the answer you're looking for. But it's the truth."

I think the matter came into focus when he realized that he wasn't dealing with robots. I said, "Fay, you've got to expect an umpire to miss a pitch from time to time. But that's no reason to string the guy up." I said that job one should be keeping each strike zone consistent. Hitters and pitchers can deal with a strike zone in any shape or size as long as it's not floating around like a helium-filled balloon.

Of course, we've had our laughs about the strike zone through the years. I used a couple of elastic knee supporters to keep my shin guards from rubbing my kneecaps. One day, umpire John Hirschbeck dug into my locker and pulled out those knee supporters, which are about five inches long.

On the top of the elastic, John wrote "strike zone." On the bottom, he wrote "too low." In the middle, he wrote "don't know." It was just a little joke about the supposed shrinking size of the strike zone.

Peter Ueberroth, in his five years as baseball commissioner (1984–89), didn't run the league from behind a desk. Ueberroth had made the 1984 Olympics a smashing success as president of the Los Angeles Olympic Organizing Committee and I know why. He was a guy who'd roll up his sleeves and rub elbows with the real people. The man's got tons of personality, and I really think that baseball was a fun experience for him. Shoot, he liked to go out to the ballpark, eat a hot dog, smell the fresh-cut grass, and talk to the grounds crew. I wouldn't have been surprised to see him out there raking the mound or lining the field.

The commissioner was a regular around the umpires' room. He liked to come in and just flop down and talk. He was a great leader because he was a grassroots kind of guy. One afternoon, we were sitting around in the Anaheim umpires' room when he noticed my little knee supporters with all of John Hirschbeck's artwork and he just fell over laughing.

Then he scooped them up and took off down the hall, and I think he showed them off to everybody in the ballpark. Every time the commissioner and I were in the same ballpark, he'd come down to the umpires' room and grab my knee wraps and take off down the hall, waving them for everyone to see.

Jokes aside, a good umpire will work long and hard at determining exactly what his strike zone should be. There's no question that calling strikes and balls is really the essence of the job and the reason umps get paid the big money. But think about this. Major league baseball doesn't issue you an instruction book for the strike zone, and everybody knows we don't follow the rule book. Once upon a time, a league president tried to fix the strike zone, and he was told to sit down and shut up. So what is an umpire to do?

I started trying to define my strike zone the first day I got to spring training back in 1972. I walked around the Chicago Cubs camp asking every umpire I could find to draw me a strike zone. I got some good advice. I was told to set my knees on the outside part of the plate. Any pitch thrown inside my knees, and also above my knees, would be a strike. Then I was told to set my eyes at the level of the batter's belt buckle. Any pitch above eye level would be a ball.

For years, I've looked a little funny behind the plate because I extend my balled-up fists from my body kind of like a kung fu fighter. But there's a reason for this madness. I set my eyes on the top part of the strike zone, and if the pitch is above my mask, then it's a ball. Unlike most umpires, I set up over the top of the catcher's head because it gives me a better view. Most umps like to stay behind the catcher and look over his shoulder. They view strikes and balls from a place we call "the slot."

A lot of people ask me why I have such a large strike zone, while some umpires in the American League are more conservative. When I came to the major leagues in 1977, the American League was just doing away with the big balloon chest protector that was held in front of you. Umpires were going to the inside chest protector. Because A.L. umpires had been looking over the top of the big balloon for years, their strike zones were a cut higher and they didn't call as many low strikes. So I came into the league at a time when the strike zone hadn't been pushed down by a couple of inches.

But there's actually a larger reason for my strike zone, and it's built on my philosophy about baseball. Fans pay good money to see players play, not to see umpires ump. They don't pay money to see pitchers issuing walks. Baseball has to be a game of action, and it needs to have a rhythm and a flow. If batters aren't sometimes forced to take the bat off their shoulder, the games will never have a flow. It's not below me to bark at a batter, "If you don't like my strike zone, get the bat off your doggone shoulder."

If hitters aren't going to swing the bat, why do they wear $30 batting gloves? Why do they rub that sticky pine tar on their bats all the way up to the label? Why do they carry bats that cost $150 apiece? Why do they need hitting instructors? My advice to every hitter in the American League is simple: If you're going to bring the big lumber to the plate, use it.

I also have a strategy that I use for my strike zone. In the early innings, I want to get the message across to the hitters that they need to come up swinging. I want some action and I want an up-tempo game, so I'll stretch the strike zone just a little in the first three innings. I'll hear the manager over in the dugout yelling, "Durwood, that pitch was three inches outside.'' But he doesn't realize that I'm trying to get that hitter to swing the bat.

As we get into the fourth inning, I'm going to shrink the strike zone just a little bit. I'll keep it fairly tight through the sixth inning. In the seventh, eighth, and ninth innings, I'm going to expand the strike zone again, and I'm going to keep it out there. Now don't get me wrong. I'm not calling un-hittable pitches strikes. Again, I want the message to be that the hitter, not the umpire, is going to decide this game, so you might as well come up hacking and hacking early. If the hitter gets behind in the count early, it's not my fault. He's just not paying attention to what is going on around him.

I've always enjoyed watching a pitcher try to manipulate my strike zone. A real master was Tommy John, who left the game in 1989 after pitching for six teams and surviving reconstructive elbow surgery. Tommy would start every game by throwing his first pitch an inch outside. He wanted to see just how big my strike zone was that day, and he had the stuff to do it. If I called that first pitch a strike, he'd throw the next pitch two inches outside. If that pitch was called a strike, he'd go a little farther outside with the next one, just to test me. By the third or fourth pitch, Tommy knew exactly where my strike zone would be that day. Generally, my strike zone will extend about an inch and a half off the outside part of the plate, and about a half-inch on the inside part.

According to our rotation, I go behind the plate every fourth game. In the old days, there was a guy named Bill Klem who wanted the plate every night, but nobody in today's game wants that kind of stress, nor can you find one with that kind of ego. Umpires rotate clockwise from third base to second base to first base to home.

Every base has its built-in problems. At first, you've got the bang-bang plays on ground balls, and that's because everything that's hit starts with running to first. The more plays that come your way, the greater the chance that you'll make a mistake. Sure makes sense to this old Texan. Second base is a little easier than first, but you've still got the sweep tags on stolen bases and those require good positioning by the umpire. At second base, the ball comes from every angle on the field and that means you have to work around the second baseman, the shortstop, and even the centerfielder. Third base is the easiest of the three. However, you must remember when the tough play comes, it's only ninety feet from home. You botch a call at third base and it could mean that a run scores that wasn't deserved. The closer the play to the plate, the tougher the call.

Home plate, as they say around the umpiring room, is hell.

As I strap on the chest protector and slip into the steel-covered plate shoes, I can be sure that I'll see about 310 pitches. Some will be hit. Some will be fouled. Some will be obvious balls and strikes. Then there will be thirty to forty pitches that will be right on the borderline. Those are the ones you've got to be dead-solid right about. The outcome of the game may be riding on those pitches.

I estimate that I've seen more than a quarter-million pitches behind the plate. Just like hitters, plate umpires go in and out of mental zones. If I'm in the zone, I'm certain about every pitch that comes down the pipe. I'll go weeks and weeks just knowing that my plate calls are right on the money. I'm like a machine back there, and I'll never hear a single complaint from either team. Then I'll slide out of the zone for a while, and just like a hitter, I'll struggle with some of my decisions.

After a game behind the plate, I can go back to the umpires' room and distinctly remember the fifteen or twenty pitches that could have gone either way. I'll focus on those pitches and ask myself, "Did I get those right?" I'll carry those fifteen or twenty pitches back to the hotel with me, and on occasion, they'll wake me up in the middle of the night.

Bill Kinnamon, who was the chief of my umpiring school back in 1972, said that an umpire is allowed to miss one pitch per inning. That means you can miss nine pitches per game. I don't subscribe to Mr. Bill's thinking on that one. You wouldn't be a very good umpire if you missed that many pitches in one game.

This is the kind of pressure I put on myself. Just before the pitcher releases the ball, I say to myself, "If this were the last pitch ever thrown in your career, how would you call it?" By doing that, I'm examining every pitch to the best of my ability. I'm not allowing my mind to drift somewhere else, and I'm forcing my eyes to home in on the baseball. At this stage of concentration, I become mesmerized with the baseball and the strike zone. I push myself into a mental zone where everything else on earth is blocked out. I don't hear the crowd. I can't hear the managers in the dugout chirping at me. I don't worry about the tractor being broken down back in Hooks.

Because working the plate is such a tough task, an umpire will usually change his entire routine that day. I'll get to the fitness room in the hotel, but my workout will be light. I won't eat much during the day. If it's a day game, I'll have waffles for breakfast because they give me energy. Because the work requires great mental focus and can be physically grueling, the plate umpire needs plenty of rest. Eric Gregg from the National League and Richie Garcia from the American League try not to even talk during the day before they've got the plate.

Walk into the umpires' room an hour before the first pitch and it's easy to pick out the guy who's working the plate that night. He's usually over in the corner doing some peaceful meditation. The plate umpire won't be doing much talking. The others will be watching TV or playing cards, and they'll be a lot louder than the plate man. After spending most of the day thinking about my strike zone, I will have visualized it long before I walk onto the field.

When Dick Butler was the supervisor of umpires, he had a little game he'd play in the play-off games. Instead of going strictly by the rotation, he'd assign the plate umpire just hours before the game. He had a funny way of doing it. He'd arrive at the umpires' room early and set the plate shoes in front of the locker of the man who'd call balls and strikes that night. I asked him about it once and he said, "I want you guys to be able to get a full night's sleep. If you automatically know you're going to be working the plate the next game, you won't sleep that well.'' I thought Mr. Butler's thinking was right on the mark.

The best balls-and-strikes umpire I'd ever seen is sadly no longer with us. That is a general consensus of all the umpires who worked with him. Steve Palermo, my great friend, still walks with a cane after being gunned down on the streets of Dallas back in 1991. He's valiantly tried to make a comeback to umpiring, but it wouldn't be realistic to believe that he can.

With the count three-two, and the pitch a quarter-inch off the plate, Steve would confidently call ball four. And there wouldn't be a peep from either dugout. He had a perfect strike zone, and he really was the exception to most rules in plate umpiring. It's just sad that we'll likely never see him back there again.

I know that I attract a lot of attention on the field and some people think I'm a hot dog out there. I'm not trying to detract from the game, and God knows that I believe that umpiring is more important than entertaining. But that didn't keep *USA Today* in 1993 from naming me baseball's most stylish umpire at first base. Not many people know this, but I made such a wild gesture one night at first base that I temporarily threw my right shoulder out of its socket. According to the national newspaper, I also ranked among the top three most stylish umpires behind the plate, along with Richie Garcia and Frank Pulli of the National League. That's pretty good company.

My signature in umpiring is that I use both hands to call strikes and outs. When my right hand does something, it seems my left hand doesn't want to be left out. I'm probably the most mimicked umpire in baseball. Ballplayers practice and practice my two-handed strike call. A lot of them have it down and that's really a compliment to me. It's fun watching those fools from the corner of my eye.

Just about every player in the American League can impersonate Durwood. George Brett started it. I was behind the plate in Kansas City in 1984 when I heard him yelling, "Hey, Durwood! Hey, Durwood!" He was crouched over in the dugout, doing my two-handed strike call. Everybody on the Royals bench was doing it by the third inning. I guess it was the first feeble attempt at the macarena. A lot players call me "Naked Gun" after the umpire in that movie who made all of his calls with two hands.

Walking to home plate for the exchange of lineup cards before Royals games, George would be over there doing Durwood's double pump. It started spreading to other dugouts. Some of my more conservative colleagues might have been agitated, but I thought it was funny as hell.

Umpiring the bases, I do the same double pump. I'll bend over, raise one foot off the ground, and throw the quick right-left combination, kind of like a prizefighter. My hat usually flies off, and fellow crew member Rocky Roe says, "Durwood's our Tasmanian Devil. When he's done, his hat is liable to be on the ground and he may be facing the scoreboard. But you can be sure that the call came from the heart."

Of course, I love to be animated, and people wonder why I pace up and down the right field line when I'm umpiring at first. People who say I'm imitating Oscar Mayer don't really know me, and they probably don't know baseball. Shoot, I learned about pacing from Marty Springstead, a twenty-year umpire who just so happens to be my boss now. I used to say, "Spring, why are you always moving around so much?" And he'd say, "Dur, think about it. The first thing you've got to do at the crack of the bat is move. So you might as well be working your feet over there at first."

Going from a dead stop to a sudden start will throw you out of sync. That's why I'm staying light on my feet over at first base. Sure, I'll pause right before the pitch reaches the plate. But I'll be in position to move in any direction. My pacing must be working, because there are very few calls at first base that I ever felt that I needed to give back.

I've been compared for more than twenty years to the late Ron Luciano, who got out of umpiring in 1979. He was probably the most animated umpire in the history of the game, and Ronnie called me his heir apparent. There were some plusses and minuses to that. I really felt that Ronnie got run out of major league baseball by the American League office, and I'm not so sure that was fair. He still had some skills, and I thought he was a good umpire. But let's be realistic about Ronnie and his style. It didn't work, even for him.

Don't get me wrong, because I love umpires who work with enthusiasm, but Ronnie went too far. He thought he had to umpire and entertain at the same time. I really think the pressure to be a comedian is what burned him out and was the biggest reason that he started losing interest in umpiring. Ronnie decided that instead of just calling a man out at first base, he had to shoot him. He'd point his index finger at the runner and start firing away. Some of the players liked it, and some of them mimicked him. Ronnie's biggest problem was that he spent too much time with his eyes in the stands and his head in the clouds, and even though he was funny at times, enough was enough.

It got to where the fans expected a circus performance every night out of Ronnie. I really don't believe that Ronnie had fun his last couple of years. The bosses were on his case, and even some of his fellow umpires wanted him to tone it down. But fans will always remember Ronnie's style.

One of the most important jobs in umpiring, though, is selling the call. Not only must you convince somebody that they're out or safe, you've got to avoid the big argument that will lead to an ejection. You've got to be a part-time psychologist and full-time diplomat out there.

A lot of times, my hat will fly off when I make one of my big sweeping out calls, especially at second base. I want the boys over in the dugout to be saying, ''Boy, he's got confidence. He really believes in his calls.'' Players and managers can detect insincerity, and they know when you have second thoughts about your call. An umpire who hesitates is lost. That's one of the big reasons that I call strikes and outs with a double-fisted pump.

One Sunday night during the 1997 season, though, I didn't do such a great job on one of my strike calls. It was a nationally televised game on ESPN between the A's and the Twins early in the season. I committed the cardinal sin on a called third strike against Jose Canseco when I hesitated. In calling balls and strikes, you're taught to see it, hear it hit the catcher's mitt, and call it. As soon as that pitch explodes into the catcher's mitt, you're supposed to either call it a ball or a strike.

This is what I did wrong against Jose. In my mind's eye, I was trying to get a second look at the pitch because it was real close to the inside corner. Minnesota's Brad Radke was on the mound, and he threw a badass sinkerball that did all kinds of funny things around the plate. I studied the catcher's glove to see where the pitch had come in, and I instantly knew it was a borderline call. Since Jose had two strikes, and I had doubts about the pitch, I probably should have called it a ball. Instead, after a brief pause, I rung up strike three on him. It really wasn't bad umpiring, but it did go against all of Durwood's principles about selling the call, and I knew that I had a fight on my hands.

As you might expect, Jose whirled on me and hollered, "What's the hesitation for, Durwood?" Then from the A's dugout, I heard, "Ewwwwwwwwwwwwwhhh." I knew that Jose and I were about about to go several rounds. Let me tell you that Jose and I've had a good relationship through the years, and like some other players, he'll come down to the umpires' room before the game to shoot the bull.

"That couldn't have been a strike, Durwood," Jose hollered. I stared him down and shot back, "Jose, I've been calling that same pitch on you all night. I've called four strikes in the same place in this same game."

Jose gave me that little smirk and said, "I ain't going nowhere." I knew right then we were in trouble. Instead of dragging this thing out, I yanked off my mask, started hopping on my right foot, raised my right hand, and tossed his butt right out of the game. *Ka-boom!* He was finished. Adios, Jose. Get to the showers, amigo.

Deep in my heart, I knew that Jose wanted me to throw him out of the game. On this particular night, he was playing with some pain in his back, and he wasn't really happy about being in right field. But with Matt Stairs out with an injury, the A's were forced to play Jose in the field. As longtime Canseco observers can testify, making him play the field can be a big mistake. Jose was feeling gimpy and acting wimpy, so I had no reservations about sending him up the tunnel. The funny part is that as he ran down the steps, he banged his head against the dugout roof.

The baseball writers came down after the game for a few comments. I said, "We just reached an impasse." They laughed all the way back to the press box.

People ask me all the time if it bothers me when I miss a call. Actually, it eats me alive and I find, as I grow older, it bums me out even more. I can't sleep well after a botched call. This might sound really shocking, but my appetite subsides and I tend to get very quiet after a bad call. Other umpires have told me over and over that I shouldn't burden myself with it all. But I can't help it. I know that I won't feel any better until I get to the next game when I can make some good calls and start putting the bad one behind me.

Former major league manager Bobby Bragan, who was my boss in Double-A baseball, tells a story about confronting umpire Babe Pinelli over a bad call at first base. Bobby sprinted from the dugout and started yelling, "Babe, dammit, my guy was two steps past first base when you called him out." Babe grinned and said, "Ain't that a shame."

Another time, when Bobby was hitting for the Brooklyn Dodgers, plate umpire Bill Klem called a ball. Klem, who's in the Hall of Fame, took very little lip from anyone. He ejected the pitcher, the catcher, and the manager in a period of about thirty seconds. After the new pitcher warmed up and Bobby dug back in at the plate, Klem said, "Now, Bobby, why would you take such a beautiful pitch as the last one?"

* * *

The use of instant replay in football didn't work because it took too long for the official in the press box to describe something he'd already seen. Duh. Football continues to study ways to make the system easier on the blood pressure and the digestive tract.

My opinion on instant replay will go against the grain of the so-called base purists, and it's going to fly up the noses of the Baseball Lords. But I really believe the doggone system would work in baseball if they could iron out some of the technical kinks. My ego just isn't big enough that I don't believe the umpires could use some help on the base paths and for some confusing calls in the outfield.

First, let me set the record straight that I don't believe we could use the TV camera to call balls and strikes. Many of the TV networks have already proved that by setting their cameras at a cockeyed angle and then letting loose cannons like Tim McCarver second-guess the umps from the press box. For one thing, the TV camera compresses everything it focuses on. So pitches are naturally going to appear to be higher than they really are. Second, we've already experimented with mechanical ways of calling balls and strikes and it hasn't worked. So let's eliminate that aspect of instant replay from the equation.

But using cameras out in the field is a horse hide of a different color. There are times when an umpire can't get a good angle on the swipe tag, one of the toughest calls in all of baseball. Other times, the ump is blocked from the action and has to guess. Then there is the situation we had last year in the play-offs at Yankee Stadium when a twelve-year-old boy, who was skipping school, leaned over the wall and caught a fly ball that was destined to land in the glove of Baltimore's Tony Tarasco. Tell me that umpire Richie Garcia couldn't have used some help with that call. He didn't see the kid in the stands catch the ball, and ruled it a home run. That call by Richie was the boo-boo heard round the world.

One of the toughest calls in all of baseball is the trapped ball in the outfield. Did the outfielder catch it, or did it one-hop into his glove? Sometimes only God knows for sure.

Even if the Baseball Lords are too stiff and stodgy to consider replay umpiring for the regular season, at least give it some thought for the postseason, where one wrong call can turn the whole thing around. But then again, I might be expecting too much progressive thinking from a bunch of guys asleep at their desks.

Just about everywhere I go these days I hear about the combative relationship between umpires and players/managers. You'd think that the umpires were out to get the bad guys. Let's study the issues.

Ejections almost doubled in the first month of the 1997 season because umpires were still seething about Baltimore second baseman Robbie Alomar spitting on John Hirschbeck. We felt that justice hadn't been served since Robbie got to participate in the '96 play-offs, his owner paid his fine, and his five-day suspension wasn't served until the following regular season.

Umpires were even more upset when interim commissioner for life Bud Selig promised to crack down on umpire attackers and then failed to do so. That's just Bud, I guess. Therefore, we took matters into our own hands in the first month of the season and enacted what was then called "zero tolerance." The bullshots were over, as far as we were concerned.

When April ended, though, it was business as usual. The rash of ejections stopped, and I really feel that most umpires stopped pressing the issue. At the season's conclusion, the numbers revealed that ejections really tailed off after April. In fact, overall suspensions were up only 10 percent from 1996 to 1997. Me, I finished the year with a measly three and a half sacks. I had to share one of those with fellow crew member Davey Phillips.

The umpires over in the National League got a black eye for some of their calls in the championship series. Eric Gregg took a beating from the broadcast boys for his gigantic strike zone in game five. One of the managers supposedly called his strike zone an "embarrassment." But you've got to realize that Eric's had that same strike zone for years, and the players know all about it. Besides, Atlanta pitcher Greg Maddux said that he thought Eric missed just one of his pitches in the entire game.

I'll say, though, that the umpires didn't take a lot of real grief in the postseason, even though Mike Hargrove and Davey Johnson did argue a couple of calls in our games. The biggest reason that we didn't have managers in our faces is because our union chief, Richie Phillips, drew a line in the sand before the start of the play-offs and said that if anyone got within an arm's length of us, he'd be gone. That was a reaction to Robbie Alomar getting a wrist-slap for spitting on John Hirschbeck. Our feeling still is that if you're going to do the crime, you've got to pay the fine.

Late in the 1997 season, Bill Koenig of *USA Today Baseball Weekly* wrote a story about the snits going on between the lines. He quoted Chicago White Sox broadcaster Ken Harrelson thusly: "Umpires are like players. You have good ones, bad ones, and mediocre ones. What I hate to see are the good umpires—guys like Ken Kaiser and Durwood Merrill—lumped into the same category with the bad ones.

"Most of the guys getting into these arguments are the bad ones who are having trouble anyway. I've seen ejections today where a guy gets run without saying a word. He just looked at the umpire the wrong way."

Harrelson is a former player and ex–general manager who's been around the major leagues since 1963. I really appreciate what he said about me because he's got the experience to back up his opinion.

Here's the problem with umpiring as I see it. All umpires are capable of calling balls and strikes, and most of us know when the runner is out or safe. We all know the rule book or we wouldn't be here. What separates good umpires from everybody else is dealing with people on the field. It's being able to convey your call to them and sell it without making them mad as hell.

I think that most baseball people will look back at the 1997 season and say the umpires were fair, even though we were mad as hell about the Alomar-Hirschbeck episode. What really perplexes me, though, is that it seems we're destined to forget the incident altogether. Let me tell you why it's important that we keep the memory of it all pretty handy.

I don't blame American League president Dr. Gene Budig for his decision to let Robbie play in the postseason, because he merely acted according to the accepted guidelines of baseball. He had a precedent to guide him. No player had ever been suspended in the postseason for his actions in a regular season game. So I'm not blaming Dr. Budig. But, at the same time, I think it's time we stop leaning on stupid precedents and start using some common sense. Some of these outdated guidelines need to be run through the paper shredder. Robbie committed a heinous act. He should have paid for it during the play-offs, plain and simple. He had no right to spit in an umpire's face, regardless of his frustration. Our system has got to change.

I know that a lot of people are laying some of the blame at John's feet because, on the day after the spitting incident, he charged into Baltimore's clubhouse and tried to get to Robbie. First, you must understand how John felt after some of Robbie's postgame comments. Robbie told a large gathering of reporters that the ejection was somehow related to the 1993 death of John D. Hirschbeck, who was John's eight-year-old son. Little John had died from a rare and inherited blood disorder that also afflicts the family's other three sons. When Robbie started talking about death in the Hirschbeck family, and blaming it on an umpire's outburst, he stepped way out of line.

If I'd been there, John would have never reached the clubhouse and started yelling those things at Robbie. I would have tackled him and held him on the ground. I would've hog-tied him if I'd needed to. If John Hirschbeck had made it through the clubhouse doors that afternoon, he would've had me riding on his back.

I've liked John since he broke into The Bigs in 1984. He's got the movie-star looks, and he's not ugly like the rest of us. So he kind of stands out on the field. John has always been able to handle himself on the field, even though some people say he has a hair-trigger temper.

As for John's behavior, he was wrong in saying he was going to "kill" Robbie. I doubt that he even knew he said it. He was being driven by a powerful emotion. It's too bad that the word "kill" ever was uttered.

But it's still appalling to me, and to every major league umpire, that Alomar was not properly punished. Major League Baseball can't say that Alomar was dealt with properly. Another thing that bugs the heck out of me is baseball's antiquated system of fines and suspensions that should have been retired with Babe Ruth. Baseball, it seems, never allows common sense or changing times to detract from its goofy set of rules and standards.

For one, it takes forever for a suspended player to serve his sentence. When a player's suspended, the union normally appeals it. Union chief Donald Fehr and company make sure of that. In baseball, they say the player has a right to a hearing before he serves a suspension. But the system is a joke. That hearing usually is held the next time the player goes to New York. So there's no telling when the suspension will actually begin, meaning the player is right back on the field.

Basketball, on the other hand, moves swiftly and with an iron fist. When Dennis Rodman kicks a sideline cameraman and is suspended for eleven games, that suspension begins the next day. And, buddy, there is no turning back the clock. When the Knicks and the Miami Heat went to war during the '97 play-offs, they suspended five New York players, including Patrick Ewing, and one player from the Heat. They started serving those suspensions the next game—right there in the middle of the play-offs. There's no telling what the NBA might do to a player if he spit in the face of one of their referees. I doubt that he would be pampered like Robbie Alomar and told he could take his vacation next season.

David Stern, the commissioner of the NBA, wields a mighty stick over there. Or should I say that Rod Thorne, the vice president who determines the punishment, is a man with some clout. The NBA has it all together when it comes to punishing their players.

Some critics say that baseball is screwed up on fines and suspensions because we don't have a full-time commissioner. Wrong. League presidents dole out the punishment in baseball. Now, I'm not laying the blame at the feet of Leonard Coleman over in the National League, or Dr. Budig. I'm just saying the system is seriously flawed.

I really get a laugh when some knucklehead in New York says baseball's fines and suspensions are justified because "we don't have that much violence in our game." Have they ever seen one of baseball's bench-clearing brawls when cleats and fists and bats are flying? Have they ever seen twenty guys in a dog pile, fighting, scratching, and trying to poke each other's eyeballs outs? Have they ever seen me pin Lou Piniella to the ground? Have they ever seen one of our thirty-minute free-for-alls when a couple of guys get sent to the hospital? Did they see Juan Marichal crack Johnny Roseboro in the head with a bat? There was blood flying everywhere that day.

For that matter, have they ever seen one of our beanball wars? Do you know how much damage you can inflict with a 95 mph baseball aimed at the batter's chin? Maybe we should drag a few executives out of their New York offices, and a few owners off their yachts, and let them stand at home plate during a beanball war. Talk about reality therapy. I can't think of a better way to finally get the Baseball Lords back in touch with the game they run.

Breaking Me Like a Bronc

THEY SAY THAT BASEBALL is a game of power brokers. And I'm not talking about the kind of powerful stuff that propelled Mark McGwire to fifty-eight dingers during the 1997 season in spite of switching leagues in mid-July and having to wake up every morning wondering where the heck he was.

When I first got into the major leagues in 1977, the umpires, and especially the ones from the American League, were scared to death of the Baseball Lords. We didn't have a strong union, and we got kicked around like a bunch of yard dogs because we didn't stick together. The bosses knew that our union would split like a piece of dry wood if they threatened to send guys back to the minor leagues. So the only way to fight back was to hire a gunslinger lawyer to lead us. While he was interviewing our next union boss, Davey Phillips told Richie Phillips, "We've had leaders who'll point the gun. Now, dammit, we need somebody who'll pull the trigger." Fact of the matter is, we needed a bully to run the union.

To this day, the owners and baseball bosses still get Pepto-Bismol stomachs when they see Richie swaggering into a bargaining room. Some people say that he's a loose cannon but, by gosh, that's what the umpires needed back in 1979 when our collective backbone didn't amount to a couple of herniated disks.

Richie was a man of action when he started leading our

little posse, and job one was breaking our existing contract with management. He'd found a loophole in the collective agreement and decided to draw down on our bosses. Now, the closest I'd ever come to a real union man was when I'd eat lunch down at the Hooks truck stop and one of the Teamster truck drivers would walk by. When Richie started talking strike, I thought he meant the kind that pitchers threw. I didn't know that we were going to come out with guns blazing and try to take back the Alamo in one day. Sure, I knew that the umpires needed to do something drastic to get their attention. But after just two seasons in The Bigs, I was feeling a little empty inside when I walked off the job with my fellow comrades. Still, the most important lesson I'd ever learned in sports was the value of teamwork, whether you're carrying the ball, hitting the ball, shooting the ball, or calling balls and strikes. As I saw it, my loyalty should be to the guys who'd struggled through the horribly lean years without any days off. I'd been umpiring only two full seasons at the big league level, but I already knew that you were dead tired after a 162-game marathon that included just three days off at the All-Star break. I'd already seen how that kind of grind had wrecked home lives and destroyed marriages. I'd never seen a sadder man in my life than Jerry Neudecker on the day he reported back to work after the 1985 All-Star break. He'd been served with divorce papers at his own house, and now he had half a baseball season to think about it.

Thanks to the outdated rules of baseball, I didn't get to attend the high school graduation of my son, Mickey, and the wedding of my daughter, Maria. I practically begged for those days off and was effectively told to sit down and shut up. I didn't even get to go home when Maria was having surgery. Umpires were always asking for days off for graduations and marriages, and they were reminded by Dick Butler just how lucky they were to be in the major leagues.

So here I was, walking away from the game that I loved and the job that I'd dreamed of most of my life. I kept asking myself, "What in the world am I going to tell Mama?" I knew she could handle it okay because my wife, Carolyn, is one of the real troupers. She'd worked long hours and suffered many headaches down at the Red River Army Depot while I was away from home six months straight and pulling down peanuts in the minor leagues. I made $1,800 that first season in the California League, and it didn't get much better my next three years in the minors. Shoot, I was only drawing $15,000 a year as a major league umpire, and I was still selling cars in the off-season. Without Carolyn and her iron will to fight the wars right alongside me, this umpiring thing would have never happened.

On the day we went on strike, the paychecks stopped and the first wave of anxiety washed over us. Management really had us by the short hairs because we only drew our pay during the season. That would soon change, and now we get our paychecks twelve months out of the year. Back then, umpires would put their money in the bank during the season with hopes of riding out the storm during the winter months. So walking off the job was almost like committing financial suicide. Some of the guys who had mortgages and car payments were too broke to pay attention.

With the strike in full swing, about twenty of the umpires were invited to meet at Davey Phillips's house in St. Louis to discuss our strategy and to share some of the pain. I actually had to borrow money from a neighbor in Hooks to get there. How comical to see twenty grown men sleeping on the floor all over the house, not to mention some of the sounds that emanated during the night. We didn't go hungry, though, and I still think about those big breakfasts every morning with eggs and bacon and biscuits and shortcakes. All of that good food did a lot for morale.

On the third morning at Davey's house, the phone rang and big Dutch Rennert, one of our National League brothers, was summoned to the phone. As he said, "Uh-huh," Dutch's face was turning as white as a ghost. When he said, "Oh, my God," I knew that the news wasn't good.

Gathering all of us around the big room in the basement, Dutch tried to speak, but his voice kept breaking. "Boys," he said, "that was my wife on the phone. I'm sure that you guys will be getting calls from home soon. Our bosses have just dropped the hammer on our asses. They've sent telegrams to all of the missuses, informing them that their husbands are no longer employed by Major League Baseball.''

I could see it coming. Right before I left Hooks, I'd gone down to apply for a new driver's license, and I'd worn my umpire's hat for the picture. At least if the strike cost me my job, I wanted my grandchildren to someday know that I'd umpired in the major leagues. As Dutch delivered the bad news, I pulled my driver's license out of my wallet and reflected on my short but sweet life in The Bigs.

Big Bruce Froemming was a tougher-than-nails kind of umpire who's still around after twenty-six major league seasons. When Bruce started crying that morning at Davey's house, I had to battle just to control my emotions. Bruce had spent seventeen brutal years in the minor leagues trying to fulfill his dream, and he had every reason to bawl like a baby. Then Dutch started crying, and I could see a few more tears around the room. All I had to do was close my eyes to see Mama back in Hooks, opening that telegram and breaking into tears.

We didn't need a degree in psychology to tell us what the bosses and the Baseball Lords were up to. They had hammer in hand, and they were pounding the umpires into the woodwork. In a few days, they would send out another telegram to inform the wives that all insurance benefits had been cut off. Furthermore, the games were continuing with a bunch of lowlife scab umpires. The Lords figured that if the fans continued to show up at the ballparks, then to hell with the real umps.

At first, taking on baseball's power brokers was like playing a pair of deuces against a full house. This might seem surprising, but the other side wasn't playing fairly at all. This battle had nothing to do with ethics and everything to do with intimidating tactics.

Before the strike, I was always getting calls from Dick Butler, who'd say, ''Now, Durwood, didn't I do you a big favor by bringing you to the major leagues? How would you like to be back in Oklahoma City, doing a game with the Triple-A scrubs? How'd you like to be eating your lunch at Denny's instead of the best steak houses in New York? Think about that, big boy.'' Actually, I should have told Mr. Butler that I liked Denny's very much and that he still wasn't paying me enough for a big salad in New York City.

Mr. Butler and everybody else at 350 Park Avenue in New York had plenty of cards up their sleeves. They'd call up one of the crew chiefs and say, ''Look, we're thinking about raising the salaries of all the lead guys. If you just wouldn't mind getting all of the guys on your crew to stop talking all of this union crap, we might be able to get that raise to you right away. Whaddaya think?''

For years, American League umpires were known for splitting ranks right at crunch time because baseball bosses were practiced and pretty doggone effective at dealing from the bottom of the deck. Back in 1968, when major league umpires Bill Valentine and Al Salerno were trying to organize the union among the American League umps, league president Joe Cronin got wind that a vote was coming. Valentine was about to umpire a game in Cleveland when a call came to his hotel room from Cronin. ''Go home,'' Joe said. ''You're not a very good umpire.'' A few minutes later, Valentine heard a knock at the door and it was Salerno, who'd been told the same thing by the A.L. boss. Both of those guys were banished from baseball with no notice and no one to back them up.

In 1979, we knew that the owners viewed us as something between a country club caddy and a wash boy. Shoot, when they built County Stadium in Milwaukee thirty years ago, guess what they forgot? The umpires' dressing room.

Guys like Marty Springstead and Nester Shylock, who'd had been busting their backsides for twenty years in the major leagues, were making a top salary of only $50,000 and were getting three days off during the 162-game schedule. If not for the All-Star break, umpires might have been working straight through for six months. If you don't think there's a mental grind, come walk in my shoes for a few games and let the fans and the managers and the players yell at you and call you names and see if you don't feel some stress. Do that for six straight months with no break and you'll wind up on the funny farm. What our bosses were doing to the umpires back in 1979 was pure insanity.

Our per diem that year was $52 for taxis, meals, and hotel rooms. I remember laughing my ass off when Mr. Butler told us one day, "Now, boys, don't be saving your fifty-two bucks with hopes of buying a car." Just how stupid did he think we were?

What the power brokers didn't know was that the umpires were ready for a fight. The deeper they backed us into the corner, the tougher we got. Hiring Richie Phillips was a wise move, even though I don't agree with a lot of his tactics. Richie does some wacky things during bargaining sessions, like breaking coffeepots and throwing chairs through windows. Personally, that's just not my style, and I don't approve when other people do those things. Also, I still don't understand why Richie has to take three limousines to World Series games at the cost of the union.

Richie really is two people. One minute he can be a charmer and the next he's Satan. When it comes to going toe-to-toe with anybody, he's an absolutely fearless man. I really don't think that he ever even heard of the word "surrender." His game is being an intimidator, and he laughs in the face of intimidation. What has impressed me through the years is that there's no phase of baseball he doesn't know when it comes to his men. If it concerns an umpire, you can bet the farmhouse that he's going to be on top of it.

On the flip side, the man can turn colder than a blue norther rolling through Amarillo just after sundown. He's about as aloof as they come. Sometimes I think it would be easier to get ahold of the president of the United States than to get Richie on the phone.

Richie's two favorite words are "F—— 'em." This was never more obvious than during the 1996 play-offs when the Rangers were due to open up in New York against the Yankees. That day, a judge had ruled that the umpires would have to work in spite of our protests over the handling of the Robbie Alomar spitting incident. Even though Robbie had treated John Hirschbeck to a saliva shower on the final weekend of the regular season, he was still ruled eligible for the postseason by American League president Dr. Gene Budig. The umps found the whole scene to be disgusting and we threatened to walk.

So the pitchers had warmed up and the umpiring crew was ready to take the field at Yankee Stadium when Richie put up a human blockade in front of the dressing room door and started telling jokes. We all knew that Richie was stalling because he wanted the Baseball Lords to know that the umpires would come out when he said so. But there's an unwritten law in baseball that once the pitchers are warmed up, the umpires should start the game. You don't want them to warm up again and risk hurting their arm. We were starting to run that risk as Richie continued to blab.

It's hard for a bunch of umpires to say "Richie, get out of our way. We've got to go work this ball game." The game was supposed to start at eight, and at eight-fifteen, Richie was still telling jokes. Five more minutes passed, and a Yankee executive was pounding on the door. Five more minutes passed, and Richie was still telling jokes. Finally, crew chief Jim Evans looked at me very sternly and said, "Dur, lead us out onto the field." I pried open the door and the other umps filed out behind me, and far down the hallway, I could still hear Richie cackling at his own punch line.

The umpires may have thought that Richie was about half crazy, but we followed him in '79 because we knew that loyalty to the cause was the only means to kicking butt. At this point in baseball history, the players were starting to make big bucks, thanks to their union boss, Marvin Miller, and it just seemed that a pissed-off attitude permeated the game. Maybe it went back to Curt Flood fighting the reserve clause or something. But the natives were restless, and the Baseball Lords were about to have a fight on their hands.

Because Richie had done his homework and knew the battleground, he could predict that the scab umps would fail miserably and that the players and managers would beg for the return of the regular umpires. He demanded that we stick together this time and that we fight back. About a month later, the real umpires went back to work with an improved contract and with renewed dignity. I've never seen the players and managers so happy to see us after playing about thirty games with those scab umpires who should have been working games in the Cal League. Thanks to the fact that the umpires finally stood up for their rights in 1979, things changed. Today, the top salary is five times what it was then and our per diem is $230. We get vacations during the season, and I even got to go home for one of my grandsons' eighth-grade graduation. Glory hallelujah.

Now, I know that some people will say that major league umpires don't deserve big bucks and vacations and nights at the Hyatt instead of the Red Roof Inn. But, after all, this is a billion-dollar industry, and I'd imagine that people who officiate the games should be both capable and compensated well. But there is another large reason that umpires are making a generous living these days. It goes back to 1979 when the Baseball Lords showed no compassion for their employees and wouldn't even let us go home for family events. A little more give-and-take and we wouldn't have needed a hired gun named Richie Phillips. From years of frustration was born a union boss that pulled umpiring out of the dark ages. Instead of doing the right thing back in the 1970s, now the owners must deal with a hardhead who breaks things and throws tantrums and cuts doggone good deals for his umpires.

When Ron Luciano retired after the 1979 season and then proclaimed me to be his heir apparent, I knew that I was on the highway to hell with my bosses on Park Avenue. They never could control Ronnie, and they sure as heck didn't want another Luciano cavorting around their ballparks. I really think that all of the frustration they felt for Ronnie through the years was passed along to me. I felt like the poor groom who married the divorcée who was still looking for a place to vent her anger against her ex-husband.

I still couldn't figure how I was going to be the next Luciano when umpiring boss Dick Butler never let me within nine miles of the man and I'd never worked on his crew. How could I be the new Ronnie when I hadn't had the time to study his style?

I guess my first few years in The Big Show must have scared the bejeebers out of the power brokers. My hat was always flying off and most people thought from the get-go that I had Oscar Mayer written all over me. I'm not blaming anybody for my badass attitude and my flamboyance during my early years in the majors, but I did learn from The Master. When it came to throwing backsides out of the game, nobody did it better than my friend Marty Springstead. It's ironic that Marty's been my boss since 1986.

Those early years on Marty's crew, I tossed guys out of games for chewing the wrong brand of tobacco. Marty's theory was if they gave you any trouble, get rid of them. Eventually I became the enforcer of the crew, and I really felt good about sending guys to the showers. Back in the throw-'em-out days, I was also influenced by Davey Phillips, who today is one of the most mild-mannered umps in the game. Davey is often praised for showing the restraint of a nun. But in his younger days, Davey could rage with the best of them, and when he got riled, mister, you'd better run for cover. Davey would take you to the woodshed, and you might not come back.

So here I was in the early years, tossing out Billy Martin and Earl Weaver and getting applauded by my fellow umps. When an argument flared, I always got the final word. I let my hair grow out a little, and I wore nothing but shiny snake-skin boots on the road. The boy from Nowhere, Texas, was starting to get a reputation for having an attitude and I liked it.

At first, Dick Butler would say to me, "Durwood, when you start to learn that you don't have to fight with everybody, you're going to be a good umpire. And when you find out that you don't always have to have the last word, you're really going to be a great umpire.'' Boy did those words sail through the wind tunnel that connected my ears.

While I didn't shoot the runners at first base like Ronnie did, I was developing a style on the field, and I loved to interact with the fans and the sporting press. I loved talking to the people in the seats whenever I got the chance. One night in that tight little bandbox called Fenway Park, I raced over to the third base stands, where Red Sox third baseman Butch Hobson was leaning into the crowd to make a catch. When I threw up my big right fist to signal the batter out, a little ol' lady barked at me, ''If you were my husband, I'd feed you poison!'' I looked at her scrawny husband and said, ''If I were him, I'd take it.''

For years, the National and American League bosses had been putting the hammer down on the umpires for so long— from salaries to per diem to how you walk to what you wear to what you say—that they were starting to worry that we were finally coming out of our shells. They wanted us to be seen and not heard. Well, brother, that was changing fast with Richie Phillips now on the scene. Richie used to tell them, ''You're not going to treat the umpires like a bunch of cretins any more. That baloney is over.''

I've never really thought it was wrong if umpires could entertain just a little bit. Besides, what else happens between pitches, and between innings, other than a bunch of grown men out there scratching and spitting? So what if I lean over the rail and say something funny to a fan or sign an autograph or tell a joke. So what if I walk over to the seats and pitch a baseball to a kid who's probably going to hold on to it until the day he dies. I got this letter dated August 14, 1980, from a fan in New Rochelle, New York: ''Dear Mr. Merrill . . . On Sunday, August 10th, your fortuitous personal actions brought a great deal of happiness not only to a youthful Yankee fan, but to his entire family. My grandson, George Newsome III, was actually speechless when you walked over from first base and placed the baseball in his little glove. He wanted to thank you but explained, as an excited and surprised youngster would, that he didn't have a chance to do so. Witnessing this unsolicited, thoughtful deed on your part and reveling in the joy and delight of my grandson compelled me to extend a personal and very sincere salute of thanks on behalf of George and our family.''

I doubt that Mr. Butler or Dr. Brown ever got a letter like that.

Of course, I'd be lying if I said didn't strut my stuff a little around the ballparks and just about every place, for that matter. I was born with an outgoing personality, so why not use it? On top of that, I'm a big guy and I don't like wimping around and acting like I'm not really there. Many times I told Mr. Butler, ''I'm big, so I have to umpire big.''

But I guess all of my fun-loving antics finally started getting to my bosses, because they started cracking the whip and making me stay in line. They even made me start dressing differently on the road. Back then, I owned nothing but western clothes. I liked to wear my shiny boots and long dusters, and I know that I probably looked like one lost cowboy when I came strolling through LaGuardia Airport. When sportswriters quoted me, they always mentioned my getup and how it made me look like a Wild West gunfighter. One day I got a call from Mr. Butler, who had the gall to tell me that it was time for me to start dressing more like a stockbroker and less like Tom Mix. For six years, my bosses in New York took away the clothes that I really enjoyed wearing. I still don't know how they got away with that in a free country. But even Richie Phillips himself couldn't help me on this dress code issue.

They could take away my boots and jeans and dusters, but they couldn't nix my attitude. I was still battling on the field, and I was sending them down the tunnel and to the showers faster than you could call me John Wayne. So, quite naturally, when the *Sporting News* printed their list of Roughneck Umpires in 1985, my name was right at the top, along with Richie Garcia. At the time, we were leading the league in ejections. Thanks to the Baseball Bible, I got to take another trip to see Mr. Butler the next time I was in New York.

It's a good thing that they don't print the *Sporting News* in hardbound copies because I might have ended up with a pretty big bruise. As soon as I walked through the door, Mr. Butler threw the *Sporting News* and it caught me on the shoulder. I didn't know he had that kind of arm. "I told you, Durwood, that if you kept up this stuff, it was going to catch up with you," he yelled.

I never got suspended or fined or put on probation, and they never cut my pay. But I still feel certain that my free-wheeling attitude kept me out of the World Series in my early years because I know I was grading higher than most of the guys qualifying for the Fall Classic. Not until 1988 did I finally make it to the World Series. But it wasn't Dick Butler who sent me. It was my mentor and former partner Marty Springstead, who'd become the executive director of umpiring in 1986. Marty understood the wild side of me because he'd basically umpired the same way for twenty years before getting the big promotion. Marty recognizes that you've got to step out and have some fun because there are too many umpires who are acting like they're about to go to the electric chair. My bosses used to tell me that I was acting like I was having too much fun, and I told them they were turning baseball into a funeral.

I'm trying not to let anything sour my memories on all of the great years in baseball. And I'll admit that much of the advice that Mr. Butler gave me during those early years turned out to be right. He said that when I learned to relax, and stopped demanding to have the last word, I'd become a better umpire. He was right.

I knew that deep inside, Dick Butler would rather have an umpire with a lot of fire than no backbone at all. You can't always build a fire inside a man who has no spark. He figured that if he could tone down and refine me, he might eventually be able to fit me into his mold.

It is truly amazing how much I've mellowed after more than twenty years in the major leagues. If a team gets on me, I'll just walk over to their dugout, put my arms out, and say, "What the hell is this? Kick Durwood's ass day? Here, start kicking.'' Then they'll laugh about it. In my earlier years, I would say, ''Who wants to be first? Who wants to fight first?'' I think mellowing has helped me be a better umpire. Do I think that Dick Butler was right? In some respects, he knew what he was talking about. Shoot, I had only three and a half ejections during the 1997 season, and I had to share a sack of Mike Hargrove with Davey Phillips. Those numbers should tell you something about the man who once toted the fastest gun in the American League.

Back in the late 1970s, Chicago's Comiskey Park was a place that was serving up more than just baseball. They had a shower in the outfield where fans could wash off, and they had Harry Caray broadcasting some of the day games from the bleachers, and they had an exploding scoreboard and the first real up-tempo music offered by a major league park. Since I'd come from a small town where the center of our social life was the Dairy Queen, I really didn't know much about being hip. But I still appreciated that Bill Veeck was cooking up something fresh.

Bill was a baseball maverick who once sent a midget to the plate. Three-foot-seven Eddie Gaedel pinch-hit for Veeck's St. Louis Browns in 1951, and people are still talking about it. Bill had a peg leg, and you always knew he was coming because you could hear that *thump-thump-thump*. The White Sox owner dressed up his players in softball-type uniforms and even sent them onto the field in shorts a few times.

Bill's thinking turned a little too radical one night when the White Sox decided to sponsor Disco Night at Comiskey Park. For 98 cents and a few disco records, a fan could see the White Sox and the Tigers play a twi-night doubleheader. According to Veeck's promotion, a disc jockey was going to blow up the records between the games.

I knew that we were in trouble when I heard the promotion on the radio that afternoon. Long before the first pitch, I knew we didn't have your typical baseball crowd at Comiskey Park, because instead of families and kids, I saw a bunch of hard rockers with long hair and spacy-looking eyes. I could smell marijuana from the moment I walked onto the field, and wondered if you could get high from secondhand smoke. From the looks of things, I figured ZZ Top was setting up in center field.

I put my hand on the shoulder of umpiring supervisor Nester Shylock and said, "Nester, old buddy, I believe that we're going to have some trouble tonight. Something tells me we won't be playing two."

From the first inning, the White Sox hitters were hammering the Tigers' pitching, and it seemed that Sparky Anderson was out of the dugout every five minutes. I thought they were going to wear that exploding scoreboard out. The crowd continued to grow restless, and you knew they didn't come to see baseball. They were waiting for the show between games when a local DJ was going to blow up all the disco records they'd brought into the stadium. This was going to be a real revolt by the hard rockers against John Travolta and all that fresh disco stuff that'd been playing on the radio for years.

By the seventh inning, the inmates were throwing their records onto the field. I'm sure it must have seemed like fun because those records traveled like Frisbees and would float on the air from the baselines far into the outfield. Pretty soon I found myself dodging vinyl projectiles and paying more attention to the stands than to a ball game that had also gotten way out of hand. In the eighth inning, Sparky came out to the mound, and from my post at first base, I could tell he was getting agitated. My job was to signal the Tigers bullpen for the next pitcher Sparky was willing to sacrifice. "Hey, Durwood!" he shouted. "Think you might get me another pitcher out here?" I shook my head and said, "Sorry, Sparky. I guess I'm worrying more about saving my life than your pitcher."

Thank God the first game finally ended so we could run for cover underneath the grandstands. About the time the umpires and players made their exit, the fans started coming over the rails. They were running toward center field where the DJ was set up, and pretty soon the whole scene looked like a jailbreak. Bill Veeck's so-called fans were smoking dope and pulling up chunks of grass and threatening the DJ with his life if he didn't hurry up and blow up more records. I stood in the corner of the dugout and watched as battles broke out on the floor of Comiskey Park.

Naturally, the umpires did the logical thing. We holed up in the umpires' room and locked the door until we heard a heavy pounding about the time the second game was scheduled to start. Nester opened the door to find Veeck out of breath and looking like he'd been inhaling thick clouds of pot. The man had crazy eyes and some even crazier ideas. Veeck started stomping around the room with that peg leg, looking like a besieged Captain Hook when he blurted, "You guys have got to get out there so we can start the next game. You can't just sit in here on your butts when we have a baseball game to be played!"

Nester then tried to explain the rules of baseball to Captain Veeck. "First of all, we can't do anything to endanger the safety of the ballplayers," Nester said. "Second, I can't do anything to endanger the safety of the umpires."

"F—— the safety of the umpires," Veeck bellowed. "I've got fifty thousand people out there who want to see baseball!"

I enjoyed a good hearty laugh, and Veeck's face turned crimson red.

"Look," I said. "I've got a wife and kids back in Texas. And I'm not going to risk my life with those crazies who've commandeered your damn stadium."

Veeck's behavior turned from wacky to bizarre.

"To hell with your wife and kids," he muttered.

That sealed it for the captain. After that remark, there was no hope that the umpires would even consider walking back onto the field that night.

Nester pointed to the door. "Those are your people, Bill. Now go get them off the field."

Bill had a three-part game plan to get the fans back into the stands. First, they would play the national anthem with hopes there were some patriotic people among the twenty thousand nuts lying on the outfield grass. When that failed, he grabbed the microphone and headed for the pitching mound, where he pleaded with the fans to disperse. "Get off the field, you old man," they yelled back. Then he went to his only real ace in the hole, Harry Caray. Harry had developed a cult following in Chicago, and even the longhairs thought he was pretty cool for an older guy. Harry liked to sing and drink beer, and just like the rockers, he was a free spirit. So Bill thought his fans would relate to Harry when he walked to the pitcher's mound and, with microphone in hand, started asking for the rioters to return to their seats.

"Hey, everybody, how about getting off the field?" Harry said. He even sang a few verses of "Take Me Out to the Ball Game" and that didn't work. By now the rowdies were tearing up the turf and throwing records in all directions. The real baseball fans had run for cover and were pledging never to come back to Comiskey Park.

Veeck returned to the umpires' room, and since his game plan had failed so miserably, he was far more humble this time around. He called American League president Lee MacPhail in New York. Veeck was told to give up any hope and to call off the second game.

In all of my years in baseball, I don't think I'd ever seen a more mentally beaten man than Bill Veeck. He sat in the corner of the umpires' room and buried his face in his hands for several minutes. Until Disco Night had blown up in his face, the other owners were really starting to pay attention to the sizzle he was serving at Comiskey Park. Now the very future of his franchise was in jeopardy, and it would take years for the real baseball fans to come back.

Being the curious person that I am, I sneaked back down the tunnel and took a seat in a dark corner of the dugout. I wanted to see just what the crazies were going to do next. Thousands and thousands had just taken seats on the outfield grass, and some of them were chanting, "Hell, no, we won't go." A cloud of smoke wafted above the stadium, and I wished for a gas mask. They were digging up home plate, and another couple of so-called fans were peeling the rubber off the mound. I could see that Harry and Captain Peg Leg were really respected around this place.

I knew that it was going to take one helluva effort by the Chicago cops to get these people out of the stadium. But, after all, they got some pretty good practice with these kinds of gatherings during the 1968 Democratic National Convention.

About eleven o'clock, the large gates in center field swung open, and I knew it was show time. The riot cops on horseback started riding through the outfield fence. They were toting clubs the size of baseball bats, along with their shields and their guns. The horsemen were followed by the foot soldiers who were dressed in full riot gear. They had massive German shepherds on leashes. The last thing that Bill Veeck needed that night was to have cops busting heads and dogs chewing on the paying customers, but that's what it had come to. Most of the folks who had commandeered the stadium ran like the devil when they saw the cops on horseback. It was really starting to look like a war zone out there.

I'd never experienced anything like it in my life. I remember sitting there thinking, My whole life I've dreamed of stepping onto a major league field. And look what happens. My third year in The Bigs and the nuts are running the place. I just wish some of the Baseball Lords and my bosses could have been sitting there with me that fateful night in Chicago. They would have seen that my job isn't as easy as they think. Dealing with the great unwashed every night wasn't all it was cracked up to be. For a while, baseball wasn't the same on the South Side of Chicago, and much time would pass before I would begin to view our national pastime with the same reverence. I'm just glad that I wasn't walking in Bill Veeck's shoes—I mean, shoe.

If I Were the Commish

SOME PEOPLE SAY THAT our interim commissioner for life Bud Selig is a little wooden, and at times, I've considered him full-blown plastic. Check the guy out during a TV interview. He looks like he's in terrible pain, and you'd hardly say he's the Great Communicator like Peter Ueberroth. Because Bud is an owner, you always expected his decisions to favor the owners.

Then came Bud the Bulldog when he started leading his grand crusade to reconfigure baseball. We heard more than just a bark, and for a while, we actually saw some action. Here was a man with a plan on the table and an eye on the future. I saw a chiropractor at work, cracking joints and trying to give baseball's backbone a realignment.

At one point, Bud had a grand scheme whereby fifteen teams would switch leagues with hopes that baseball finally would have all of the natural rivalries that we'd been dreaming of—Mets versus Yankees, Cubs versus White Sox, Royals versus Cardinals, Rangers versus Astros. But when it came to vote-getting time, the owners managed to water it all down to a point where realignment was really just a rubdown.

I know that Bud and the boys failed in their dreamscape, and that's too bad because baseball really needed an overhaul, an oil change, a lube job, and a new attitude about doing business. For years, we've needed to chuck all of the traditionalists and the purists in favor of leaders with an eye set on the twenty-first century. We're finally making some progress, but you've got to wonder how much longer we'll have to wait before baseball is no longer just a dead game walking.

I still think that the biggest problem with baseball are the people with their eyes in the back of their heads. For those who think that baseball shouldn't change, I give you the TV ratings and the overall decline in interest. I give you the NFL boom and the NBA explosion and that whooshing sound of wind generated by the other leagues as they've blown the doors off baseball the last two decades. I give you that musty old smell that still emanates from our game. I give you Bud Selig before he finally woke up and smelled disaster.

What gives me hope, though, is that at least we have an interim commissioner who's willing to stick his neck out for the game. The last time something like this happened, then commissioner Fay Vincent got his head lopped off by the National League owners back in 1992. Raise a toast for Bud for overcoming his wimpy self and at least trying to do something good for baseball, even though only one team changed leagues after the 1997 season.

Oh, I guess we'll always remember Bud Selig as the man who stood before the microphones and the cameras back on September 14, 1994, and announced that the World Series was off. Bud still gets blamed for facilitating the 232-day players' strike, and rightfully so. In the absence of a real commissioner, he was willing to become the pump station that fueled the gasoline fire between players and management. Even if Bud really does become full-time commissioner, and even if he straightens out baseball, I'm always going to have trouble watching his painful press conferences.

I'll say, though, that I almost gave the man a standing ovation when he said he wasn't going to rest until realignment was done. I got even happier when I realized we might be closing in on the death of the designated hitter. When American League president Joe Cronin introduced the designated hitter to baseball in 1973, he called it "an experiment." The idea was to see how many runs and how much excitement the A.L. could generate by taking the bat away from the weak-hitting pitcher and putting it in the hands of an over-the-hill slugger whose fielding skills were comparable to those of a dead fish. Even though the DH went against every principle in baseball, our leaders were willing to try anything in the '70s, when it seemed the whole world was experimenting with something. Problem is that twenty-five years later, we're still suffering from Joe Cronin's grand experiment.

You've still got to wonder how the DH has hung tough all of these years when you've got so many purists banging on their beat-up drums. Let me give you one big reason that's spelled U-N-I-O-N. Seems the union boys don't want the DH to go away because on the average he's hitting between twenty-five and thirty home runs and making $4 million a year. The removal of the DH would mean a sudden deflation of the average team salary in our league. Union boys don't like to see that.

Owners have proposed that, in doing away with the DH, they would add a twenty-sixth player to the roster. We all know, however, that roster spot would be assumed by some kid making $200,000 a year. The union wants nothing to do with another utility infielder who'll never make it to his arbitration year.

I have no use for the DH because it's a gimmick way past its time. Not only does the DH take strategy out of baseball, it lengthens the A.L. game and makes it a lot more unwieldy. Over in the National League, where the games are shorter, I hear they've actually got some players who can still bunt. The last time an American Leaguer bunted successfully, Jimmy Carter was still in the White House. No wonder manager Tony LaRussa wanted to get to the No-DH League where he could exercise some strategy and strut some of his cerebral stuff. The use of the DH not only cuts out the bunt, it does away with double switches and a few other strategical maneuvers.

There's yet another reason for eliminating the DH that makes way too much sense. By making the pitcher hit, you virtually eliminate the beanball wars. Make a pitcher grab some lumber and stand in the batter's box and he'll stop plunking the other team's players. Once he becomes the object of retaliaton, he'll wise up. Pitchers, like most players, don't like to get bruised. Now, I'm not saying that pitchers are the smartest people in the world. But they're still bright enough to figure this one out.

When I think about all of the problems of baseball, I like to quote one of baseball's great quipsters, Bob Lemon, the former pitcher and manager. I guess he needed a sense of humor and a calm mind to work for George Steinbrenner all those years. Bob liked to say that baseball is a kid's game that grown-ups have screwed up.

For years and years and years, baseball hasn't been sold properly. I've seen watermelon seed–spitting contests in East Texas that were marketed better. The Baseball Lords have believed for decades that they could open the gates and the fans would come. They had their heads stuck in an Iowa cornfield, still believing *Field of Dreams* was still playing at local movie houses.

Since I came into the major leagues in 1977, owners have been madly grabbing for quick fixes, using Band-Aids when they've needed tourniquets. Back in the '70s, when The Show started going bad, they started giving away things at the gates like balls and bats. They thought that if they threw umbrellas and wristwatches at the fans, they'd keep coming. They had Farm Night when players got to milk cows and throw eggs at each other. They even had that stupid Disco Night in Chicago when fifty thousand drug-crazed fans showed up and almost burned down Comiskey Park.

Yes, I know that some of those promotions worked. Then the fans started throwing their souvenir baseballs back onto the field, which proved that you can lead a fan to the ballpark, but you can't make him behave.

Our owners, our presidents, and our interim commissioner for life need to realize that the greatest marketing tool is a player himself. Those players need to get off their butts and start signing autographs. They need to get out there to the stands an hour before the game begins and sign those baseballs, caps, and little slips of paper. Those players need to meet the kids and their parents, and they need to perform community service. Do you know what the fan in the stands thinks of the player on the field? They think the players are cold and distant and, in some cases, faceless. Fans are saying to themselves, "Who are these guys?" They really don't know the players anymore. That's why so many fans long for the old days and players like Mickey Mantle and Ted Williams and Joe DiMaggio and Yogi Berra and Stan Musial.

Players these days can be as aloof as a cat after a big lunch. You almost have to give blood these days just to get an autograph. You have to get in your car and drive down to the local Kmart on a Saturday afternoon when a couple of obscure utility fielders are signing from noon until two. Or you must peruse the sports section to find out that three ex-players are signing autographs for a couple of hours at the local convention hall. All you need is fifty bucks to get you and the kid through the front door.

No. No. No. Baseball stars should be signing between batting practice and the first pitch, when the real fans are in the ballpark. Every team could alternate their players every day, but you need to make darn sure that at least five or six of them will be there every night. The kids need to reach out and touch the players once again.

Late in the 1997 season, the Texas Rangers asked me to come tell a few banquet stories at their monthly luncheon. Of course, I obliged for a free meal and a pittance. I ate my lunch at the same table with catcher Pudge Rodriguez and pitcher Darren Oliver and a few other players. On the banquet circuit, I always love to speak right after players because they're always talking about "Me, me, me." They tell the audience about their great stats and the fabulous season they're about to have. Then I get up, tell the crowd that I had a flat tire on the way to the luncheon, and I zap them with funny stories. I blow those ballplayers right off the stage.

As the key speaker, I followed the players that day and I had the place roaring. Then I walked over to a side table, and as the four hundred or so fans filed out, I signed autographs. After a few autographs, I looked around and said, "Where are the players?"

Those guys who'd showed up in their suits and ties for their "appearance" were long gone. So the fans had to stand in line to get an autograph from a real umpire instead of their real heroes. Boy, does baseball know how to screw up a good thing.

The first thing I would do as commissioner is to call a meeting. It wouldn't be just the owners in that room. It would be the general managers and the promotions people and the marketing people and the public relations people and the community service people. First, we would see if we could do more family-oriented things. We would plan more Little League Nights, and I'm not talking about bringing the teams to the park and having them sit in the nosebleed section. I'm talking about good seats down by the baselines where the kids can actually see the game. I can't tell you how many times I've walked onto the field for Little League Night and the Little Leaguers were so far way I could barely see them. We need to give them better seats so they can at least yell at the umpires.

A few years ago, the baseball geniuses came up with a nifty little promotion for youngsters who attended the games. They decided to let the kiddos go out on the field so they could run the bases right after the game. Only one problem with this game plan. The players would be long gone, so the kids would be out there running the bases by themselves. Why not let them run the bases before the game while they players were still around?

After getting our promotions squared away, I'd take a cab over to the NBA office in New York and knock on commissioner David Stern's door. He seems like a bright guy, and I know he had a lot to do with the revival of a game that was drowning back in the '70s. There was a time when the NBA was on its back and gasping for air, and then along came Larry Bird and Magic Johnson, and ever since, they've been kicking our butts at the box office and in TV ratings.

Here is my question: Why can't baseball do the same thing with superstars like Junior Griffey and Larry Walker that basketball did with Bird and Magic? If you've ever been around Walker and Griffey, you know they're two of the nicest and most engaging people you could ever meet. But I think those guys get more real exposure from their TV commercials than they do from playing the game. If not for those creative Nike ads, there's no way that Junior Griffey would be the superstar he is today.

Another marketing mystery about baseball: Why did it take the Baseball Lords fifty years to finally realize the impact Jackie Robinson had on the game? Jackie Robinson was a star from the moment he stepped onto the field. It took baseball half a century to retire his number and sing his praises.

People ask me all the time if I'm a purist-traditionalist or somebody who believes in change for the sake of it. Since I'm conservative in nature, and I'm a hick from the sticks in Texas, I would naturally gravitate to the side of the traditionalists. But not this time. This is going to sound radical coming from an ol' boy from East Texas. But baseball needs a revolution. Now.

The game is going to have to act fast and move forward if it's to survive, much less succeed, in the next century. That's why I'm so worried about the men who are leading baseball and their unwillingness to move off dead center. They need to take a long look at football and basketball to see how they're recruiting new fans and making sure the young ones aren't turned off by the stale air. I don't know much about MTV or the Internet or the video games that kids are playing these days. I do know, though, that my grandkids like some of that stuff, and believe me, my friend, they *are* the future of baseball.

There are just too many people who believe we shouldn't

be tinkering with baseball because somehow, they say, we'll kill the goose that laid the stupid egg. These are the same people who would have the players back in wool uniforms and the umpires back in coats and ties.

Like a lot of fans, I think the game has hardened me through the years. This doesn't mean that I'm not proud of my profession. I'm proud of what I do and of the accomplishments of the players, umps, and everyone who steps on the field. But I certainly don't understand the business side of baseball, and it's frustrating to watch our leaders at work. Because I see the game on a day-to-day basis from such an up-close perspective, that frustration often eats me up.

I really don't understand why the game of baseball—a billion-dollar industry—has decided to sail on a rudderless ship. The Lords of baseball have decided they don't want a full-time commissioner. So what happens? Bud Selig becomes the acting commissioner for life.

Think about the changes we've seen in the game over the last twenty years and maybe some of my points will come into focus. They used to say that it was taboo for players to even pick up a weight because it might destroy a hitter's natural swing. That thinking went out the window with forty-two–ounce bats. Today, players are pumping iron and putting stuff in their bodies they wouldn't have thought about using forty years ago. And I'm not talking about Scotch, bourbon, and vodka. When the games are over, the players don't head for the bars anymore. They head for the weight room.

Television has changed the game so much that it's almost impossible to tell when the games are going to start. But we've been willing to flow with those changes because it's meant more money in the owners' coffers. If baseball is willing to make those changes, it should be willing to destroy the lines between American League and National League and make the game more adaptable to the twenty-first century. It's time to wake up and smell the horse manure.

If we could break up the American and National Leagues, it would give the small market teams a better chance to compete because they're going to have better rivalries and more interesting games. The TV revenues would be higher because the game would sell better. If we regionalize the rivalries, your favorite team won't be playing two time zones away. You won't have to sit up until midnight to see the end of a game. Of course, I guess this makes too much sense.

I think the interleague play was a success, and you certainly could feel the excitement in the air for the first-round games. But, at the same time, I really believe that interleague play is just a Band-Aid for solving the problems right now. It's not the cure-all.

I firmly believe that one of the greatest problems in baseball is keeping the fan in touch with the game, in spite of the ka-zillions that are being thrown around in baseball. How does an ol' boy working a blowtorch for a living identify with a player who'll easily make more money in one game that he'll make that year? The high costs of baseball have been passed down the money chain to the fans. Since 1991, baseball's average ticket price has risen 39 percent. Part of the reason is that the owners have been trying to recoup the estimated $850 million in operating losses during the eight-month strike. So instead of taking the financial hit themselves, they pass it along to Joe Fan.

How do you expect the fans to relate to baseball when we don't even stage a World Series in 1994? I'll never understand how baseball survived World War I, the Great Depression, World War II, the Korean War, and the Vietnam War without ever missing a World Series. And then 1994 comes along and, *ka-boom*, the players walk out on August 12. No wonder the fans stayed away from baseball in droves the next season. All you had to do was listen to talk radio to feel the fans' rage.

If I were commissioner, one of my first jobs would be to speed up the game. My good buddy Steve Palermo was hired by Major League Baseball to make some suggestions on quickening the pace of the game. He had several great ideas, like keeping the batter in the box during his entire at-bat. He suggested that we eliminate the act of throwing four silly balls for an intentional walk. Just tell the umpire that it's an automatic walk and send the batter to first base. I think the pitching coach or the manager should be allowed only one or two trips to the mound per *game*. Most of the pitching changes can be made from the dugout. The manager doesn't need to saunter out to the mound and then stand there scratching himself on national television before deciding to go with the left-hander.

All of Palermo's ideas were great. But you know what the Baseball Lords did with Stevie's blueprint? They just kicked it over in the corner and forgot about it. What a pitiful waste.

Those boys over in the National League would be in big trouble if I were ever elected commissioner of baseball. At my first press conference, I'd tell the National League to sit down, shut up, and stop acting so doggone uppity. National League arrogance has no bounds, and I think we found that out in the first year of interleague play. It was enough to make you want to dip snuff.

Wally Joyner had ten outstanding seasons in the American League before moving to the Padres in 1996. Somehow, though, he's still stereotyped as an American Leaguer, which, I guess, is a dirty rotten name. Last season, Wally got called out on strikes by N.L. umpire Bob Davidson and Wally felt like arguing. Davidson, who's been around since 1983 hollered, "Get that weak American League s—— out of here." Wally had every right to get tossed out of the game over that one. Before it was over, Davidson had to throw out Padres manager Bruce Bochy. It just goes to show the condescending attitude over in the National League.

Thanks to the radical realignment debate, I think a lot of stomachs were turning over in the National League at the thought of becoming an American Leaguer. Truth is, the National League is not a cut above the American League, and it's really just a case of them being overhyped by their public relations people. I call it propaganda. The National League walks around with its nose in the air, and sometimes it makes me sick.

I've had baseball owners tell me that the National League's pompous attitude spills over into their meetings. The National League Lords try to dominate the meetings because they feel superior to the A.L. boys. The National League, because they were the first in existence, wants to treat us like a bunch of juniors and that's not right. How can you call us the Junior Circuit when we've been around for 97 years? Shoot, they've only been around for 123 years. That's like saying that a ninety-seven-year-old man is a pup compared to his one-hundred-and-twenty-three-year-old neighbor.

I'm tired of the National League acting like the blue bloods. There are times when I really think the N.L. umpires consider themselves better than us. Well, they're dead wrong, brother. I think the N.L. umpires of the day got their pompous attitude from old-timers like Al Barlick, who went into Cooperstown in 1989. There was a another guy named August Donattelli, who was in the league from 1950 to 1973 and thought he was the greatest ump to ever walk the face of the earth. He wasn't.

The National League umpires through the years have told their young umps to act superior to us. In our union meetings, there are certain umpires who act uppity. I really think that the National League teams were shocked during interleague play at just how good the American League umpires are. The ballplayers from the National League would say, "Boy, we've never been able to talk to the umpires before. We really enjoy talking to you guys."

I know this is a tough subject to broach, and I don't mean to put down the umpires from the National League. But I think that we all need to get our attitudes on the same page. After all, we are just umpires.

As far as the players go, I think that the National League proved during interleague play that they have better pitchers, but that's about all. I still think we have better sluggers and better infielders than they do. As a matter of fact, as I go back in time and name players like Ted Williams, Mickey Mantle, Ty Cobb, Cy Young, Joe DiMaggio, Babe Ruth, and

Lou Gehrig, I can think of only two words—American League. When I think of the great dynasty in the history of baseball, I think of the New York Yankees, another team from the Junior Circuit. Sure, the National League got the first black players in the '50s and they had a pretty good run in the '60s. But that's about all they're really known for.

About the only thing the N.L. has going for it is that its games are shorter. Granted, on the average, their games run about five or six minutes under ours. But they do play a lot of games thirty to forty-five minutes faster, and they are the quicker-paced league. Of course, any league could play faster games if you didn't have the DH and all the pitching changes we have in our league. You look at the American League games, and you'll see scores like 11–9, 9–8 and 7–6. Look at the National League and you'll see 4–3, 5–1, and 2–1.

We were getting ready for a game in Baltimore one afternoon, and the umpiring crew was standing at home plate when Orioles manager Davey Johnson walked up. Davey knows a lot about both leagues. He managed for seven National League seasons with the Mets and played for the Braves, Phillies, and Cubs. Davey looked at me and Davey Phillips, Rocky Roe, and Dale Scott and said, "You guys are getting screwed. You ought to be getting double the pay the umpires over there are making. You work longer games, you see mores runs, and your job is just a helluva lot tougher." Needless to say, we all agreed.

Anaheim manager Terry Collins, who managed the Houston Astros for three seasons, echoed some of Davey's thoughts. He said, "Those umps in the National League are calling strikes way off the plate. As a matter of fact, they call pitches off the plate that have no business being strikes. You guys are a lot better." Again, we totally agreed.

One of the toughest decisions you'd ever face as commissioner of baseball would involve the eligibility status of Pete Rose. You've got to love a guy they called Charlie Hustle, and I thought his approach to the game as a player was unmatched. But I hold one lasting memory of Pete and it's not a pretty one.

It was spring training of 1988, and the the Reds and the Tigers were scheduled to play that afternoon in Lakeland, Florida. Rocky Roe and I were sitting just outside our little umps' dressing room, enjoying the sunshine and waiting for the game to start.

I noticed a ten-year-old boy and his father standing near the players' entrance, waiting for the Reds bus to arrive from Plant City. The little boy was holding a Post Toasties box that had Pete Rose's picture on it. Rose, then the Reds' manager, came bouncing off the bus just as you would expect him to. The boy ran up to Pete and said, "Mr. Rose, Mr. Rose, will you please sign my cereal box?" Pete grabbed the box and heaved it into the air. Needless to say, the kid didn't get his autograph. I watched as the father tried to compose his crying child, and then I picked up the cereal box and headed into the Reds clubhouse. I walked right up to Pete and said, "Hey, how about an autograph?" Pete looked at me, winked, and said, "Hey, Durwood, are you working our game today?" He signed the box and gave it back to me, and I didn't mention what I'd seen outside the clubhouse. But Pete seemed uneasy about the whole thing, and he probably knew I saw his stupid little stunt.

I gave the boy his cereal box with Pete Rose's autograph right across his Reds uniform. He smiled and thanked me. But I'm sure that Pete Rose didn't mean that much to him anymore. Pete probably lost a pretty big fan that day. I know that he lost a big fan in me a long time ago.

It will be a sad day for me and, I think, a sad one for baseball, if Pete is ever reinstated and elected to the Hall of Fame. He was suspended for gambling on sports on August 24, 1989, by commissioner Bart Giamatti. Pete agreed to a settlement with the commissioner, and according to their pact, Pete would walk away from managing the Reds if he could apply for reinstatement in one year. The commissioner agreed not to release formal findings from his gambling investigation on Pete. We will never know how Giamatti felt about the prospects of bringing him back. The commissioner died a week after the suspension.

Before he died, though, Giamatti told the media it was his opinion that Rose did bet on baseball. Rose had ample opportunities to deny it at the time. He didn't. As Johnny Bench said back then, "If Pete hasn't bet on baseball, then why doesn't he just come out and admit it?" I wondered the same thing. If Pete had nothing to hide, he should have been singing his story to the media every day of the week.

Investigators hired by the commissioner's office uncovered plenty of dirt on Pete. They found betting slips belonging to him and estimated he was betting up to $2,000 per game while managing the Reds. Allegations still persist that Pete bet on the Reds while their manager from 1985 to 1989. We're not talking about somebody betting a couple of hundred bucks every so often for recreational purposes. We're talking about somebody with a chronic habit.

It's hard for me to understand how a man like Pete Rose could have gotten that immersed in betting. Pete had the world by the tail, and he had talent and fame and riches and the respect of the community. For more than thirty years, his name was synonomous with baseball. He broke Ty Cobb's hit record. He had a forty-four–game hit streak. He broke twelve major league records and won three National League batting crowns. He was such a public figure that when he got kicked out of baseball, the news conference was carried on live television from coast to coast.

Pete has applied for reinstatement, and I really hope that he's denied. You see, he doesn't deserve to wear a major league uniform again, and he certainly doesn't belong in Cooperstown. Pete stained his integrity by betting on the very sport that he was intimately involved in. Managers and major league players shouldn't be betting on baseball. It's not right to gamble on something when you are capable of directly affecting the outcome. That just flies in the face of the public trust.

Now, I know that I'm pretty conservative when it comes to something like gambling. I've never been to a Las Vegas casino. I don't frequent horse tracks. When I hear young kids quoting betting odds straight out of a newspaper, I get worried.

If Shoeless Joe Jackson can't get into Cooperstown, I find it hard to make a case for Pete Rose. Shoeless Joe admitted to a grand jury in Chicago that he accepted $5,000 from gamblers to consort in fixing the 1919 World Series. But there was no evidence that he actually helped throw a game. He batted .375, broke the World Series record with twelve hits, and didn't commit an error. Joe, like the other seven White Sox who were banned from baseball, was not prosecuted. But even though he was one of the greatest players in the history of the game, you'll never see his name in Cooperstown.

I've studied the case of the White Sox betting scandal. And there's one important element of the story you must understand before you publicly condemn the "Eight Men Out." They were getting screwed financially by the owner, Charles Comiskey. He paid the players peanuts while he stuffed his own bank account and lived the high life. Joe and the other boys deserved better salaries. If Joe can't go to the Hall of Fame, then neither should Pete.

Given our lack of leadership in baseball, I'm sure the day will come when Pete Rose again wears a major league uniform and, perhaps, manages once more. I'm sure the day will come when he'll make his triumphant speech from the steps of the Hall of Fame. And I also feel certain that baseball will continue to bumble along into the twenty-first century without direction or purpose. The purists will probably continue to get their way. What will I say when all of this happens? Nobody asked me.

My Calling

NIGHT HAD FALLEN ON CHRISTMAS EVE,
and I knew there was some rough sledding ahead. From the
north, I could see the low clouds sweeping across the Red
River like black angus herding across the sky. Sleet was
bouncing off the hood of my pickup, and I knew that if I
didn't get out of the river bottoms soon, I was going to end
up spending Christmas morning with icicles hanging from
my earlobes.

I was mentally and physically drained, and I was about
half lost as the truck rolled along the dirt road that angled
toward the river. It had been a hellish four weeks, gearing
up for the Hooks Christmas charity that would mean toys
and food for families that otherwise would have little or
nothing. The last few days before Christmas are always the
panicky ones because you suddenly realize you're short on
bicycles or turkeys or candy or dolls. And the thought
smacks you upside the head that some needy family is going
to get zero for Christmas. A poor little boy with holes in his
shoes once told me, "Christmas don't mean nothing to me
because I know I'm getting nothing." Since that day, I've
been working like the devil trying to make sure that everybody gets something.

I'd been down this old dirt road many times before. Shoot,
I've lived in this part of East Texas for more than forty years,
and I know every back road and shortcut through every farm
and hunting ground from Texas to Oklahoma to Arkansas to

Louisiana. How I'd become so disoriented on this night, I'm not sure. I guess I was just stressing out over Christmas plans for about sixty families.

Since 1979, when I found a family nearly starving to death in the river bottoms, I've been a man chasing the impossible dream. Folks from my hometown will tell you that I've been obsessing over this Christmas thing for almost two decades, and I get downright dingy around the holidays. But the Good Lord gave me a fine army of volunteers, and they have a good amount of common sense about them. They know when ol' Durwood's gears are slipping and when to steer me out of the ditch.

The deeper I traveled into the river bottoms, the darker the night became. Ice marbles were now rattling the truck's rooftop like rocks on a tin plate. We'd been warned about the ice storm that was slicing down from the north, and everybody but me had gotten back to town before winter blew its frosty breath across Texas. I could hear the truck's tires churning up the ice cubes and the crazy flapping of the windshield wipers as they labored against the gnarly little projectiles. This voice in my head kept saying, "Turn back. Turn back, you big dummy." But I swear it seemed the truck was pulling me along toward something or somebody just over the next hill. My eyes were welded to the road and I could feel a strange gravity at work.

Through the flickering headlamps, a figure appeared about a hundred feet in front of the truck and I swore it was a ghost. Goose bumps started springing up all over my skin. Mama had warned me that this was going to happen; that the eighteen-hour days of working for the Christmas needy would finally drive me over the madman's cliff. I'd been working too many frantic hours and toting too much emotional baggage. If some kid or some family got left out, it would stick in my craw until the next Christmas.

The ghost was now waving. I rolled down my window and said a little prayer that I hadn't wandered into the land of Looney Tunes. Then I saw the woman standing in the middle of the road with ice balls dancing around her ankles, and I felt my heart sinking into my shoes. My worst night-mare hadn't come in the midst of some restless night as I fretted over the final details of the Christmas charity. It was happening right then and there. You see, my truck, which had been filled with turkeys and bikes and skates and toy soldiers, was now empty with the exception of a few small boxes on the passenger seat. I'd been delivering the goods for hours to houses along the river bottoms, and now I'd come up one family short.

"Do you have anything at all left?" the woman said. She had three small children standing around her waist, and they were shivering in the cold night. My mind's eye photographed their faces because these were the people I'd really come to help. To define our Christmas mission in Hooks was to look into those eyes.

My mouth had gone dusty dry as I said, "Ma'am, all I have are these boxes of Jell-O. I'm so very sorry. I ran out of stuff a few houses back. Believe me ma'am, this wasn't supposed to be." As I handed her the Jell-O boxes, the children began to stir. "Oh, Mama, you mean we can have Jell-O tonight!" one of them said in glee. "This is great."

As I turned the truck around and headed back into town, I started to cry again. The Hooks volunteers often say to each other at Christmas time, "It's okay to cry. You're supposed to cry. If we didn't cry, we wouldn't have the emotional energy to get through this."

The next morning, I loaded up the pickup with toys, candy, and food, and I headed back down that road to find that family that had been left out on Christmas Eve. I wanted to see in the daylight the faces of those children who'd been so happy to have the simple pleasure of Jell-O.

Hooks is a fine little town of about four thousand people that is tucked into the right corner pocket of Texas. All around us are the state lines of Oklahoma, Arkansas, and Louisiana. Warren Hooks used to transport cotton on paddlewheel boats along the Red River when it was flowing and passable back in the mid-1800s. Those boats would head east before turning south through Louisiana. Near Simmesport, the Red River hooked into the Mississippi River en route to New Orleans.

A lot of people know us as a truck-stop town along Interstate 30 halfway between Dallas and Little Rock. But we're far more complex and confusing than that. Even though I've lived in Hooks since 1961, I have trouble describing the place to folks who've never been there. It'd be better if you'd just stop by some time, and I'll drive you around town in my pickup. Maybe we'll stop off at Jimmy D.'s for a chicken-fried steak lunch, the best you'll ever have.

There's been a bit of controversy around town since I started promoting the Hooks Christian Service back in the early 1980s. We're a year-round fund-raising group that sponsors the Christmas charity and helps send several needy kids to college. One of my jobs for several years has been to promote the charity on radio talk shows all over the country. ESPN ran a long feature on efforts back in 1992. We were the lead feature in the Christmas issue of the *Sporting News* in 1996. In fact, newspapers all over the country have run stories for years about all the hard work we do for our needy families. Jerome Holtzman writes something about us almost every year in the *Chicago Tribune*. The result of all of this free publicity has been thousands and thousands of dollars in charitable contributions from Maine to Los Angeles.

In Hooks, especially around the river bottoms, we have a lot of dirt-poor people who need a helping hand. As my good friend and popular Dallas talk-show host Norm Hitzges says, "Hooks has people so poor that even the government doesn't know about them."

True. We have people living in shacks and shanties with boarded-up windows and busted-out floors. We have people who heat their homes and cook their food with wood-burning stoves. We have people who've never dreamed of such luxuries as electricity or gas. It's that bad.

On the flip side, we've got a lot of successful citizens

who live in fine brick homes and drive around in brand-new trucks. A few blocks from a row of shanties you'll find a brand-spanking-new subdivision complete with cul-de-sacs, weed-whacked yards, and sprinkler systems. At one of our Friday night football games, you'll see a shiny muscled-up Chevy truck with an extended cab and CD player parked next to a '63 Ford Fairlane.

Now, I know I get my nose in a snit when I hear people around Hooks say to me, "Durwood, you paint too bleak of a picture of us." I had one of our town mayors walk up to me once and say, "Durwood, you've got everybody in the country believing that we're nothing but shacks." The people saying these things are the ones who aren't helping me. They don't want to come with me down in the river bottoms because they don't want to see it. They would rather have their heads buried in the sand. Besides, I've never said that Hooks is the ghetto, and I've never bad-mouthed the good hard-working people of the community. Hooks is full of real salt-of-the-earth types, but my little town also has its share of uppity people who don't know about the hardships of others because they've never even taken the time to drive to the wrong side of town.

Of course, I know there are places in this country where there is worse poverty. I've been in places in New York and Baltimore and Cleveland and Dallas where people have it worse. I've been through places where I've said, "Oh, God, I hope they've got some volunteers around here who will help these people." Truth is, though, volunteerism is basically dead in America, and the only place you're going to find it anymore is in towns like Hooks.

When potential donors come to Hooks, I drive them around and show them just how bad it is. If you don't want to go face it, then so be it. Just don't criticize me for doing it. If you want to play uppity, then play uppity. I could walk around town and say, "You know, I'm Durwood Merrill. I'm the umpire. Look at me." But I don't want to do that because that's not me. I'd rather be one of the people trying to help than one of those doing all the complaining. I think that most of the good people around Hooks will tell you that Durwood Merrill will crawl in the dirt to reach you if you need help. I'll never look away from anybody. That's the way I want to be known, and it's the way my friends really know me. I don't carry my nose so high in the clouds that I can smell the rain all the way to Oklahoma.

Enough about the different attitudes in Hooks.

The real heroes are the volunteers of the Hooks Christian Service, who've been there from the beginning and will be there until the final turkey and last toy have been delivered. They work long hours during the holidays and never whimper when they're tired or hungry or when they're ready to go home.

I have three schoolteachers—Evelyn Yeager, Diana Melton, and Susan Henderson—who work virtually year-round preparing their lists of needy kids and then buying the stuff. People say that I'm the linchpin in the operation and that's probably true. But take away those three ladies and the charity starts spinning out of control. Nobody knows the kids, and what the kids really need, better than a teacher who will see them every day.

I might hear from one of the teachers that a kid at school just can't read without glasses, and we'll pull some money out of the fund because the family can't afford them. One of the principals told me once that our little organization had helped 50 percent of the kids who'd come through Hooks High School.

In any volunteer organization, you've got to have somebody who knows where everything is at all times. That's Evelyn. Furthermore, she's one of the greatest motivators I've ever seen and probably should give halftime pep talks to the Hooks Hornets football team. I was feeling sorry for myself one day when I said, "You know, maybe I'll just go on home and make sure that the Merrill family has a good Christmas and I won't worry about everybody else." Evelyn looked at me and said, "You're just not working like you used to. Get yourself fired up again." She was right. I got my butt back to work.

For all the work that you do, there is nothing more beautiful than the day it all comes together. Evelyn will call me and say, "We're going to bag the gifts on December twenty-second. Be down at the church that day because we're going to deliver the gifts on the twenty-third." There is no sweeter music to my ears.

Of course, it's people who do something for nothing that gives all of this such a purpose. Tony Cofer has been my Santa Claus for almost twenty years, and he's worn out three suits. Jimmy D. Norris, the owner of Jimmy D.'s Restaurant, provides boxes and boxes and great food for all the volunteers. Somebody once asked Jimmy D. what he would do without me around. He said, "First, I would go out of business. The charity would go down the tubes. And I'd have nobody to talk to."

When the subject of the charity comes up, people are always asking, "How many meetings do you have? Where do you meet? Where are your offices?"

I got a call one day from a representative of the United Way who'd been alerted to our project by some workers at the Red River Army Depot. Seems the employees wanted their money to be donated to the Hooks Christian Service. So when I got on the phone with the United Way, the questions started coming.

"Mr. Merrill, how big is your office?" she asked.

"Well, we do some work in my garage," I said. "But there are some paintbrushes and gas cans and a big lawn mower we have to contend with. Actually, I'd rather think of the back of my pickup as my office."

"How many typewriters do you have?"

"Say what?"

"How many rolls of paper do you have?"

"Come again?"

Finally, I said, "We're not going to get any money, are we?" The next sound I heard was a dial tone.

Over the years, I've received checks from doctors, lawyers, bankers, ballplayers, businessmen, nurses, farmers, and state highway workers. Tony Phillips, who's considered one of the real bad boys of baseball, is a big donor every year. I was really surprised to receive his check one year after I called him out on strikes three straight times in one game. The next night, I was working third base when Tony came sliding in with a triple. Luckily, I called him safe. He looked up and said in that rapid-fire Tony-speak, "What are we going to do for the kids this year? I hope you're still working for the kids. Have you got everything lined up? I told my wife to send you a check. You'll be getting it pretty soon. I better not hear that you've stopped working for the kids!" As promised, we got a $5,000 check in the mail.

This is not going to be a popular opinion. But I'd like to see Tony Phillips get another chance in baseball. I know that that he got busted with some crack-cocaine and that's nothing to be proud of. Still, I like Tony Phillips because he's a guy who grew up poor, just like me, and he pulled himself up by his bootstraps. I think that with some therapy, he can get his life back in order.

Tony is just one of many charitable people who've helped my organization. An anonymous donor from Dallas sent us two great computers a few years ago. I have a doctor in Texarkana who sends us a check every month, and whenever I get into a bind, he'll come running with more help. Norm Hitzges of KLIF in Dallas is one of our great campaigners, and he's had me on his show during the holidays for thirteen years. You wouldn't believe the response out of Dallas. Every year, those cars come rolling in from the southwest with volunteers, food, and gifts. It's almost as if Norm's show has created a cult following for us all over North Texas. I'll be in Dallas and somebody will have found out my name and and they'll say, "You're the umpire I'm always hearing on Norm's show. You're the one doing the big Christmas thing up in Hooks."

The first year I was on KLIF, 1985, Norm and I had planned to just talk about baseball. But a caller asked what I did during the off-season, and, of course, I mentioned the Christmas charity. So we batted that around a little while before moving on to the next caller. After his show that day,

Norm got about five calls from people who wanted to know how they could donate money to the Hooks Christian Service. By the end of the week, he'd received more than twenty-five checks. The next year, Norm had me on the show and he received over fifty checks. This is an estimate, but I know we've received at least $100,000 from his listeners over the years. That doesn't count the furniture that we've gotten, along with the bicycles and everything else. Each year, we have over thirty people who make the 170-mile drive from Dallas to Hooks because they've heard about us on KLIF.

These days, Norm loves to talk about the Hooks Christian Service. He likes to say, "You can get awfully jaded in this business. Every day, I come into the radio station and I read stories about gambling, strikes, and drugs. Every once in a while, you run into something like this and find a human heart. Then you find out there are loads of human hearts out there who are really ready to respond. This is not about people donating money because of a tax deduction. This is about people going into their wallets. I get letters all the time from listeners that would just cut your heart out. I had one listener who wrote a two-page letter and enclosed a dollar. He wrote, 'I may be poor, but I'm not that poor.'"

Another great friend and donor is Merle Harmon, the nationally known broadcaster who's retired now. He loads up his Suburban with toys, basketballs, footballs, and bats every year and comes to Hooks. His truck is so loaded down that it looks like the tires are going to pop. We've had entire church congregations show just to help. Carloads of college kids have arrived unannounced because they want to do something for the community. Scores of people I've never heard of or met send checks every year and never ask anything for return.

Oh, we received some nice big donations. But I've also received checks for $1.39 and one for $1.10. And we've written those people thank-you notes just like they sent us $500.

*   *   *

The phone rang around noon that Christmas in 1979 as Mama was preparing the Christmas turkey while my son, Mickey, and daughter, Maria, were trying on their Christmas clothes. I'd just completed my third full season in the major leagues, and life was getting a little easier around the Merrill home. As a matter of fact, Mickey's Christmas present that year was a brand-new silver Grand Prix. He was seventeen and Maria was fourteen. After years of struggling to make ends meet, I was now bringing home a nice paycheck and there were plenty of gifts under the tree.

I'd done a little Christmas charity work for the Lions Club, but nothing that required weeks and weeks of preparation and a pot full of money to make it happen. I was very aware that there were some poor folks and some impoverished families around Hooks, especially down along the river. Shoot, even Billy Sims, who'd won the Heisman Trophy a year earlier at Oklahoma, had been forced to work long hours at the Conoco station during his high school days to keep food on the table. Billy had been raised by his great-grandmother on one of our typical dirt roads in Hooks. Every day was a struggle for that family, but they always handled it.

Mama was about to set the table for a big lunch when I was told that Hooks mayor Clyde Alridge was on the phone.

"Durwood," he said. "I've been informed that there's a family down in the bottoms that is starving. I really don't know what to do. It's Christmas Day and every doggone store from here to Dallas is probably closed. Shoot, Durwood, I don't even know if we can rustle up a food basket on a day like this."

It's not that the mayor didn't have the wherewithal to figure out a solution to our problem. It's just that most people around Hooks know that I have a way of getting things done on short notice, so they're not afraid to call me, even on Christmas morning, to ask for favors. My phone has been ringing for decades with people in need. So I gave our little predicament some serious thought and agreed with the mayor that there wasn't much we could do. But the word "help" hit me in the heart like a sharp hunting knife. The woman told our mayor that her refrigerator was empty and that she had nothing to put on the table that day.

After a quick lunch, I grabbed Mickey and we headed out to the river bottoms, where I wanted to check things out. I wasn't sure what the game plan would be as we pulled up in front of the little shack, which I call an East Hooks bungalow. As we walked through the front door, I realized we had a much larger mess than I'd first estimated. Over in the corner of the house was a little scrawny tree that had no gifts underneath. The woman opened the refrigerator door and it was plumb empty. Those folks didn't even have a quart of milk, a loaf of bread, or a scrap of food in the house. She opened the pantry and there was nothing but a few bugs crawling around. My hands started shaking because I knew I'd just come face-to-face with one of the saddest scenes you'd ever want to lay your eyes on during the Christmas season. She had three hungry kids and a husband who was off somewhere on a bad drunk. The woman stood in the middle of the kitchen, and big tears were rolling down her cheeks because her children needed help.

"I'll think of something," I told her, patting the poor woman on the shoulder. "Just hang tight and we'll be back just as quickly as we can."

Mickey and I drove back to the Merrill house, and I headed straight for the back bedroom, where I shut the door, sat down, and started crying. It wasn't that we didn't have the time or the money to help her. But a short-notice rescue in the middle of Christmas Day was going to be next to impossible, even for me.

My mind drifted to the 1940s and a year in the Oklahoma dust bowl when the rains didn't come and the cotton crop failed and the Merrill farm fell upon a miserable time. I remember the look on my dad's face as Christmas was approaching because he knew there wasn't much a poor family could do when your one and only source of income had dried up like a brown summer weed. We had a Christmas tree that year, but nothing under it. I knew that Santa Claus wasn't likely to bring bicycles or BB guns, and I doubted that we were even going to get a basketball or a baseball. I wasn't even counting on a new pair of blue jeans. I knew that Grandma would be making shirts for the boys from flour sacks. But that might be it for us on Christmas morning.

Those times were tough, but our pain was eased by the fact that everybody in the county was poor. In life, you generally measure your financial status by the size of the house and the car next door. Our house and our car were just about like everybody else's where I grew up.

In 1979, though, a young child only needed to turn on the TV to realize just how poor he was. The Christmas ads would tell him about the great ten-speed bicycles and some of the electronic gadgets that were coming on the market. Most likely, that little boy had walked through a mall and had seen stores that were stuffed with toys. Or maybe he had just walked down the street on Christmas morning and seen the new stuff the other kids were playing with.

As I lay there with those thoughts running through my head, Mickey walked in and said in a stern voice, "All right, all right. Stop crying. You're not doing anybody any good just laying back here. We need to figure out what the heck we're going to do. Get up and let's get going."

I said to myself, "If Mickey is strong enough to face this thing, so can I." So I picked up the phone and called Mrs. Parker, who owned a variety store in town. She was about the only hope for getting any kind of Christmas gifts, and, thankfully, she agreed to open the store. The local grocer also said he would leave his family for a while to open the door to his store.

I walked into the variety store, and there was a pretty little Christmas tree with lights and everything sitting in the window. So I grabbed it. We loaded up dolls and toys and all kinds of stuff that children would want. Then we headed down to the grocery store where we loaded up turkeys and potatoes and candy and green beans and pies. The Merrill family car was stuffed to the roof, and we had toys hanging out of the window as we drove back to the woman's bungalow. By about four that afternoon, Christmas had done an about-face for that mother and her three children. At least they had plenty to eat for several days, and they weren't going to live in misery while a lot of people in Hooks walked around with big smiles on their faces. Mickey and I went on home, and I remember the Christmas dinner tasting a lot better that evening.

I guess you could say that our charity got its start in 1979 when Mickey and I extended a helping hand to that very needy family. The next year, a small group of volunteers helped about five families, and the next year we added about five more. Our service group grew out of the Missionary Baptist Church, and it became known as the Hooks Christian Service. Every year, our little group grew and grew, and the addition of the teachers—Evelyn, Diana, and Susan—made it really start to click.

There would be times, however, when we wondered if we could keep going as the job got bigger and the list of needy families grew. You have to remember that we had no office, no typewriters, and no rolls of paper. So we had to network over the telephone, or just by driving to each other's homes. In some regards, we were kind of like an underground radical group moving quietly through the streets.

Every year, when I look at the list of all the families we're going to help and see what all those kids need, I'm just overwhelmed. I go over and sit by myself in a quiet place, and I say, ''Dear Lord, I really don't think I can do it again this year. God, can you please help me just one more time because this time, Lord, it looks impossible?''

There was a Christmas Eve when the snow was blowing and sleet pounded the windowpanes and the roads were shutting down. Darkness was falling and I felt weaker than a starved calf. I looked around the room and blurted, ''We can't get the Christmas presents out. There's just no way we're going to make it in time.'' That's when Susan got on her soapbox and started giving her little Knute Rockne. ''We've got to make it,'' she said. ''How are you going to feel in the morning if you're having your Christmas at home, and you know these people are out there with nothing!''

We loaded up our trucks and I headed down into the river bottoms. I walked into a house where the mother was standing on the porch and crying her eyes out. ''Oh, dear God,'' she said. ''I thought we were going to be completely forgotten on Christmas. And then here you come.''

Most of the windowpanes had been shattered, and I saw that the snow was blowing into the house through cracks in the walls. As I carried the heavy sacks through the front door, I stepped on a rotten piece of wood and fell completely through the floor. I quickly realized that nothing was broken but my heart. I resolved right then that I would never stop trying to help these people.

We find some sad situations every Christmas where people are living with bare cupboards and nothing under the tree. Nothing is sadder, though, than to show up at somebody's house with a bag of toys and a basket of food and find that they've been evicted. So many times we've tried and failed to find people who've been kicked out of their homes at Christmas. It just breaks your heart.

By the mid-1980s, the charity was growing in leaps and bounds, thanks to the publicity we were getting out of Dallas where KLIF's Norm Hitzges and WFAA-TV's Dale Hansen, the top television sportscaster in town, were blowing our horns. The money was rolling in, and we were adding pages and pages of needy families to the list. We were helping more than a hundred people, and the Hooks Christian Service was working feverishly from November 1 all the way through Christmas Eve. The pressure was starting to mount.

On top of that, Mama was starting to get a little concerned that I wasn't paying enough attention to the Merrill family. When you spend almost two straight months worrying about the needs of others, you start overlooking the people who are closest to you. I understood Mama's worries, and I promised to be more balanced in my Christmas planning.

I have a tendency to get worked up when I'm going at full throttle and giving a job every ounce of energy I've got. One December morning as Mama was getting ready to leave for her job at the Red River Army Depot, she said, "Now, Durwood, don't try to do too much today. Just make yourself a little list and try to get those things done today. Then you can make yourself another little list for the next day."

Well, it didn't quite work out that way. As soon as Mama left for work, the phone started ringing. "We're going to be about ten bicycles short," one of the volunteers was telling me on the phone. Then I got another call. "Durwood, we're running out of money. I don't see how we're going to buy all of these gifts unless we come up with some more cash today." As soon as I hung up, the phone rang again and again and again. My nerves were getting jangled, and my little list of things to do had just spilled over into page two.

I showered, dressed, and was ready to leave the house when I realized that I couldn't find the keys to the truck. I was frantic as I moved through the house, looking beneath newspapers and pillow cushions. I rifled through a couple of drawers, and then I grabbed the phone and called Mama down at the depot. I yelled, "You've got to come home because I've lost the keys and now my mind is blank."

Mama had a big job at the depot as the disbursing officer, and she had a staff of five. Leaving work in the middle of the day could knock the operation out of kilter, but she headed home anyway. I was sitting on the couch with my head in my hands when she half jogged into the living room and plucked the keys from the coffee table, about two feet from my head. I guess that I'd become blind with all the stress.

Really, I could cite you hundreds of reasons for worry. Experience has taught all of the volunteers through the years that we have to be careful with the gifts because we want to make sure they fall into the right hands. That's why Evelyn, Diana, and Susan are especially valuable because they see the kids every day and they know their needs. We also know that their parents might try to take advantage of us if we don't use some safeguards.

With the new bicycles, we sandpaper off the serial numbers so the parents can't return them to the store for cash.

We take labels off clothes for the very same reason. Some of the moms and dads have been known to take the gifts back to the stores in exchange for cash so they can buy a bottle of whisky, or they drive over to Shreveport to spend their money on the gambling boats. Sad as it might sound, these things happened on a frequent basis until we started exercising some safeguards.

Of course, most of the folks are extremely thankful for all that we do for them. We have received hundreds of letters through the years from people we have helped. I got a letter a few years ago from a woman who wrote: "Dear Mr. Merrill. Thanks to you and the group there in Hooks, I managed to survive some pretty tough years. I've managed to get through four years of college and it won't be long before I'm in the working world. As soon as I make some money, I plan to be a regular contributor to your cause." We started receiving a regular check from her a few years ago.

I was shopping in a Wal-Mart store a few years ago when an elderly man approached with a big warm smile and stuck out his hand. I thought I'd recognized him from years of making my rounds at Christmas. The man put his arm around my shoulders and said, "Durwood, you've been coming to my house now for about ten years with that wonderful Christmas turkey. My family and I have enjoyed that turkey for so many years that I was just wondering, how about bringing us a ham next year?"

In 1992, I got a call from Robin Roberts at ESPN, and she told me she would be flying into nearby Texarkana just before Christmas to do a story on our Christmas charity. We picked her up at the airport and took her and the ESPN crew down to the Fellowship Hall at the First Baptist Church.

Of course, I've seen Robin on the network for years and knew about her talents as a sportscaster. What I didn't know is that she's a fine athlete, too. There's a basketball court at the Fellowship Hall, and she showed some our local kids some moves that I don't think they'd seen before. Robin, along with being a beautiful woman, is also charming and engaging. You just want to hug her every time you see her. She has tremendous presence, both in person and on TV. Little did Robin know, however, what she was getting into that day as we prepared to deliver the Christmas bags to our needy families around the area. She knew that she'd hit upon a good Christmas story that the network could run for a few days during the holiday season. But going down into those river bottoms was going to be a different matter, as she soon learned.

As we started making our rounds, I asked Robin if she'd like to help deliver food to some of the families. We hit a very poor area of town, and she carried food into the shacks and shanties and put it away in the refrigerators and the pantries. All was going pretty smoothly until we walked into a house that had gaping holes in the walls and hardly a floor. These people were so poor that I'm not sure they had running water. The mother of four children met me at the door, threw her arms around my neck, and, as she sobbed uncontrollably, said, "Oh, thank you, sir, so very much. I just had no hope that we were going to have a Christmas in our family. I just had no hope at all."

I looked over at Robin, and she was starting to cry. She covered her face, and then she turned away and walked out into the yard. I caught up with her and said, "Now, Robin, there's one thing that you've got to learn about our little charity here. Everybody cries sooner or later. I guess you could say it's just part of the experience. If you've never cried, you've never really been part of this thing."

With tears still welling in her eyes, she said, "Durwood, I grew up around some pretty poor people in Mississippi. But, God, I've never seen anything like this in my life. I didn't know that people could be this poor."

The piece that ESPN produced that Christmas even brought tears to my eyes. I still hear people talking about it, and we're still reaping financial benefits from the public exposure. Thank God for Robin Roberts.

One of the first large news outlets to do a major story on the Hooks Christian Service was WFAA-TV in Dallas.

Sports director Dale Hansen, who's really made a big name for himself in Dallas–Fort Worth, heard about us in 1985 from one of our needy families who'd been getting some assistance. Dale said, "I just love stories where somebody's giving something back to the community. That's the story that always pulls at your heartstrings. A lot of times, I get call from PR agents who are trying to boost the image of their star player. Well, this wasn't the case in Hooks. This was somebody who was dead serious calling me about some help they'd received there in Hooks. It was a wonderful cause and it made a great story."

Dale sent reporter Mike Capps to do the story. Mike is gregarious guy who would go on to become a news reporter at CNN before the baseball bug bit him. He wrote an excellent book on longtime scout Red Murf. When Mike came into Hooks with his cameraman, I never suspected he would become emotionally overwhelmed. But as we started making our rounds in the river bottoms, I noticed that Mike was no longer a chatterbox. He'd become quiet and withdrawn, and I noticed that he'd walked off from the group. Big Mike needed to have a moment to himself, and he'd decided to go out and cry behind a tree.

He came to Hooks as a shaggy-haired little seventh grader in 1968, and we really didn't know what we had when Billy Sims hit town. We heard he came from the St. Louis projects, where his mother had struggled to make ends meet and to keep Billy out of trouble. Billy's mother finally gave up the fight and sent him to his great-grandmother, Miss Hattie, who lived on one of our dirt roads just down from the schoolhouse in Hooks.

My coaching career was about over when Billy started playing for the seventh-grade team under coach Jim Griffin. I was still the high school head football coach when Jim walked up to me one day and said, "Durwood, we've got a little kid over here who's pretty shy, but I really think he's going to be something special. Just from looking at him a couple of days, I can tell he's got a lot of talent. Kid's prob-

ably going to make you a doggone good running back one
of these days.''

If I'd known just how good Billy was going to be, I might
have had second thoughts about leaving coaching and going
off to umpire pro baseball. He would put Hooks on the map
by winning the Heisman Trophy at the University of
Oklahoma in 1978.

I think one of the reasons that Billy had the drive to excel
in football is that he was treated just like one of the kids
back in Hooks. In return for his meals at school, he slopped
the trays in the cafeteria. You'd find him working during the
afternoons, and on the weekends, down at the Conoco Station on Interstate 30. Miss Hattie was a fine lady and there
were times when they needed a little money. Mama was always sending quilts and blankets over to Miss Hattie's house
to make sure they were sleeping warm at night.

I was home one winter during the baseball off-season
when I told Oklahoma coach Barry Switzer about Billy. I
had gotten to know Barry from a high school banquet, and
we struck up a friendship when he found out I was from
Oklahoma and a big Sooners fan. Barry just laughed about
Billy because, he said, kids from small 2A schools just
weren't good enough to play for a powerhouse like
Oklahoma, which had won back-to-back national championships. Barry said, ''Durwood, you've taken too many foul
tips off the noggin.'' That was before Barry got a good look
at Billy.

I've always thought that Barry was the greatest recruiter
in the history of the game because he knew he was really
selling himself to the mama and papa. I've always said that
if Barry could get into the kitchen and get his elbows in the
Karo syrup, he'd walk away with that ballplayer. Barry
would be back in the kitchen helping the mama cook the
fried chicken and then he'd wash the dishes afterward. That's
the biggest reason he got Billy, because he knew how to talk
to Miss Hattie.

Barry had a few other tricks up his sleeves. One afternoon,
when the Sooners were whipping the snot out of Colorado,

he didn't even worry about helping with the halftime strategy. He got on the phone in the locker room and called Billy back at the Conoco station in Hooks. They talked for the entire halftime, and Billy couldn't believe it. "Are you listening to the game?" Barry said. "Yeah, coach," Billy said. "And I can't believe you're calling me at halftime."

People still say that I hand-delivered Billy Sims to the University of Oklahoma, and I'm not sure that's completely the case. I'm proud that he went there and of all of his accomplishments, including the Heisman Trophy. Billy had a fabulous career when you consider his college feats, along with three All-Pro seasons with the Detroit Lions before he tore the anterior cruciate ligament and they had to reconstruct his knee. When Billy realized that he wasn't going to be the same player as before, he decided to hang up his spurs.

After he'd won the Heisman Trophy, and before he took over for Detroit, we decided to have a Billy Sims Day in Hooks so we could name a street after our hero. What better street to name after Billy than the one that ran right in front of Miss Hattie's old house?

When Howard Cosell got wind of the event, he flew down to Hooks and brought a crew from ABC Sports. He wanted to scoop the world, so he came down several days before the ceremony. Now, I don't know what he was expecting, but Hooks is not Queens or the Bronx.

It was one of those fiercely cold days when the rain was turning to sleet and the wind sliced through you with a keen blade. That old road in front of Miss Hattie's house looked like two miles of pig slop.

Howard had come to Hooks to do the classic story on the black kid who had punched his ticket out of the ghetto by becoming a mean motor scooter on the football field. Howard practically had the script written when he realized that he and his crew would have to walk down that muddy road to reach Miss Hattie's house, where Billy was waiting. I'm not so sure the U.S. Army could have maneuvered that road on that raw winter day. Howard had on a pair of alligator shoes, and when he took his first step into the cold muck, he let out an oath you could hear all the way to Oklahoma. I've never heard such cussing in my entire life. Howard would take a step and he'd cuss. Then he'd take another step, and he'd berate everybody from God to somebody's mother we'd never heard of. That muck was up over his ankles, and I thought somebody was going to have to carry Howard on his back. But nobody in Hooks cared that much for him. Even those New York cameramen and producers were laughing their butts off.

Howard finally made his way to the old broken-down house, and he got his interview with Miss Hattie and Billy, and then he left town in a New York minute. I never could understand why we never heard from him again.

For several years after signing his big pro contract, Billy had a beautiful white ranch house on forty acres in Hooks. There were times when you'd go out there and you'd find twenty gorgeous brand-new cars. He lived like a king, and I guess that's what happens when you're so dominant in your sport for so long. I really think that if Billy hadn't torn up his knee, he might already be in the Pro Football Hall of Fame.

In college, and on the pro level, they teach you how to run the football. But they don't teach you how to save your money or make wise investments or simply hang on to the millions they're paying you. I think that Billy must have gotten some bad advice, because when his empire faltered, it burned all the way to the ground. He filed for bankruptcy in 1991, and he lost the beautiful ranch house in Hooks. A group of investors tried to save the house for Billy and his family, but it was too late.

It may be a while before Billy gets his life back on track. He's been doing some token PR work for the University of Oklahoma.

Last football season, I was doing the public address announcing at the Hooks football games when I felt a pat on the shoulder. There stood Billy right behind me with that big wide grin on his face. I grabbed him a chair and made him my spotter. I had to be careful to keep the microphone shut off between plays because Billy was doing so much yelling. His son Brent is a quarterback, and B. J. plays safety for the Hornets.

We were drinking a soda pop and eating a moon pie not too long ago at the old country store in Hooks when Billy said, "Coach, I was happy when I had nothing. Then I was a millionaire. I had enough money to live the rest of my life. But things have happened and I'm poor again. But I'm still happy."

Billy has been through some hard times, but he's still a hero in Hooks, where he can walk down the street with his head held high. You don't hear many people around town talking about his problems because we'd like to remember him as the great player he was. Billy will always be a celebrity to us.

As I drive around the streets of Hooks these days, I think about how much things have changed and how much they've remained the same. I guess the little town has walked the same path as Billy Sims, just kind of going in a big circle. We've conquered a lot of problems in Hooks the last two decades, but we still haven't broken the chain of poverty. Just like anything else, we'll have to keep rolling up our sleeves and getting the job done the best we can.

A lot of people would have changed drastically if they'd walked in my shoes the last twenty-one years. Still, I think the people around my little town will tell you that Durwood's the same ol' boy. I don't do anything fancy, and I still hang around with the same friends that I had when I first went into umpiring. I still eat some of my meals at Jimmy D.'s Restaurant, and you can be sure to catch me at just about any athletic event around Hooks. If you've got a problem, and I can help you, I'll be there as quickly as my pickup will go.

When I left for umpiring school back in 1972, my son, Mickey, was ten and my daughter, Maria, was seven. Today, I have eight grandchildren. From Maria's family I have Dustin Durwood Kahler and Dylan Kahler, along with Ryan Hughes, Jason Hughes, and Garrett Hughes. From Mickey's family, I have Brandon, Matthew, and Shari Merrill. I look into their eyes and I see the past, but I also see a brilliant future.

Mama still wants to know when I'm going to hang it up from umpiring. I really think I've got a couple more good years in me. My bosses tell me that I had a great year in 1997, and I keep hearing from some pretty smart baseball people that I'm as good as they come in the American League. They say that you'll know it's time to retire when you don't feel like walking out on that field anymore. Well brother, that time hasn't come, because I still feel a rush of adrenaline whenever I walk to home plate for the exchange of lineups. Every time they play the national anthem, I still get goose bumps.

If you're ever driving through Texas, why don't you stop in Hooks and say hello. Or, if you ever pass me on the street, please stop me and shake my hand. There's something I need to tell you: You're out and you're ugly, too.